1880 CENSUS:

CARTER COUNTY, TENNESSEE

Transcribed by:

Byron Sistler and Barbara Sistler

JANAWAY PUBLISHING, INC.
Santa Maria, California

1880 Census: Carter County, Tennessee

Originally published, Evanston, Illinois
1979

Reprinted by

Janaway Publishing, Inc.
732 Kelsey Ct.
Santa Maria, California 93454
(805) 925-1038
www.JanawayPublishing.com

2006, 2012

ISBN: 978-1-59641-034-3

Made in the United States of America

IMPORTANT INFORMATION

You cannot utilize the material in this booklet at all effectively unless you read the following.

This booklet is an exact transcription of the county schedule, household by household. A transcription in sequence from the schedules is very useful in placing the relationships of neighboring families. When the county by county transcription is completed, a state-wide index of heads of household and of individuals whose surnames differed from that of the household head will be prepared to be used either with the printed transcriptions or the microfilm.

Surnames appear in capitals. Where a surname does not appear before the person's given name in a family listing he has the same surname as the entry immediately preceding him. Given names were copied as read with the exception of Francis--Frances to indicate sex of person. Where there is a doubt about gender of a name we have followed it with (m) or (f).

Age of each person is listed after his name. Unless indicated by (B) (Black) or (Mu) (Mulatto), the person is Caucasian (W). In a household, unless a symbol for race appears after a name, person is of same race as the preceding household member(s).

Occupations were shown on the schedules for all persons but young children. These are listed in our transcription with the following exceptions--farmer or farm labor for men and housekeeping for females. Thus, if no occupation is given, farmer or housekeeeper can be assumed.

Illnesses and infirmities at time of the census enumeration are shown as indicated on the schedules.

The place of birth of each individual was to be included on the schedules along with place of birth of each of his parents. We have used standard Post Office abbreviations for the states, except where Tennessee is indicated we simply use a T. If the individual and both parents were born in Tennessee this item is omitted. Also in households where the parents were born in other states but the children were born in Tennessee the birthplaces of the father and mother are not repeated unless there is a discrepancy.

Relationship of all persons in the household to the head of household was to be indicated. We have omitted this where it was obvious that the second person was the wife and succeeding individuals were the offspring of the father. Where identification in this fashion seemed unclear we entered what we thought were appropriate notations.

An example from the transcription (fictitious entry) should be informative:

> SHELTON, George 47 (T AL GA), Susan 37, Bettie 20, Narcissa 18, Mary 15 (KY), Ada 13 (blind); WALKER, Caroline 40 (sister) (widow) (T AL GA), George 21 (nephew); MAXWELL, Eli (B) 35 (farmhand), Louisa 28 (servant); SCRUGGS, Henry 28 (W) (boarder) (schoolteacher), Josie 24 (Henry's wife), Mamie 3 (Henry's dau)

This translates into George Shelton age 47, a white man born in Tennessee whose father was born in Alabama and mother in Georgia; his wife Susan age 37, born in Tennessee and parents also born in Tennessee; George's children Bettie, Narcissa, Mary and Ada. The first two were born in Tennessee, Mary in Kentucky and Ada in Tennessee. Ada is blind. George's sister Caroline Walker lives with the family with her son George (though conceivably George Walker is not Caroline's child). A black man, Eli Maxwell, lives here and works as a farmhand for George Shelton. Louisa Maxwell, listed as servant, is probably Eli's wife, but she could be a sister. The Henry Scruggs family is made rather clear in the schedules, as noted above; they were Caucasian.

Keep in mind that this is a copy from handwritten schedules. Although the condition of the schedules and the handwriting is much improved in 1880 over earler censuses, it is still quite possible to misinterpret individual names (or letters).

Byron & Barbara Sistler

Page 1, Dist. 1

1. MOURLEY, David 32 (T T NC), Sarah E. 34, William W. 12, Robert C. 10, Rosa C. 8, Arta A. 6, Dicy I. 3
2. PIERCE, Francis M. 47 (T NC T), Sarah Ann 43, Sarah J. 24; DUGGER, Nancy 69 (mother in law) (T NC T)
3. PIERCE, William C. 44, Sarah J. 42, Margarett C. E. 14
4. PIERCE, Griffin 25, Nancy L. L. 17
5. VAUGHT, James (B) 25, Angeline 25
6. PHILIPS, Wm. O. 27 (distiller of whiskey) (IN OH IN), Loueasy A. 20 (wife); STOUT, Lemuel 5 (ttok to Rase); VANOVER, Maron 22 (servant--works in distillery) (NC NC NC); GRAGG, Daniel 18 (servant--works in distillery) (T NC T)
7. COOK, W. A. D. 44, Sarah E. 35 (wife) (T T NC)
8. PIERCE, Henry C. 55 (T NC T), Frankey 54 (wife) (NC NC NC), Noah W. 21, Minnie A. 19, John F. 17, Eliza L. 13, William R. 6 (g son); HAZLEWOOD, N. J. 6 (g dau); OBERHOLSER, James 20 (boarder) (cabinet maker)
9. PRESSNEL, Alfred 22 (NC NC NC), Amanda E. 26 (wife) (T T NC), Henry H. 1; PIERCE, Samuel 4 (stepson) (T NC T)
10. TIMS, James A. 26 (NC SC NC), Sarah S. C. 28 (T T NC), William W. 1; PIERCE, Lillie I. 4 (step dau)
11. SMITH, Francis M. 36, Nancy C. 29, Henry T. 13, George P. 8, Pheby A. 6, Ruthee C. 4, Julia M. 1
12. JAENKINS, R. J. 29, Martha E. 22, George E. 1

Page 2, Dist. 1

13. CARRIGER, A. T. 56 (m) (T ___ NC), Margarett D. 24 (dau), Eliza J. 18
14. PLESS, James I. 29 (NC NC NC), Amarader 24 (wife) (T NC T), Ellaetter E. 5, Thomas C. 6/12
15. SMITH, Robert L. 36, Mary C. 35, Mary O. 13, Cililie E. 11 (dau), Robertie A. 9 (dau), Sarah E. 7, William W. 5, Edward 3, infant (f) 1/12; CAMPBELL, W. J. 25 (servant) (m) (T T NC)
16. WHITE, Thomas C. 42 (Rev collector), Mary A. 40, Elizabeth R. 16, Henry T. 14, Ezekiel G. 12, Sarah S. 7, Lawson A. 5, Martha C. 2
17. CAMPBELL, C. N. 59, Bethany 40 (wife) (NC NC NC), Martha 8, Luvina E. 5, James Z. 3
18. SMITH, Ezekiel 69, Elizabeth 63, Hamilton W. 5
19. SMITH, W. G. B. 29, Alice 18 (wife)
20. SMITH, John H. 64, Loueasy 28 (dau), Hamilton 22, David 6 (g son), Ader 1/12 (b. Apr) (g dau)
21. TIMS, Amos 64 (SC SC SC), Sarah 50 (NC NC NC), Rebecca 24, Jane 20, Mary A. 17, William 15, James 5 (g son) (T NC T), Donna B. 3 (g dau) (T NC T), William 1

Page 3, Dist. 1

22. TEAGUE, Robert A. 30 (cabinet maker) (NC NC NC), Dicy M. 25 (NC NC NC), Ida A. 8 (VA), William A. 6 (VA); TRUMAN, Aline 20 (servant) (T T NC)
23. TRUMAN, J. R. 26 (NC VA NC), Susan 38 (wife), Nancy 70 (mother in law) (NC NC NC); JONES, John A. 21 (sp son) (school teacher)
24. GRIFFITH, Thos. D. 25 (T NC T), Mary E. 22 (NC NC NC), William L. 4, James P. 4/12 (b. Jan)
25. SMITH, Lawson M. 59, Hily J. 53 (sis); MILLER, Alice 18 (servant)

Page 3 (cont'd)

26. BOWLIN, Hugh 53 (NC NC NC), Sophia 75 (mother) (NC ___ ___); HESTER, Sally 14 (niece) (T NC NC)
27. SMITH, F. J. 62, Mary 58, Micheal E. 21, Mollie O. 17, Samuel (B) 21 (servant), Penelope 11 (servant)
28. TEAGUE, Avery 37 (NC NC NC), Nancy 21 (wife) (NC NC NC), Mary C. 7/12
29. SMITH, Mary E. 62 (widow), Sarah A. 40, Margaret J. 35, Emla C. 31, George A. 26
30. SIMERLEY, George (Indian) 36, Nancy (W) 35, Eliza J. 11, David H. 10, Nathaniel 8, John F. 6, Samuel A. 2 (these children all listed as half-breeds)
31. PIERCE, Joseph 39, Deleena L. 42, Anderson K. 17, Daniel T. 14, Arthur C. 9, Julia A. K. 4
32. CAMPBELL, J. A. 76 (widow), Eliza J. 44 (liver disease), Celia Ann 36, James M. 21 (g son), Delceny C. 19 (g dau)

Page 4, Dist. 1

33. DUGGER, Susan C. 46 (widow) (bad cold), Cornelia E. 19
34. CARDEN, Jas. W. 53 (T NC T), Anna M. 43 (T NC NC), Ellen S. 28 (dau), Rhoda 23, Susan 20, Ancil G. 17, Polly 15, Anner 13, Mary 9, Minnie 7, Randolph 4
35. WILSON, James M. 48 (NC NC NC), Mary A. 51 (T NC T), David L. 23, William R. 21, Sarah E. 18, James L. 16
36. OLIVER, William I. 25, Nancy A. 23 (T NC T), James M. 5, Luvina J. 3, Eva 1 day (b. May)
37. OLIVER, George 47 (piles) (T NC NC), Jane 42
38. CAMPBELL, C. 37, Sarah E. 36 (wife), Maredith M. 13, John 11, Anna J. 9, Martha E. 7, Eva L. 5, Andrew F. 1
39. DELOACH, Saml. C. 35 (minister gospel), Martha L. 36 (NC NC NC), Margarett 13, William V. 10, Sarah 5, Celia A. 3, Julia A. 5/12
40. CAMPBELL, Nay? 48 (widow), James 19, Sarah C. 16, Eliza C. 10
41. CAMPBELL, S. G. 58, Sarah 54 (wife) (NC NC NC) (crippled), Sarah A. 15
33. (out of order) CARDEN, Samuel 4 (apparently this individual belongs in a family, perhaps with James Carden)

Page 5, Dist. 1

42. GLOVER, William 25, Ellen S. 23 (T T NC), Dora B. 2, Samuel M. 2/12 (b. March)
43. CAMPBELL, Thos. 19 (T T NC), Elizabeth 22, John S. 2
44. GLOVER, James H. 24, Mary E. B. 22, John A. 2, Charles F. 8/12
45. GOODWIN, Nancy 59; CAMPBELL, C. 2 (g son)
46. GOODWIN, M. D. 22, Delcena V. 20, Andrew B. 1
47. GOODWIN, J. L. 36, Nancy J. A. 22 (wife), Virginia ___ 7, Celia A. 6, Mollie 4, Nancy 3, Roderick R. B. 1, James L. 9/12
48. HATHAWAY, E. C. 54 (works in forge), Luviey E. 35 (wife); CAMPBELL, J. C. 20 (stepson); CLAWSON, Amanda 17 (servant)
49. ESTEP, Harvy 25 (VA T NC), Martha E. 20, Alice 1
50. CAMPBELL, G. F. 29, Nancy J. 25 (wife), Etta 5, Orle 3
51. MOURTON, M. Y.? 65 (T SC NC), Barbary 51 (wife) (T SC T)
52. CARDEN, Emla C. 38 (widow), Nathaniel T. 12, James L. 9; GOODWIN, M. A. 18 (dau), C. A. 14 (dau)
53. LEWIS, William L. 39 (T NC T), Celia A. 31 Nancy E. 17, Naomy E. 14, Melvin G. 11, Martha L. 7, Lawson G. 4 (son), Celia E. 2

Hh#	Page 6, Dist. 1

54. CAMPBELL, G. A. 23 (T T NC), Nancy M. 21 (wife), Matilda E. 6, Mary A. 3, Sarah 9/12 (b. Aug)
55. SMITH, Hamilton W. 35, Celia J. 42, John A. B. 14, Robert W. 12, Melissa I. 9, James R. E. 8, Lawson L. 5, Nancy C. 3, Columbus W. 1
56. CAMPBELL, Elizab. 71 (widow)
57. SMITH, D. H. W. 28, Salley E. 20 (wife), Hily Jane 9/12
58. CARDEN, Vinson 25 (NC NC NC), Cassa A. E. 22 (wife), Susan 3, Henry W. 1
59. CARDEN, Ripley 65 (NC NC NC), Glatha C. 60 (wife) (NC NC NC), Martha A. 19
60. WHITEHEAD, Wm. C. 48, Nancy E. 42, John A. 19, Hannah J. 17, Loueasy C. 15, Celia T. H. 11; HILL, Alexander 20 (servant)
61. LEWIS, Susan J. 40 (T NC NC), Mary C. 17 (dau), Rebecca A. 11, William H. 3
62. STOUT, Mary A. 28, James C. 3 (son)
63. HOLAWAY, J. A. 32 (NC NC NC), Mary A. 31 (NC VA NC), George A. 8, Edna A. 7, John A. 4, Nancy E. 2, Mary S. 28 days? (b. May)
64. WHALEY, Rachel 46 (T NC T), Sarah 48 (sis) (T NC T), Dicy Caroline 14 (niece), Joseph W. 12 (nephew), James A. 10 (nephew); WHITEHEAD, Mary C. 13 (dau)

Page 7, Dist. 1

65. WILLIAMS, John B. 52, Rebecca C. 55 (T T NC), James H. T. 27, Robert L. 19, Sally J. L. 17, Nancy L. E. 13
66. WILLIAMS, P. J. 25 (artist) (widower), Mary A. 8, William B. 3, Rebecca C. 1; GILREATH, Enos (B) 47 (servant--black smith) (NC T NC)
67. SMITH, N. T. 35, Mary A. 39 (wife), John G. S. 12, Mary E. 10, Sally A. 8, Ezekiel 6, Nancy J. 5, Hetty 3, William D. D. 11/12
68. BAILEY, John B. 22 (T NC NC), Mary A. 19 (T NC T), Loretta V. 4, David C. L. 3, William B. 1
69. WORD, Keren H. 49 (widow) (NC NC NC), Abraham L. 18 (T T NC), Thomas T. 16
70. BAILEY, Henry L. 57 (T NC NC), Mary J. 55 (NC NC NC), Josiah M. 24 (T NC NC), Martha E. 20 (T NC NC); SMITH, Sarah S. 28 (dau) (NC NC NC), Lafayett 5 (relationship omitted) (T T NC)
71. FORD, Millie C. 37 (widow) (NC NC NC), William 7 (T NC NC); HAMBY, Elizabeth 20 (niece) (T NC NC)
72. HAMBY, Allen 70 (NC NC NC), Mary A. 39 (wife) (NC NC NC); SIMS, Martha 12 (step dau) (NC NC NC), Francis 9 (step son) (NC NC NC), Emmer 3 (step dau) (NC NC NC); RADER, Rebecca 11 (step dau) (NC NC NC); THOMPSON, Rebecca 40 (dau) (epilepsy) (insane) (NC NC NC)
73. CLEMONS, Martha 65 (widow) (crippled) (T NC NC), Martha C. 39 (g dau), Cintha L. 21 (g dau) (T NC T), Levi 5 (gr g son), Mary Jane 2 (gr g dau); DUGGER, Mary A. 18 (g dau), Martha 20 (g dau)

Page 8, Dist. 1

74. MATHERSON, Wm. A. 50 (NC NC NC), Delcenee E. 49 (T NC T), Mary E. 20, Ellen F. I. 16, George W. 10, Celia A. A. M. 7, Edda M. D. 5
75. MATHERSON, John C. 34 (NC NC NC), Rhoda A. E. 30 (T NC T), Mary E. 10, Martha J. 8, Nola E. 6, Sarah E. 3, David V. 3 (twins)
76. SMITH, Jacob A. 65, Celia 60, Lawson E. L. 24, James C. 20
77. SMITH, Melissa C. 33 (divorced); WHITE, Boston C. 11 (son), John A. 8, Daniel L. 6
78. WHITE, John V. 31, Nancy J. 25, Martha E. 7, Leannah 5, David L. 2

Hh#	Page 8 (cont'd)

79. MESSIMERE, J. A. 40 (T NC NC), Nancy 44 (VA NC VA), Margarett J. 14 (NC), Celia E. 8 (T), Mary A. V. M. 5, William H. L. 3, Nancy V. 1, Jane 60 (Mid-wife) (NC PA NC)
80. McNEELY, Square 65 (NC NC NC), Nancy L. 40 (NC NC NC), Minerva E. 20 (NC), Ensor M. 19 (NC), Martha L. 17 (NC), John P. 15 (NC), Sarah J. 12 (NC), Square N. 9 (NC), Robert F. H. 7 (T), Lillie B. 3
81. GOODWIN, L. H. 44, Lorinda 45 (wife) (NC NC NC), Tobias 8, Robert C. 6, Chales 4

Page 9, Dist. 1

82. LEWIS, Lawson L. 46 (brown ketus) (T NC T), Sarah A. 37 (T T NC), Millard F. 19, Martha J. 15, George W. E. 9, Edna M. 7, Wilbern G. 4
83. LEWIS, Wm. M. 20, Nancy J. 22
84. LEWIS, Mary 72 (widow) (T T NC)
85. LEWIS, Mary J. 36 (F disease) (idiotic) (T T NC), Daniel R. 18 (son) (T __ T), James A. A. 5, Ida Alice 1/12
86. GOODWIN, R. E. (m) 41, Tempa E. 32 (T NC T), Lemuel L. 12, John A. 10, Robert L. 7, David E. 5, Nathaniel H. 2, Cora A. 1; WHITE, David W. 35 (boarder) (mechanic) (divorced)
87. WAGNER, N. C. 48 (widow)
88. DONNELLEY, M. E. 26 (dau--of 87?)
89. WAGNER, David A. 20 (son--of 87?), Susan B. 17 (wife)
90. WAGNER, Nancy N. 17 (sis--of 89?)
91. PLOT, Caroline 60 (widow) (NC NC NC), Margarett S. 30 (NC NC NC)
92. CROSSWHITE, J. H. 28 (T T NC), Nancy C. 27 (wife) (T NC T), William R. 5, Lucinda I. 4, Abraham G. 10/12; MESSIMERE, Jane 69 (relationship omitted) (NC PA NC)
93. LEWIS, Gieon? 65 (NC NC NC), Matilda J. 69
94. LEWIS, Thomas G. 22 (T NC T), Sarah A. 22 (NC NC NC)
95. HAZLEWOOD, Pleas (m) 27 (VA VA VA), Nancy Jane 26, Elizabeth 8, William 6, Robert 3, Alice 9/12; PAINE, Mary A. 16 (servant) (T __ NC); HICKS, Samuel 20 (NC NC NC)

Page 10, Dist. 1

96. VUNCANON, A. 47 (NC NC NC), Pollyann 48 (wife) (NC NC NC), William A. 21 (NC NC NC), Jaems G. 15 (NC NC NC), Mary M. 13 (NC NC NC), Alice 7 (NC NC NC), Anna A. 5 (T NC NC)
97. WAGNER, Jas. I. 24, Sarah M. 24 (NC NC NC), John M. 1
98. HATELEY, John F. 42 (NC NC NC), Mary M. 39, Mary Caroline 12, William W. 11, Sarah E. 8, Alexander C. 6, Sabia Ann 2
99. WHITE, Sabry 54 (widow), Martha 35, Thomas J. 22, Angeline L. 15, Juliann 8 (g dau)
100. WHITE, R. C. jr. 31, Josaphene 20 (wife) (NC T NC), Graville W. 2, Rosa J. 3/12 (b. Feb)
101. WHITE, Lawson 24, Eda C. 19
102. KINNICK, John 66 (NC MD NC), Mary 54
103. KINNICK, J. C. 23 (T NC T), Loretta 20, Riley 2, Minnie B. 9/12 (b. Sep)
104. COOK, Thomas H. 29, Sarah E. 32 (T NC T), Ida E. 4, Charles E. 1
105. CALAWAY, A. A. 24 (NC NC NC), Hannah 23 (T NC T), Maryann 4 (T NC T), Joseph L. 1 (T NC T)
106. FINNEY, Philip 56 (NC VA NC), Catharine 35 (wife) (NC NC NC), Alice 14, George W. 13, Jaries E. 10 (dau), Mary N. 8, Caldona 5, Alvin W. 3

Page 11, Dist. 1

107. LEWIS, James L. 24 (T NC T), Sarah Ellen 22 (T T NC), Nancy Ann 3, Mary A. 2, Luvina 5/12 (b. Dec)

CARTER COUNTY

Hh#	Page 11 (cont'd)

108. GRAGG, James 60 (NC NC NC), Logina 46 (wife) (NC NC NC), Buenavista N. 18 (NC), Logina L. 16 (NC), Saphrona C. 14 (T), Nelson 10, Margarett L. 8, Celia C. 3
109. HIKS, Mathias 47 (NC NC NC), Martha J. 28 (wife) (NC NC NC), Mary L. C. 9, William A. 8, James M. 7, Matilda E. 4, Mathias F. 3, Noah A. 1, Sarah Edna 24/30 (b. May)
110. GRAGG, N. E. J. 25 (f) (NC NC NC), Barbary D. 3 (dau) (T __ NC), Scott 3/12 (b. Feb) (T T NC)
111. LEWIS, Ann 42 (widow) (T NC T), George M. 19 (T NC T), Solomon E. E. 16 (T NC T), Arzilla C. 8 (T __ T); ANDERS, James 16 (servant) (NC NC NC); BUNTEN, E. J. 25 (servant) (f); CAMPBELL, W. H. 33 (m) (boarder)
112. ISAACS, Marion 29 (NC NC NC), Mildred C. 26 (T T NC), William A. 6, Maryann I. 5, Amanda M. 4, Joseph D. 3, Eliza Ellen 1
113. GRAGG, James C. 20 (NC NC NC), Mary F. 20 (NC NC NC), Elias W. 1; GREENWELL, F. E. 62 (mother in law) (NC NC NC)
114. PARDUE, Lurand 51 (widow) (T NC T), Sarah Jane 14 (T NC T), Rachel S. 11 (T NC T)
115. POTTER, Elihu B. 29, Naracissa 31, Eliza Ellen 6, Amariel O. M. 4 (dau), Emma J. 1; CAMPBELL, A. O. 13 (step dau), S. S. 11 (step dau), J. F. 9 (step son)

Page 12, Dist. 1

116. SHEETS, Young 51 (NC NC NC), Margarett 47 (NC NC NC), Mary E. 27 (NC), Sarah J. 16 (NC), Joseph D. 15 (NC), Abraham L. 14 (T), Rachel A. 10, John 7, Wiley 9/12 (b. Aug), Eliza 7/12 (b. Oct) (g dau) (T T NC)
117. SHEETS, George 24 (NC NC NC), Mary 16 (wife) (NC NC NC), James W. 3/30 (b. May)
118. PARDEW, Genetta 56 (widow) (NC NC NC), Malinda 17 (T NC NC)
119. CABLE, Cornelius 45 (divorced)
120. SHUFFIELD, W. S. 26 (T T NC), Clacey? J. 25 (wife) (NC NC IN), James E. 3
121. PARDIEW, Cilas 67 (NC NC NC), Melvina 35 (wife), James E. 10 (T T T), Mary A. 8 (T NC T), Sarah Jane 4 (T NC T), Rosabell 3/12 (b. Aug) (T NC T)
122. SHUFFIELD, John C. 45 (T NC NC), Nancy Jane 42 (NC NC NC), John H. 16, Willard 13, Mary E. 10, Robert H. 8, Alice Ann 5, Oscar 2
123. SHUFFIELD, Wm. E. 40 (T T NC), Clara L. 36, Elender F. 17, James W. S. 12, Amanda V. 9, Lawrance L. B. 6 (dau)
124. SHUFFIELD, A. X. 24, Mary L. 22 (wife) (T NC T), Celie D. 3, Oshmon P. 2
125. SHUFFIELD, George 76 (T __ T), Elizabeth 66 (NC NC NC)

Page 13, Dist. 1

126. BLACK, John J. 59 (NC NC NC), Elendar 53 (NC NC NC), Caroline 28 (NC), Jessee 22 (NC), Robert 20 (NC), John L. 18 (NC), Thomas M. 12 (T), Ellen 3 (g dau) (T NC NC)
127. CAMPBELL, J. R. 30, Sarah L. 23 (NC NC NC), William M. 7
128. EGGERS, Alexander 46 (NC NC NC), Sarah Jane 44 (NC NC NC), Martha A. 20 (NC), Sarah M. 16 (NC), Emla V. 13 (T), James M. 11; SIREY, George 11 (servant) (NC NC NC)
129. HATELEY, W. S. 33 (NC NC NC), Catharine 30 (wife) (NC NC NC), Julia Ann 13, Martha C. 9, William D. 6, Sarah M. 3, Luzena 1; SMITH, Elbert 35 (boarder) (NC NC NC)
130. GREEN, David C. 33 (NC NC NC), Eliza Jane 35, James N. 10, Julia 10, Mary E. 8, Dolly 5, Sarah M. 2, Allissa A. 10/12

Hh#	Page 13 (cont'd)

131. WHITEHEAD, Marth J. 42 (widow), Elijah 21, Sarah Jane 19, Thomas J. 10, Ar J. 7, Amanda V. E. 1, C. 80 (mother law); BICE, Tennesse C. 18 (niece)
132. LUTHER, Jordan 55 (miller) (NC NC NC), Hannah 44 (NC NC NC), Cornelia 16 (Thomas W. 14 (NC), Jeramiah G. 11 (, Oreann A. 5 (NC), Charlie Alex 1 (T

Page 14, Dist. 1

133. EGGERS, Lillie A. 40 (widow) (NC NC NC), Patterson Y. 15 (NC NC NC), Esley R. (son) (T)
134. CROSSWHITE, S. A. S. 23 (T T NC), Cathatarine (sic) S. 19 (T T NC), John W. 9/12 (b. Mar)
135. PRESSNEL, Anna 53 (widow) (NC NC NC), El L. 10 (T T NC)
136. CROSSWHITE, M. E. 57 (divorced)(f) (NC NC NC)
137. GREEN, Joseph W. 34 (NC NC NC), Racheal 4 (wife), Sarah M. 13, Nora C. 10, Jame I. 8, Thomas C. 6, Minnie R. 3, Nancy 1
138. GILBERT, Edmond 25 (NC NC IN), Malissa J. 19, Dora Bell 1; SMITH, Eliza J. 52 (mother in law) (raising poltry) (T T NC)
139. DUGGER, John F. 50 (T T NC), Sarah 48, Rol ert L. 18, Nancy C. 9; GAUNT, Sarah J. 14 (niece) (T SC T)
140. DUGGER, James W. 27, Hannah R. 25 (T NC T) Enoch E. 3, John A. 2, Ulissus G. 3/12 (b. Feb)
141. BLACK, Jacob 27 (NC NC NC), Mary E. 26 (NC NC NC), Una Leona 2 (NC NC NC), Martha L. L. 1 (T)
142. VUNCANON, Nancy 73 (widow) (NC Ire Ire)
143. VUNCANON, A. B. 46 (son--of 142?) (house carpenter) (NC NC NC), Margarett 38 (wife) (PA PA PA)
144. VUNCANON, J. L. 25 (NC NC NC), Catharine C. 25 (wife) (T NC T), Victory 3 (dau) (T NC T), Alvin D. 10/12 (b. Jul)
145. POTTER, Ezel A. 30, Delila F. 27 (T NC T), Mary J. 8 (NC), John W. 6 (T), Solomon 4, Sarah E. 2, Tempa C. 6/12 (b. Dec)
146. WILLIAMS, A. M. 24, Jula Q. 18 (wife?) (NC NC NC)

Page 15, Dist. 1

147. STOUT, John R. 59, Elizabeth 45, David W. 24, Araminta 20, Cathalene V. 17, George T. 12
148. CABLE, John J. 23, Sarah E. 22 (NC NC NC), Nancy C. 4, William 3, Alvin G. 8/12, Mary 62 (mother) (T NC NC), Gilliland B. 14 (nephew); POTTER, Martha 16 (servant)
149. KINNICK, H. H. 44 (T NC T)
150. POTTER, Peter H. 50, Sarah 40, Sarah Fina 15, Louisa I. 13, Godfrey D. 10, John R. 8, Elizabeth 6, Mary S. 10/12 (b. Jul)
151. HEATON, G. W. 52, Elizabeth A. 43, Lurana 18, Joseph 16, Granville 13, Catharine 12, Evaline 10, Luthena 7, Rachel 3, Daniel 25 (divorced)
152. STOUT, James R. 33, Sarah Jane 39, Emma C. 11, Amarader 10 (dau), William M. 8, John Alex 5, Mary A. 2, Rhinaann E. 1/30 (b. Jul)
153. BASH, Susan 50 (NC NC NC); HARTLEY, Cal 26 (son) (NC NC NC), Elvira 19 (dau) (NC NC NC), Jas. 2 (nepew) (T T NC)
154. HARTLEY, Albert 24 (NC NC NC), Mary E. 21 (sis) (NC NC NC), Lorusy 2 (nephew)
155. MORGAN, John 20, Martha E. 24, Della Jane 4/12 (b. Jan) (relationship omitted) (T NC T)

3

Hh#	Page 16, Dist. 1

156. MORGAN, W. C. & Son 52 (NC NC NC), Velissa 42, Eliza Jane 18 (NC NC T), Mary C. 15 (NC), Nancy E. 13 (NC), William L. 9 (T), John F. 6 (g son) (T T NC)
157. GUINN, A. J. 21 (NC NC T), Lutitia 18 (T NC NC)
158. HATELEY, William 72 (NC __ NC), Anna 66 (NC NC NC), Sarah E. 26 (NC)
159. HATELEY, Wm. C. 19 (NC NC NC), Clemma A. 18, Mary E. 1
160. POTTER, Johnson 74, Martha B. 39 (wife), Daniel 11 (son), Clara 49 (dau) (T T __)
161. POTTER, Mary A. 49, William S. 14 (son)
162. STOUT, Logan 21, Martha S. 21
163. MEGINNIS, Newton 38 (NC NC NC), Maryann 25 (wife), James W. 5, George L. 2
164. POTTER, John M. 54, Louisa J. 50; PERKINS, J. L. 6 (g son)
165. CLAWSON, R. E. 67 (VA VA VA), Elizabeth 40 (wife) (NC NC NC); DUGGER, Caroline 13 (step dau) (T T NC)
166. STOUT, John L. 19 (NC T T), Evaline 15 (NC NC NC), Blakely A. 1/12 (b. Apr) (son)
167. BAIRD, Benj. 22 (NC NC NC), Cordelia A. 22
168. CLAWSON, James L. 20, Edna Jane 18, Sarah M. 2/12 (b. Mar)
169. HARMON, A. J. 42 (NC NC NC), Susan 42 (NC NC NC), Rebecca L. 9, Mary C. 7
170. MORCANGAS, D. 25 (T nC T), Hettyann R. 29, John Taylor 11, William R. 5, Robert L. 9/12 (b. Aug)

	Page 17, Dist. 1

171. HICKS, David 67 (NC NC NC), Emla 44 (wife), William R. 15 (NC), Emanuel R. 11 (T), John P. 7, Nancy A. 4
172. FINES, Thomas 20, Elizabeth 15 (NC NC NC)
173. CLAWSON, Wm. A. 24, Charlotta 29 (NC NC NC), Sarah E. 3, James T. 1
174. CLAWSON, J. L. sr. 46 (blacksmithing) (T VA T), Sarah E. 47, Lillie J. 14, John 10
175. HICKS, M. A. R. 18 (f), George W. 1 (son) (T NC T)
176. DUGGER, Charlotte 35 (widow), William L. 12, Mary E. 6, John M. 4 (T NC T), Nathaniel 4/30 (b. May) (T NC T)
177. POTTER, Noah J. 40, Sarah A. 32 (NC NC NC), Martha L. 17, William H. 12, Mary Jane 10, Rebeca C. 8, Cordelia A. 5, Carie N. 2 (son)
178. POTTER, Peter 81 (T __ __), Lourany 43 (wife), Alice R. 7, David E. 4, Daniel S. 2
179. CHESTER, C. E. 43 (NC NC NC), Mary E. 27 (wife)
180. LUNSFORD, A. (f) 20 (servant of #179) (NC NC NC), Joseph 3/12 (b. Feb) (VA NC NC)
181. LUNSFORD, Enoch 62 (NC NC NC), Temperance 66, William H. 31, Hannah 79 (mother) (NC NC NC); PILKINTON, C. (f) 23 (servant) (NC NC NC)
182. GOODWIN, J. M. 33, Nancy Caroline 34 (wife) (T NC T), Hannah E. 11, Temperance C. 9, Julia M. 8, Solomon L. 2, Martitia V. 11/12 (b. Jun)

	Page 18, Dist. 1

183. PILKINTON, Letha 50 (widow) (NC NC NC), Polly 18 (NC NC NC), Esther M. 16 (NC), Rutha 11 (T)
184. WILSON, James F. 20, Hannah C. 22 (NC NC NC); PILKINTON, Enoch 26 (boarder) (NC NC NC)
185. SHEPPHARD, L. J. 30 (NC NC NC), Margarett 27 (wife) (NC NC NC), Luvena A. 9 (NC), Amanda J. 8 (NC), Thomas W. 6 (NC), Mary M. 4 (NC), Cora Ellen 2 (NC)
186. CABLE, Richard 39, Melinda 24, Sarah J. 4, Stephen 2
187. CABLE, Noah 33, Esher M. 21 (wife) (T NC T), Mary E. 5, William L. 3, Sarahann 1

Hh#	Page 18 (cont'd)

189. GOODWIN, A. L. 64 (T T NC), Malinda 55, Alfred S. 21, Celiaann B. 19, Martha R. S. 12
190. LUNSFORD, Mary F. 22 (widow), Temperance M. 6
191. GOODWIN, S. H. 24, Martha T. 20 (wife) (T NC NC)
192. GOODWIN, T. M. 31, Elizabeth A. 31 (wife) (T T NC), Malinda M. 10, Martha C. 8, William A. 4
193. CARNUTT, John 47 (NC NC NC), Genetta 44 (NC NC NC), William M. 20 (NC), Marttia 18 (NC), Jacob 13 (NC), Calista 10 (NC), James A. 9 (NC), Harison 7 (NC), Elizabeth 5 (NC), Asa 3 (NC), Cora Alice 1 (T)

	Page 19, Dist. 1

194. WAGNER, Andrew J. 29, Sarah J. 19, Granville A. 2
195. BUNTEN, J. W. 22, Delphina 21 (NC NC NC)
196. BUNTEN, J. D. 31, Emla Saphrona 31, James R. 8, Noah T. 6, Jacob 5, Henry S. 3, William C. 1
197. CORDELL, A. D. 35 (NC NC NC), Mary H. 39 (NC NC NC), Lillie F. 10 (NC), Malona E. 7 (NC), Etta L. A. 5 (NC), James R. 3 (NC), Charles H. 10/12 (b. Aug) (T)
198. KITE, Malden 60, Tempa 65, Tula Bell 4 (step dau) (T T NC)
199. POTTER, Carie N. 34, Ellen 22 (wife) (NC NC T), Nancy Jane 12, Matilda 5, Joseph 1 (NC T NC), Thomas Alex 1/30 (b. May) (T T NC), Matilda 56 (mother) (T NC T)
200. SMITH, E. J. 34 (T NC NC), John T. 12 (son) (T T NC), William A. 11, William A. 11, Columbus B. 7, Nancy J. A. 5
201. HAMBY, Allen 56 (NC NC NC), Nancy 53 (NC NC NC), Martha J. 31, Lawson 19, Mollie 16, Matilda J. 14, Amarader 10 (dau)
202. HAMBY, Landen C. 21 (T NC NC), Nancy C. 21 (NC NC NC)
203. CAMPBELL, Jeramiah 27 (T T NC), Mary C. 24 (T NC NC), Nancy Jane 4, William L. 2, James 22/30 (b. May)

	Page 20, Dist. 1

204. CHEEKS, David 39 (NC NC NC), Nancy C. 46 (wife) (T NC NC), Susan 12, Edna C. 8
205. PERKINS, Geo. W. 24 (stepson of 204), Mary E. 21 (step dau of 204) (consumption), Florance E. 17 (step dau of 204)
206. JONES, Ambrose C. 44 (NC NC T), Celia D. 38 (T T NC)
207. CLARK, Mary 30 (divorced) (NC NC NC), David H. 9 (T T NC), Daniel W. 8, Noah A. 6, Hannah 1, Michel Leander 20 (son) (NC NC NC)
208. BANNER, H. B. 39 (NC NC NC), Ortha M. 40 (wife) (NC NC NC), Teleann 12 (dau) (NC), Emanuel L. 10 (NC), Laureann 8 (T), John H. 5, Lemuel L. 3, Daniel J. 1
209. LUNSFORD, J. E. 36 (T NC T), Clementine M. 31 (wife), Sarah J. 13, Hannah C. 11, William C. 7, Mary E. 4, Celia Ann 1
210. LUNSFORD, J. F. 38 (T NC T), Luvena C. 29 (wife), James Thomas 12, Catharine M. 10, Sarah S. 6, William H. 3, Robert C. 1
211. LUNSFORD, S. A. 26 (T NC T), Mary E. 22 (wife), Minnie A. 3, Andrew D. 2
212. MONTGUMERY, S. W. 48 (T NC NC), Mary J. 47 (wife), James H. 20, William C. 18, Martha 16, Henry S. 14, Eliza E. 12, Daniel E. 10
213. STOUT, Granville W. 60, Martha C. 47 (wife), Mary A. 20, Daniel 12, Emma J. 10, Marthe J. 2; IRICK, George W. 21 (servant) (note: George Irick was listed first in this household, but this was apparently a mistake in arrangement)

Hh#   Page 21, Dist. 1

214. POTTER, Daniel 73 (T NC VA), Margarett I. 32; IRICK, John 15 (stepson), Alice 12 (stepdau); POTTER, Andrew J. 6 (son), Elarader 1 (dau)
215. GROGAN, Isaac 53 (SC NC SC), Sarah Jane 31 (wife), Adline 12, David W. 5, Sarah Ann E. 1
216. KIRKPATRICK, J. T. 27 (NC NC T), Hannah E. A. 26 (wife), Everet E. T. 4, Estalene E. 10 (stepdau), Nancy L. A. A. 7 (step dau)
217. HAMBY, Thomas 50 (NC NC NC), Elizabeth J. 65 (wife), Arzilla 19; KELLER, James 6 (took to rase) (T __ NC)
218. HAMBY, D. M. 23 (T NC T), Fanny E. 52
219. PETERS, Rheubin 52, Nancy E. 52, Anna 11, Alfred 9
220. GUINN, Elizabeth 24 (NC NC NC), William J. 5 (son) (T T NC), Charles A. 1 (son) (T T NC), James M. 3/12 (b. Feb) (son) (T T NC)
152. GILLILAND, N. J. 18 (neace) (an addition by enumerator to previous household)
17. CAMPBELL, Wilbern 28 (son) (T T NC) (an addition by enumerator to a previous household)
81. GOODWIN, W. W. 13 (son) (T T NC), Leonades H. 11 (son) (T T NC)
221. PETERS, Thomas W. 56 (fever), Nancy 45, Margarett 20, Evaline 19, Robert M. 16, Eliza A. 13, Wm. A. 12, Zachariah 9, Bej. H. 2 (m)

Page 1, Dist. 2

1. JONES, James H. 44 (T NC T), Nancy 40 (T NC T), John B. 20, Arabella 18, Robert 14, David 10, Hamilton 8
2. DOBY, Isham 72 (NC NC NC), Nancy E. 67 (T NC NC); BORDERS, S. H. (m) 17 (ward) (T NC NC), Clara C. 16 (ward) (T NC NC); BROYHILL?, Lec 13 (ward) (NC NC NC), Daniel 28 (ward) (NC NC NC)
3. KITE, Russel 34 (NC NC NC), Sarah A. 48 (wife) (T NC NC); STOUT, Jefferson 7 (ward) (T NC T)
4. FIELDS, Wm. H. 25 (crippled) (T KY T), Nancy 26 (NC NC NC), Jordan 4 (T NC NC), Asbury 2 (T NC NC), Miles F. 9/12 (b. Oct) (T NC NC)
5. HARRISON, Henry 56 (VA VA VA), Frances 32 (wife) (VA VA VA), Ena 24 (dau) (VA VA VA), Solomon 15 (son) (VA VA VA), James 12 (OH VA VA), George 10 (VA VA VA), Mary 8 (T VA VA), Lourana 4 (T VA VA), Samuel 2/12 (b. Apr) (T VA VA), Alice 2/12 (b. Apr) (T VA VA)
6. ORR, James W. 48 (T NC T), Celia J. 28 (wife) (T T NC), Seraphina 19, William B. 18, Henrietta 2
7. RAMSOMS, John (B) 32 (NC NC NC), Rebecca (Mu) 30 (NC NC NC), Emma 9 (T T NC)
8. HARDY, Sewell (Mu) 29 (NC NC NC), Peggy 50 (mother) (NC NC NC), George 27 (bro) (NC NC NC)
9. BANNAN, Frank 45 (teacher) (NC NC NC), Camnur 37 (wife)
10. VANCE, Abner 60 (T VA T), Alexander 18 (son), Zeb 13, Jane 12, Drant 9, Thomas 6, Henry 4, Mary 3

Page 2, Dist. 2

11. SMITH, Nicholas 69, Sarah 69 (KY T PA)
12. RICHISON, Jos. H. 34 (T NC T), Charlotte 25 (T NC T), Marietta 10, Eliza J. 8, Deborah 6, Hillsbury 4, Mollie 2, Joseph 1/12 (b. Apr)
13. BUCK, George W. 39 (T T NC), Susan 33, Andrew A. 13, John E. 10, Vina A. 8, George C. 3; YOUNG, Rachel 20 (servant) (NC NC NC); HOUSTON, S. E. 18 (f) (boarder--seamstress) (NC NC NC), Mimie 3 (boarder)
14. CALLAWAY, John 42 (NC NC NC), Nancy E. 36 (IN NC IN), Emma 12 (IN NC IN), George 10 (T), Joshua 4, Amos 2, Callie J. 1/12 (b. Apr) (dau)

Hh#   Page 2 (cont'd)

15. KEATON, Peter 18 (VA VA VA), Barbara 20 (VA VA VA)
16. OAKS, Daniel 67 (widower) (T T NC), Lorina 26 (dau) (T T NC)
17. CALLAWAY, William 36, Martha 28, Mary E. 15, William D. 12, Lourana 10, Finly 7, Asbury 6, Althea 5, Cinthia 2
18. BARNETT, Spencer 53 (NC NC NC), Mary 51 (NC NC NC), David 18 (NC), Myra 16 (NC), Caroline 14 (NC), Mitchell 12 (NC), Dosser 9 (son) (NC), Anderson 6 (T)
19. COOPER, David 37 (NC NC NC), Eliza 32 (NC NC NC), Charles 12 (NC), Spencer 9 (NC), William 7 (NC), Caroline 6 (NC), John 4 (T), George 2, David R. 1

Page 3, Dist. 2

20. HAMPTON, Lauson 28 (T T NC), Josephine 24, William H. 1
21. SMITH, George W. 43 (T T PA), Jane 42 (T T NC), Celia 19, James 16, Washington 15, Hannah 13, Taylor 12, Matilda 10, Phina 8, Winsy A. 6 (dau), Delia 4, Lucy 10/12 (b. Aug)
22. HODGE, Sammy 30 (T NC NC), Martha 25 (NC NC NC), Enna J. 6, Thomas 5
23. PERRY, Albert W. 53 (T KY NC), Mary 43 (NC NC NC), Milly E. 21 (NC NC NC), Martha C. 19 (NC NC NC), Dicey L. 14 (NC NC NC), Edmond F. 13 (NC NC NC), Nancy 10 (NC NC NC), Elizabeth 8 (T NC NC), Lusiter 5 (dau) (T NC NC), Albert 3 (T NC NC), Laura D. 4/12 (b. Feb) (T NC NC)
24. BOWLING, Henry 23, Sarah 22, Alice 2/12 (b. Mar)
25. HISE, Jacob 49 (NC NC NC), Sarah 31 (NC NC NC), Laura 7, Elisha D. 5, Rebecca J. 3, Abner 6/12 (b. Dec)
26. MILLER, John S. 50 (NC NC NC), Elizabeth 49 (T NC NC), Johnson 14, George 12, Elbert 8, Nathaniel 6

Page 4, Dist. 2

27. SHELL, John A. 58 (T NC T), Eliza 28 (wife) (NC T T), Elizabeth 8, Laura E. 4, Mimie J. 2
28. RAY, Hamilton 54 (NC NC NC), Jane E. 52 (NC NC NC), James 23, Henry 21, Sidney A. 15 (dau)
29. GREER, James A. 29 (T NC NC), Elizabeth 31 (NC NC NC), William A. 10, Lucinda 8, Mary J. 6, James F. 4, Martha 2, Josephine 1; MILLER, Rebecca 22 (servant) (NC ____)
30. SNYDER, Solomon 32, Eliza J. E. 25, Rebecca A. 8, Isaac N. 5, Dora 3, Carrick? 10/12 (b. Jul) (son)
31. SHELL, Finly 50 (T NC NC), Rebecca 36 (wife) (T __ NC), Margaret 72 (mother) (NC NC NC), John A. 8, Laura 5, Nathaniel 3, Finley 1
32. CAMPBELL, Jerry 27, Mary C. 24, Nancy J. 5, William L. 3, Fletcher 1/12 (b. Apr)
33. HAMBY, Landon 21, Nancy C. 21, Mary J. 3, Nolon A. 1 (son)
34. BANNER, Jos. L. 28 (NC NC NC), Ann C. 31, Mary C. 2; HYDER, Josephine 13 (boarder)
35. RANKIN, Mary M. 54 (widow) (NC NC NC), Rosamond 27 (VA NC VA), Jennie 15 (VA NC VA), Martin 25 (VA NC VA), Houston 13 (VA NC VA)

Page 5, Dist. 2

36. SMITH, Henderson 33, Martha 38 (fever) (NC NC NC), William B. 14, Nancy L. 12, Elijah 10, Ellen C. 6, John H. 4, Albert T. 2, Lucretia 9/12 (b. Sep)
37. STREET, Simon 24 (NC NC NC), Celia A. 25 (NC NC NC), Annie 6 (NC), Spencer 4 (NC), Mollie 3 (NC), Simon T. 1 (NC), Joseph 8/12 (b. Aug) (T)

Hh#	Page 5 (cont'd)

38. JULIAN, Wm. M. 42, Myra 35 (NC NC NC),
    Chas. M. 11 (NC), Polly 10 (T), Jane
    8, Lorena 6, Johnson 4, James 2,
    Hacker 1
39. WEBB, William (B) 56 (cooper) (NC NC NC),
    Martha 45 (NC NC NC), Palmon 17 (son)
    (NC), Marshall 15 (NC), Robert 13 (NC),
    Darby 11 (NC), Grant 9 (NC), Sherman
    7 (NC), Louis 5 (NC), Amy 3 (NC)
40. HAMPTON, Francis 49, Sarah C. 50 (NC NC NC),
    Elijah 21?, William 17, Louisa C. 14;
    ELDON, Joseph (Mu) 32 (boarder) (black-
    smith) (NC NC NC)
41. BUCK, Andrew 66 (T PA T), Rebecca 56 (NC NC
    NC), David E. 16 (g son); LINEBACK, Wm.
    H. 19 (boarder--clerk in store);
    AUSTIN, Sarah 16 (servant) (NC NC NC)

Page 6, Dist. 2

42. SMITH, Carter 27, Sarah 33 (NC NC NC), Susan
    6, John C. 4, Ellen 2, Nicolas 1
43. THOMAS, Strawberry 50 (NC NC NC), Bradena
    40 (NC NC NC); WHITEHEAD, Charles 21
    (step son) (T T NC), Nancy (step dau)
    (T T NC); THOMAS, Wm. R. 17 (son),
    James E. 14, Joseph W. 11, Lucinda 9,
    Radford 8, Julia 6, Elbert 4, Alice M.
    2
44. SHELL, John L. 32 (T NC NC), Buenna V. 25
    (wife) (NC NC NC), William D. 7, James
    L. 4, Mary E. 3, Ida Bell 10/12 (b.
    Aug)
45. BOON, Jno. F. 32 (NC NC NC), Eliza 32, Cora
    14, James 12 (VA), Ira P. 10 (VA),
    Alfonso 8 (VA), Julian 6 (T), Lydia 12
46. BOON, Nathaniel 26 (NC NC NC), Louisa 15
    (wife) (KY VA VA), James A. 1 (KY)
47. BLEVINS, Nathan 45 (NC NC NC), Celia 45
    (NC NC NC), Fleming 16 (NC), Biddy 14
    (NC), Nelson 11 (NC), Axie 8 (dau)
    (NC), Walter? 4 (NC), Robert L. 2 (T)
48. HUGHES, Louis 33 (NC NC NC), Maggie 28 (NC
    NC NC), George W. 6 (NC), Elizabeth 4
    (NC), Fannie 2 (T)
49. HUGHES, Charles 60 (NC NC NC), Elizabeth 58
    (NC NC NC), Mary 18 (NC) (deaf & dumb);
    BURCHFIELD, Lydia 16 (dau) (NC);
    BARNETT, Eliza 14 (dau) (NC)

Page 7, Dist. 2

50. BUTLER, Henry 40 (NC NC NC), Caroline 35 (NC
    NC NC), Johnson 10, Kate 8, Carrie 6,
    Richard 3
51. AMOND?, William 30 (NC NC NC), Celia 26 (NC
    NC NC), Elizabeth 10, John 8, Ellen 6,
    James 4, Henry 2
52. WINTERS, Stephen 52 (NC NC NC), Caroline 55
    (NC NC NC), Benjamin 16 (NC), Caroline
    14 (NC), Martin 10 (NC), Elizabeth 6
    (NC)
53. POWELL, Joseph 32 (T T NC), Nancy 26, John
    H. 10, William H. 8, James E. 6, Ellen
    4
54. WINTERS, James A. 25 (NC NC NC), Elizabeth
    17 (T NC NC), John W. 3 (son), Eliza-
    beth 1
55. JOHNSON, Albert M. 44 (T NC NC), Mary A.
    28 (wife) (T NC T), Lorena 11, Marietta
    8, Emma 6, Ada B. 3, Oscar 1
56. BANNER, Wm. O. 33 (NC NC NC), Mintora J. 30
    (wife) (NC NC NC), Carrie 9 (NC),
    Richard S. 4 (T), Oscar F. 2; WEBB,
    Sarah (B) 18 (servant) (NC NC NC)
57. WINTERS, Martin 53 (NC NC NC), Nancy 53 (NC
    NC NC), Lydia 25, Monroe 19, Louisa 16,
    Joel 13, Alfred C. 7 (g son) (T T NC),
    HAYES, Martin W. 1 (g son) (T T NC)

Page 8, Dist. 2

58. McLEAN, Newton 23 (NC NC NC), Mary 21,
    Thomas 3 (son) (T T NC), Marietta 1
    (dau) (T T NC)

Hh#	Page 8 (cont'd)

59. CORDELL?, Russel 44 (NC NC NC), Mary C. 37
    (NC NC NC), Thomas P. 18 (NC), Benjamin
    15 (NC), Nola 13 (NC), Adolphus 11 (T),
    Nathaniel 9, Lilly 4; WILCOX, Canick
    26 (boarder--physician)
60. WILSON, W. D. 39 (T NC NC), Matilda 43, John
    8, William F. 7, Robert T. 3, Jackson 1;
    BADGETT, Catharine 22 (step dau),
    no name 1/12 (b. Apr) (g dau);
    TRIBBETT, Nicey 39 (boarder) (NC NC NC)
61. BADGETT, Elijah 24, Caroline 35 (wife),
    William 4, Mary C. 1
62. SHELL, Alfred C. 50, Rebecca 53 (NC NC NC),
    FRANKLIN, Nancy 31 (boarder) (NC NC NC)
63. TURBYFIELD, Jas. P. 49 (NC NC NC), Lavinia 45
    (NC NC NC), Mary C. 21 (NC), Cordelia 18
    (NC), Wesley 16 (NC), Jane 14 (NC),
    Joseph 12 (NC), James 10 (NC), Lavinia 8
    (NC)
64. OAKS, William A. 27 (NC NC NC), Rebecca 30,
    Abraham 8, Jackson 6, George W. 4,
    James 2
65. TURBYFIELD, John W. 19 (NC NC NC), Mary E.
    17 (NC NC NC), George 1

Page 9, Dist. 2

66. LAWS, George W. 29 (NC NC NC), Callie 21 (NC
    NC NC), John J. 2, Pauletta 4/12 (b.
    Feb)
67. LAWS, John 35 (NC NC NC), Amanda 25 (NC NC
    NC), Sallie 7 (NC NC NC), William D. 5
    (NC NC NC), Myla 3 (T NC NC), Henry
    9/12 (b. Aug) (T NC NC)
68. LAWS, James 23 (NC NC NC), Martitia 18 (NC
    NC NC), William 3, Susan 1
69. SIZEMORE, George 36 (T SC T), Rhoda 36,
    Hiram F. 14, Rebecca 10 (NC), John H. 7
    (NC), Margaret 5 (NC), Daniel 3 (T),
    Julia 1
70. LAWS, Joel 53 (NC NC NC), Myla 50 (NC NC NC),
    Nancy 14 (NC), Rebecca 12 (NC), Julia 9
    (NC), Samuel 6 (T), Cordelia 5
71. FOX, Susanna 66 (widow), Chaney 24 (dau),
    Tabitha 19, Emma 14 (g dau), Lutitia 8
    (g dau)
72. LAWS, Marion 18 (NC NC NC), Sophronia 21
    (NC NC NC), Maggie 3 (T), Joel E. 1
73. OAKS, David 51 (NC NC NC), Elizabeth 44 (T
    NC T), Eudora 22 (T T NC), Julia 16 (T
    NC T), Julius 14, David 10, John L. 8,
    Margaret 6; JUSTICE, Louisa 18 (boarder)
    (NC NC NC)
74. BASS, James C. 48 (SC SC SC), Dorothy L. 32
    (NC NC NC), William H. 14 (NC SC NC),
    James S. 12 (NC), Charlotte 10 (NC),
    Asbury F. 8 (T), Mary E. 6, Samuel G. 2;
    WORKMAN, Martha 18 (ward) (NC NC NC);
    MORGAN, Adeline 30 (ward) (NC NC NC)

Page 10, Dist. 2

75. ELLIS, David W. 40 (T NC NC), Adaline 43 (NC
    NC NC), James 18 (NC), Mary 17 (NC),
    John 15 (T), Martha 13, William C. 11,
    Thomas 9, George 8, Elizabeth 6, Joseph
    2
76. SHELL, James 22, Mary J. 22 (NC NC NC), Himy
    H. 1 (son), Finly G. 1, Chana 3/12 (b.
    Jan) (dau)
77. MILLER, David H. 28 (T T NC), Louisa 31,
    Jacob A. 8, Nathaniel 5, Isaac 3;
    GLOVER, William 15 (stepson)
78. HENDRICKSON, E. D. 37 (VA VA VA), India V.
    38 (VA VA VA), Austin C. 15 (VA),
    George A. 13 (VA), Mary S. 6 (T),
    Carrick W. 3, Nellie 1
79. JOHNSON, Alfred 69 (NC NC NC), Sallie 65 (NC
    NC NC), Thomas L. 21, Stephen H. 20,
    George W. 20
80. STOUT, Lourana 40 (widow) (NC NC NC);
    POTTER, Daniel 31 (overseer); GRIFFIN,
    James (B) 30 (servant), Sallie 26
    (servant)

Hh# Page 10 (cont'd)

81. JOHNSON, James W. 29 (T NC NC), Elizabeth 26 (T NC NC), William 5, Jacob 3, Mary 1, Mimie 4/12 (b. Feb); AVRENTS?, Martha 18 (boarder)

Page 11, Dist. 2

82. HEATON, Elkana 38, Elizabeth 26, Robert T. 2, not named 1/12 (b. May) (dau)
83. ARNETT, John 56 (NC NC NC), Mary A. 48 (NC NC NC), Hiram 18 (NC), Eliza A. 14 (NC), Martha J. 11 (T), Elbert W. 9, Hannah 6; HEATON, E. W. jr. 16 (boarder); MULER, Isabell 23 (boarder) (NC NC NC)
84. ISEHOUR, Sol 45 (NC NC NC), Amanda 45 (NC NC NC), Rachel 16 (NC NC NC), John 14 (NC NC NC), Finly 10 (T), Amanda 8, George 6; MILLER, Rachel 18 (dau) (widow) (NC NC NC), Dora 1 (g dau) (T NC NC)
85. TAYLOR, Robert 24 (NC NC NC), Mary J. 42 (wife) (T NC NC), Henry 6, Milly 3; HICKS, Louvella 7 (step dau), Mira B. 11/12 (step dau); TAYLOR, Joseph 4 (ward)
86. WEBB, John C. 27 (NC NC NC), Sallie J. 28, Rebecca 8, Sallie 6, Elbert G. 4, Fannie 3/12 (b. Feb)
87. McLEOD, Tillman 30 (NC NC NC), Martha 23 (NC NC NC), William 8 (NC), Josephine 6 (NC), John L. 4 (T)
88. VANCE, Andrew 25 (NC NC NC), Julia 23 (NC NC NC), Mary 5 (NC), Bell 3 (T), Andrew 1, John G. 16 (nephew) (NC NC NC)

Page 12, Dist. 2

89. PRITCHARD, Jerry 27 (NC NC NC), Esther 19 (wife) (NC NC NC), Mary 6 (dau) (NC), Sarah 4 (NC), Josie 1 (T)
90. JULIAN, Henry 32, Margaret 37 (NC NC NC), Lila E. 12 (NC), Mary A. 10 (NC), Amanda 8 (T), John S. 6, Viney C. 4, James M. 1; HUGHES, Mitchell 20 (nephew) (NC NC T)
91. GRAGG, Abner 25 (NC NC NC), Narcissa 27, Lucy 5, William H. 3, Elbert D. 1
92. HICKS, Nancy 49 (widow), Martha 24, Roslin O. 4 (g son), Caruck 1 (g son)
93. SHELL, Nathan 29, Sarah 42 (wife), John L. 6, Elijah F. 4, Nathaniel L. 2
94. MILLER, Francis 38 (NC NC NC), Hannah 47 (wife), George 12, Jacob F. 10, Mary A. 8, Lucy 6
95. PRITCHARD, Nathan 25, Lucinda 21, Monroe 1
96. PRITCHARD, Thre. 25, Alice E. 20, Mary O. 2, lda B. 8/12
97. HEATON, Johnson 45, Mary A. 35, Isaac 19, David 17, Sarah J. 5, Mollie 3, Henry 6/12 (b. Dec)
98. ARNETT, Thomas 21 (NC NC NC), Mary J. 16 (NC NC NC)

Page 13, Dist. 2

99. FREEMAN, Joseph 45 (NC SC NC), Sarah 36, Johnson 15, James 13, Mary E. 12, Walter H. 8, Samuel 6, Rebecca 4, William 2
100. JUSTICE, Frank 36 (NC NC NC), Celia 38 (NC NC NC), James 9 (NC), Julia 5 (NC), Lottie 1 (NC)
101. SIMULY?, William 28, Emeline 22, William 8 (son), Phoebe 6, Daniel 4, Carrick 1 (son)
102. MILLER, Jacob 27, Sarah 21, Samuel 1
103. GRAGG, James W. 28 (NC NC NC), Nancy 26 (NC NC NC), Deborah 7, James A. 6, Sarah 4, Maloney A. 3 (dau), John A. 6/12 (b. Dec)
104. TWIGG, Daniel 23 (NC NC NC), Myla 24 (NC NC NC), John 5 (NC), Elbert 3 (NC), Sarah 1 (NC)
105. TWIGG, John 56 (NC NC NC), Kate 45 (NC NC NC), Timothy 21 (NC), Jason 18 (NC), Mary 16 (NC), Henry 14 (NC), Elkana 11 (NC) (son)

Hh# Page 13 (cont'd)

106. BROWN, Bettie 56 (widow) (NC NC NC), Albert H. 22 (NC NC NC), Susan 18 (NC), Celia 16 (NC), John 14 (T); VANCE, Abner H. 22 (boarder)
107. HICKS, Wm. W. 38 (NC NC NC), Elizabeth 36 (NC NC NC), Lucinda 11, Hannah 9, Polly 7, Mary C. 4, Daniel 2, Laura V. 1/12 (b. Apr); VANCE, Sallie 17 (boarder), Jane 20 (boarder)

Page 14, Dist. 2

108. GOUGE, Allen 44 (NC NC NC), Fanny 35 (NC NC NC), Martha V. 7 (NC), John C. 6 (NC), Susanna 4 (NC), Myra E. 2 (T), Landon T. 5/12 (b. Jan)
109. MILLER, Jacob 21 (NC NC NC), Luanna 31 (wife?); ELLIS, Deborah 13 (stepchild), Dempsy 3 (step child); MILLER, Ettie J. 1/12 (b. Apr) (dau)
110. RICHESON, William 23 (NC SC T), Nancy 24 (T NC T), Sarah E. 2, Nathaniel 8/12 (b. Oct)
111. MORGAN, John 32, Eliza C. 28, Mora A. 8 (dau), Mattie J. 6, Ida B. 4, James P. 2, Joseph 1, John sr. 59 (father) (NC NC)
112. RICHISON, Linda 55 (widow), Ellen 18 (T NC NC), John 15 (T NC NC), Hillsbury 13 (T NC T)
113. WINTERS, William 59 (NC NC NC), Eliza 61 (NC NC NC), Ellen J. 23 (NC), John P. 18 (NC); CARRAWAY, Jefferson 8 (g son) (T NC NC)
114. GREER, James 26, Lottie 26, John R. 5, William D. 3, Eliza C. 10/12; COUSINS, Emma 19 (boarder) (NC NC NC)
115. McNABB, W. G. 52 (m), Elizabeth 48 (wife?), William F. 22, Henry C. 17, Marietta 15, Nathaniel 14, Ellen 11, Malinda J. 7, John B. 4

Page 15, Dist. 2

116. WILSON, Jack C. 45, Nancy 30, John 17, Amanda J. 14, William 10, Alexander 7, Robert T. 5, Benjamin 3
117. STOUT, David 26, Emma 22 (NC NC NC), Eliza J. 5 (NC), Blakely 2 (T)
118. BICE, James 40, Elizabeth 40; SLOAN, Joseph 15 (stepson); BICE, Mary 6 (dau), John 3
119. LINEBACK, Sarah (widow), Martha C. 17, DUGGER, Monroe 22 (boarder)
120. DAVIS, Jefferson sr. (B) 58 (NC NC NC), Jefferson jr. 27 (son) (NC NC NC), Cennia 50 (wife) (NC NC NC), Ann 20 (dau) (poisoned) (NC), Jerry 16 (NC), Lincoln 12 (NC), John 8 (NC)
121. DAVIS, Lank (B) 30 (NC NC NC), Charity (Mu) 20, Adeline 6/12
122. McNEAL, Thos. (Mu) 42 (NC NC NC), Josephine 29 (NC NC NC), Mary A. 10, Aldora 9, John H. 6, William 4, Joseph 2, Todd C. 3/12 (b. Mar)
123. GOINS, Jessie 56 (NC NC NC), Phoebe 50 (NC NC NC), Columbus 22 (NC), James M. 18 (T), Alexander 16, Martha 14

Page 16, Dist. 2

124. HOWARD, Dorcas 65 (widow) (NC NC NC), Nancy 37 (NC NC NC), Hester 4 (g dau) (NC NC), John 2 (g son) (NC NC NC)
125. TINNER, Alexander 34 (NC NC NC), Nancy C. 28, George W. 8, Eva J. 6, Margaret 4, Augusta 2
126. RAY, Samuel (B) 39 (NC NC NC), Alice 30 (NC NC NC), Mary E. 8, Andrew F. 6, lda Bell 3, Henry 1
127. HODGE, William R. 55 (NC NC NC), Sarah E. 48 (T NC T), William 23, James N. 19, Emma E. 16, David 13, Elizabeth 9, Cynthia 4
128. MILLER, Delilah 62 (widow) (NC NC NC), John Bell 17 (T NC NC), Emily 3 (g dau) (T NC NC)

Hh# Page 16 (cont'd)

129. CAMPBELL, Welburn G. 69, Nancy 42 (wife), Adeline 11, Susan E. 8, William 6, John S. 2
130. STOUT, Andrew L. 56, Louvana 57 (NC NC NC), William A. 21, John L. 15, Daniel S. 13, Robert C. 10, Amanda 5
131. HURLY, Ham H. 22, Celia J. 19
132. MORGAN, Thos. 25 (NC NC NC), Evaline 25, Nonie 9 (son), John 7, Mollie 5
133. ORR, Jackson 54, Nancy 35 (wife) (NC NC NC), Bell 16 (T NC T), Rebecca 14 (T T T), Shand 12, James 6, Alfred 4

Page 17, Dist. 2

134. MORGAN, James 23 (NC NC NC), Caroline 22 (NC NC NC), William 6, Audy 3
135. MILLER, Absolom 72 (NC T NC), Annie 74; McKERSON, Annie (Mu) 16 (boarder)
136. MILLER, Jacob A. 35 (T NC T), Matilda 33, Andrew 14
137. BOWLING, Jacob 58, Elizabeth 46, Elizabeth 18, Tennessee 13, Clarissa 11, Matilda 8, Jacob 5, Erleana 6/12 (b. Dec)
138. MORLAND, Mary 70, Phoebe 45 (dau), Verle? 21 (g son), Johnson 19 (g son), Martha 18 (g dau)
139. HAMPTON, Andrew C. 30, Lucretia M. 31, Lizzie R. 7, Ida Bell 5, John J. 3; OGLE, Lillie V. 16 (boarder)
140. HAUGER, Cornelius 23 (VA VA VA), Celia 22 (NC NC NC), Louisa 5, Robert 3, Desdemona 1, Elizabeth 40 (mother) (VA VA VA), Rister 13 (nephew) (NC NC NC)
141. SMITH, Lovena 56 (widow), William 16, Eustace 14 (dau)
142. LEDFORD, William 25 (NC NC NC), Phoebe 30, Alice 6, Armond 3
143. WILSON, Hannah 70 (widow), Isaac 21 (g son) (blind)
144. BURLISON, Oliver 40 (NC NC NC), Phoebe 34 (NC NC NC), Eliza J. 16 (NC), Berney 14 (NC), Terrell 12 (son) (NC), Fannie 8 (NC)

Page 18, Dist. 2

145. HANGER, James A. 25 (miller) (VA VA VA), Sarah E. 25 (NC NC NC), Fannie E. 3 (NC), James 1 (NC), Lee 1 (NC); FOSTER, Elizabeth 23 (sis) (NC NC NC), Emma 2 (niece) (NC NC NC)
146. LEDFORD, Isaac 22 (NC NC NC), Mary 22 (NC NC NC), James 3, Thomas 1
147. CALLOWAY, Giles 49 (NC NC NC), Harriet 48 (NC NC NC), Mary 20 (NC), General 19 (NC), Orfie 14 (dau) (NC), Monroe 12 (NC), Henry 6 (T)
148. MILLER, Lorenzo 33 (VA VA VA), Miralda 40 (wife), Mary 11, Annie 5, Rhoda J. 3
149. LEDFORD, Thos. 60 (NC NC NC), Margaret 63 (NC NC NC), Alethea 33 (NC), David J. 17 (NC), Margaret 12 (NC)
150. HEMPHILL, Margie 54 (widow) (NC NC NC), Peter 14 (NC NC NC), Alice 10 (NC)
151. PERRY, David A. 27 (NC NC NC), Catharine 21, Anna 1; POWELL, Joseph 4 (stepson)
152. SMITH, John K. 49, Elizabeth 44; WORKMAN, Martha 44 (boarder) (NC NC NC)
153. PERRY, Joseph 28 (NC NC NC), Sarah 27 (NC NC NC), Thomas S. 3, Thomas 72 (NC NC NC), Nancy 63 (mother) (NC NC NC)
154. HOSS, James H. 35 (T T NC), Nancey 33, George E. 13, Sarah S. 11, Ferdinand 9, Margaret 7, Andrew B. 5, Eddie 2

Page 19, Dist. 2

155. JENET, Ashbury 68 (NC NC NC), Elizabeth 67 (NC NC NC); TIPTON, William (B) 18 (farmhand); CARRAWAY, Ashbury 7 (ward) (T NC NC)
156. MILLER, Wesly 38 (NC NC NC), Eliza 30, David 17, Sarah 15, Dollie 13, Myra 9, James 7, Mary 5, Gordon 3

Hh# Page 19 (cont'd)

157. SHELL, Mary A. 35 (married), Evaline 16, Daniell 14, Thomas 11, Columbus 9, Andrew 7, Cora 4, Leonore 2 (son)
158. BUNTIN, James C. 32, Adelaide 31 (NC T T), Nancy J. 7, Helen 5, George 3, Marietta 1
159. FOSTER, Horton 30 (NC NC NC), Edie 30 (NC NC NC), John 6, Delia 4, Arthur 2, Mary 2/12 (b. Mar)
160. SHELL, Milton 39, Elizabeth 35, Sarah 13, Alexander 11, Jackson 9, Henry 8, Daniel 7, Julia 6, Hester 3
161. HARDIN, Margaret (B) 55 (widow) (NC NC NC), George 29 (NC), Pauline 25 (NC), Terrell 21 (Mu) (NC), Martha 19 (NC), Simpson 17 (NC), Ellen 15 (NC)

Page 20, Dist. 2

162. OAKS, Chas. G. 53 (T NC NC), Martha 49, Evaline 19, James 17, George T. 15, Cynthia 13, Peggy 11, Robert 9
163. SMITH, John 25, Matilda 25 (NC NC NC), James 4, Ellen B. 2
164. MEREDITH, Hugh 46 (T NC NC), Malinda 46; SMITH, Jacob 25 (stepson), Margaret 20 (step dau), Elizabeth 17 (step dau); MEREDITH, John W. 7 (son), Hester 5, Robert 3
165. JOHNSON, Henderson 34 (T NC NC), Susie 28, Mary 8, Elijah 3, Julia 2, Frank 6/12 (b. Dec)
166. SMITH, Elizabeth 37 (widow) (NC NC NC), Margaret 9 (T NC NC), John H. 7, Julia S. 5
167. JOINE, Hannah 50 (widow) (NC NC NC); MEREDITH, John 25 (son) (NC NC NC)
168. FIELDS, Elbert 22 (T NC NC), Alice 20

Page 1, Dist. 3

1. ROBINSON, Mary 46 (widow), Robert 21, Daniel 19, Samuel 17
2. PETERS, Thomas 56, Nancy 45, Marget 20, Eviline 19, Robert 16, William A. 13, Eliza A. 12, Zechariah 9, Benjamin 2
3. PETERS, George F. 25, Cealia 23, Eligah 3, John H. 1
4. JOHNSON, Andrew 24, Ellen 28, Mary E. 3
5. MORTON, George F. 69, Addle 68, Hannah 38, Carline 29, Eliza 26, Sarah 22
6. McINTOSH, Adiline 37 (widow), David H. 13, John 8, Thomas M. 5, Sarah 1
7. MORTON, Zechariah 32, Susan A. 28, Sarah L. 4, Michiel 2
8. CAMPBELL, Henerson 34, Tempa 35, John R. 16, Eliza J. 14
9. GRINDSTAFF, M. C.? 72, Sarah 70, Mary 45, Alice 9 (g dau)
10. SHAW, Drewre 51 (NC NC NC), Tempha 50 (NC NC NC), Albany 34 (dau) (NC), Zilpa L. 25 (NC), Albert T. 21 (NC), Gilford 20 (NC), Carline 5 (g dau) (T T T), William B. 4 (g son), Drewre K. 2 (g son), Sarah J. 1 (g dau)

Page 2, Dist. 3

11. JOHNSON, Rachel 54 (widow), Hester 18
12. HAZLEWOOD, John 47 (VA VA VA), Rausia 31 (wife), Corda J. 12, Elizebeth A. 9, Edward 7, Mary M. 5, George F. 1
13. JUSTICE, Elkanah 37, Sarah 36, Mary T. 19, William B. 16, John H. 14, James 12, Richard 11, Henerson 9, Charles T. 4, Samuel W. 2/12 (b. Apr), Sarah E. 7/12 (b. Nov) (g dau)
14. MORTON, Alexander 35, Mary 34, John L. 15, David 11, George F. 7, James L. 5, Malisa C. 3, William C. 2
15. GRINDSTAFF, Isaac 38, Enly 29 (wife), Sarah E. 13, Alice L. 8
16. CASEY, William 38, Leuee? 20 (wife), Charles E. 7 (son), John 5, George 11/12 (b. Apr)

8

CARTER COUNTY

Hh#	Page 2 (cont'd)

17. SORRELL, William 28 (carpenter) (SC NC NC), Eliza L. 25, Rosa D. 7, Mada O. 6 (dau), Mahala E. 3, Sterling 4/12 (b. Feb); BOWMAN, John 17 (relationship omitted)
18. HAZLEWOOD, Richard 34 (VA VA VA), Elizabeth 24, Mary J. 9, Martha L. 4, Sarah 1

Page 3, Dist. 3

19. SIMERLEY, Christey? 39, Jane 39 (T NC NC), Sarah F. 15, William G. 12, James J. H. 6, David A. 2, Charles C. 7/12 (b. Nov)
20. CAMPBELL, Zechariah C. 38 (mill right), Martha J. 31; FLETCHER, Lavinia 62 (mother in law); CAMPBELL, John 12 (nephew)
21. LACY, Sarah 90 (widow) (T Gerama--sic--PA); HAMPTON, Marget 70 (servant) (T NC NC); LACY, Richard (B) 40 (laborer)
22. CAMPBELL, Nathaniel 35, Fanney 27, Charles T. 6, Alfred J. 4, Carria A. 1 (dau)
23. GOINS, John (B) 57, Eliza 40, Mary L. 12, Marget E. 11, William R. 9, Rachiel J. 7, John G. 6, Sarah A. 4, Jula A. 2, Susa A. 1/12 (b. Apr)
24. JAMES, Nancy 77 (widow), Jane H. 35 (divorced), Kate L. 18 (g dau), William C. 15 (g son), Butler T. 14 (g son), John B. 13 (g son), Alford A. 10 (g son), Sarah J. 3 (g dau)
25. SIMERLEY, Henry 88 (T Gerama--sic--PA), Mary 80 (NC NC NC); SIMES, Salina 18 (servant)
26. HAZLEWOOD, Tabe (m) 22 (VA VA VA), Nancy 30 (wife), Anna L. 1/12 (b. Apr) (T VA T), Jane 12 (T NC T)
27. WEST, Elizebeth 60 (widow) (T NC NC)
28. SHULL, Andrew 51 (T NC NC), Jane 39
29. FANDREN, William 66 (widower) (SC NC NC), Elizebeth 38 (T SC NC), John 17 (g son), Andrew 17 (g son), Cracha 12 (g dau), Georgia A. 8 (g dau), Henry 3 (g son), Sarah J. 1 (g dau)

Page 4, Dist. 3

30. JACKSON, James 38 (shoemaker), Mary 28, Alice 10, William A. 8, Samuel 6, Alfrad 3, Robert O. 1/12 (b. May)
31. HALLEY, Robert J. 40 (carpenter), Carline 40, Sarah 21, Martha 15, Mary J. 8, James H. 6, John A. H. 4, Nancy L. 1
32. FANDREN, Albert B. 32, Martha A. 27
33. SIMERLEY, Eligah 59, Mary E. 50, Luisia 23, John B. 21, William G. B. 18, Eligah J. 14, Sarah E. 12, Cealia A. 7; MOREFILD, Thomas J. 22 (son in law)
34. TOWNSON, John 40 (NC NC NC), Jane 36, Mary 12, Nancy 12 (daughouse?), Martha 9, Samuel 6, Columbus 4, William E. 1
35. JENKINS, Samuel 29, Eliza M. 27, Eviline 9, Oda J. 5, Sarah L. 3
36. FLETCHER, James B. 33, Nancy 22, James W. 8 (son), John 7, William N. 6, Leliah M. 4, Ema L. 2

Page 5, Dist. 3

37. HAMPTON, Sarah 47 (married) (NC NC NC), Johnson H. 25 (son) (T NC NC), William T. 21, Mary M. 17, Sarah C. 14, Hily E. 12 (dau), Joseph F. 9, George W. 7
38. JOHNSON, John H. 27 (T NC T), Lavonia 21 (T T VA), Harrey D. 2, William V. 1
39. COLLINS, Elizah 49 (m) (VA NC Ire), Celina E. 46, Rebecca 22, Andrew G. 20, Peter E. 16 (T VA ___), William W. 11, Robert C. 8, Ruble A. 5 (son)
40. CAMPBELL, Sarah 52 (widow) (T NC T), Lawson 19
41. MANNING, James 28 (T VA T), Elizabeth P. 21, Nabia? M. 3 (dau), Vinia A. E. 9/12 (b. Sep)
42. FOLSOM, William J. 60 (clerk in store) (NC NC NC), Eliza E. 45 (wife), Brien 10, Mary K. 7, Flora B. 5; RENFRO, Sarah 18 (servant); FOLSOM, Sarah 28 (sis) (T NC NC)

Hh#	Page 5 (cont'd)

43. CAMPBELL, John T. 36, Mary E. 26, Levisa C. 12 (dau), Elizebeth 6, Daniel D. 4, Martha C. 7/12
44. SIMERLEY, Johnson H. 29 (treder), Laurah C. 19, Lydia B. K. 1, Anna J. 8/12 (b. Oct)

Page 6, Dist. 3

45. HESTER, John R. 27 (NC NC NC)
46. HESTER, Mary 58 (divorced) (NC NC NC), George W. C. 21 (NC NC NC), Mary A. E. 19 (T), Perline E. 14, Sarah 11
47. HYDER, John L. 42, Cathrine 52 (wife); FISHER, Cathrine 60 (servant) (Ire Ire Ire)
48. HARDEN, Eli 39, Elizebeth 39 (T NC T), Julia A. 12, William D. 9, Mary E. 6, Alvin P. 4, John N. 1
49. CAMPBELL, Susa 59 (widow)
50. CAMPBELL, Nealia 23 (dau of 49), John F. 1 (son), Samuel 3/12 (b. Mar)
51. WHITEHEAD, Andrew 30, Mary 28 (T NC T), Carter 6, Lawoll? A. 3, John I. 3/12 (b. Mar)
52. AUSBEN, John 24, Everlyn E. 24 (NC NC NC), Sarah 45 (mother)
53. WHITEHEAD, Thomas A. 50, Sarah 35 (wife), Eliza 18, David 14, William 12, Martha 2
54. WILLIAM, Russel R. 30 (VA T NC), Carline 45 (wife), Mary A. 9, Catchrine? E. 7, John H. 4, Charles M. 5/12 (b. Dec), Sarah C. 20
55. COLMAN, Francis M. 29 (NC NC NC), Harriett A. 28 (T NC NC), Nathanniel 3, John F. 2, James F. 11/12 (b. Jul); BORMAN, William 15 (servant) (T NC T)
56. MORGAN, Thomas 36, Sarah 40 (NC NC NC), Mary E. 10, William 8, Lucy S. 4, Joseph 8/12 (b. Oct)

Page 7, Dist. 3

57. WHITEHEAD, John 51 (T NC NC), Nancy A. 42, Isaac T. 22, Julia 10, Sarah 7, James 5, Henry 3
58. TEAGUE, Logan 56 (NC NC NC), Frany 54 (NC __ __), Rebeca 20 (NC NC NC), Mary (NC), Carline 16 (NC), Logan J. 14 (NC), Nervia 12 (dau) (NC), Jackson 10 (NC), William 7 (T), David 5
59. GARDNER, John (B) 40 (NC NC NC), Sarah 28 (NC NC NC), Mary 12 (NC), Joseph 10 (T), Sally 8, Elen 6, Jane 4, George 2, Henry 1
60. GILLILAND, Hamilton 58 (T VA T), Lousia 47, William S. 22, Marget J. 21, Cealia A. 16, John B. 15, Martha E. 13, Alexander 7, Emley E. 5
61. ROBERTS, William 49 (NC NC MD), Lidy 40 (NC NC NC), Elemada 20, Mary C. 15, Indinana 12 (IN)
62. WATES, Odam 24 (NC NC NC), Rhoda 16 (wife), Samuel H. 8/12
63. MILLER, Johnson 35 (T NC NC), Maneria 34 (NC NC NC), Mary 12, Susa 9, John 7, William 4, Sarah 2

Page 8, Dist. 3

64. HILL, John 54 (NC NC NC), Clersa 40 (NC NC NC), Mary 21, Rhoda 15, Emer 12 (dau), Charles 9, Sarah 9, John 6, William 1
65. GAUGE, Susa 72 (widow) (NC NC NC), Lucinda 44 (NC NC NC), Sarah 40 (NC NC NC)
66. GAUGE, John 49 (NC NC NC), Elizebeth 52 (NC NC NC), William 25 (NC), John A. 20 (NC), Jane 18 (T), Eligah 16, Swinfild 15, James 12, Alice 10; JOHNSON, Jane E. 5 (g dau), Henry 3 (g son)
67. YOUNG, Daniel (B) 32 (NC VA VA), Catchren 48 (wife) (T VA VA)
68. WHITEHEAD, James 80 (widower) (NC NC NC), Eliza J. 33 (T NC T), James 36 (son in law) (T T T), Alford T. 8 (T T T), James L. 3

9

Hh#	Page 8 (cont'd)

69. WHITHEAD, David A. 40 (T NC T), Marget 32, Dealia J. 11, George E. 9, Mary 4, Eviline T. 2
70. HILL, Ezakial 60 (NC NC N), Bidy 38 (wife) (T NC T), Alexander 22, James 20, Jinna A. 14, Mary 12, Nancy A. 9, Dicy 35 (sis) (T NC T) (insane)
71. HILL, Robert 57, Mary C. 53 (T Ire NC), Marget E. 14, CARWAY, Charles A. 5 (servant)

Page 9, Dist. 3

72. HILL, Samuel 38 (T NC NC), Elen E. 33 (NC NC NC), John H. 13, Ezlekiel 10, Alele 9 (son), Eligah 6, Luizea E. 4, James 2
73. TOWNSON, Calumbus 22 (NC NC NC), Sarah 20 (NC NC NC), Sarah M. 1 (NC), William 6/12 (b. Dec) (T)
74. COCHREN, William E. 25 (VA VA VA), Julia 25, William T. 4, Samuel 2, Charles 2/12 (b. Apr)
75. HEAD, Joseph A. 32 (clergerman) (NC __ NC), Sarah A. 27, Robert C. 6, Mary C. 5, Sarah M. 4
76. DATSON, Albert 40 (NC NC T), Mary J. 41 (SC SC NC); HEAD, Sarah C. 12 (servant) (NC NC NC)
77. CATES, David 22, Martha 20, Ida B. 7/12 (b. Nov)
78. MILLER, Hannah 33 (T PA T), Robert 13 (son), Lourae 8 (dau), Isaac 6 (son), James 3 (son)
79. MAKESSON, Spencer (Mu) 54 (NC T NC), Mary A. (B) 44 (NC NC NC), Anna 17 (NC), Julia 12 (NC), Mary L. 9 (NC), Spencer 8 (NC), Jacob 6 (T), Rachiel 4; CARPENTER, Rachiel (Mu) 86 (mother) (NC NC NC)
80. SAPES, Cahun? (B) 22 (NC NC NC), Elen (NC NC NC), Mary J. 8/12 (b. Oct); GREENLEE, Howel 21 (servant) (T NC NC); BARKER, Bemjamin 15 (servant) (T NC NC); GUIN, Andrew (W) 21 (servant); DAVIS, Charles (W) 20 (laborer)

Page 10, Dist. 3

81. BLEVINS, Hiley 61 (widow) (T NC NC)
82. WHITEHEAD, Thomas 56 (T T NC), Hannah 37 (wife) (T NC T), Catchren 12 (dau), James 9, Carter 8, Oliver 7, Lewies 4 (dau), Dealia J. 6/12 (b. Dec)
83. HEAD, Johnathan 28 (NC T NC), Martha 38 (wife) (NC T T), Porter 14 (son) (T T NC), Elizebeth 10 (T T NC), James 8 (T T NC), John 8 (T T NC), Josephean 7 (T T NC), Henry 4 (T T NC), David C. 1 (T T NC); BLEVINS, Nancy 40 (sis in law) (NC T T), John 15 (son)
84. HILL, Albert 34 (T NC T), Elizebeth 26, Mary A. 12
85. HEAD, Cement D. 58 (NC NC NC), Mary M. 62 (NC NC NC), Andrew 6 (g son) (NC NC NC)
86. CAKNIPES?, Henry 44 (NC NC NC), Eliza 35 (NC NC NC), Docter 7, Charles 6, Barbre 4, Elisah 2
87. HALLEY, James 37, Temnia 32, Martha A. 11
88. MILLER, James 36, James C. 19 (son), Mary C. 8 (dau), Jane 3 (dau)
89. WHITEHEAD, Larkin 70 (T NC NC), Elizebeth 59 (NC NC NC), Julia 22, Jackson F. 17, Nathaniel 6 (g son) (T NC NC), William N. 2 (g son) (T T)
90. WHITEHEAD, James 26 (T T NC), Julia 24, Matison 5, Larkin 4, Caswell 2

Page 11, Dist. 3

91. ROBERSON, Mosses 34 (cabnet) (NC NC NC), Marget 34, William G. 13, Nancy J. 11, Martha E. 9, John T. 5, James H. 3, Docter 1, Samuel 2/12 (b. Apr); TIPTON, Nancy 75 (mother in law)
92. MORRELL, Thomas 30, Hester 27, Hattia E. 7, John L. 6, Lavisia 5, Chestun 9/12 (b. Sep) (dau)

Hh#	Page 11 (cont'd)

93. TOWNSON, William 29 (NC NC NC), Rebecca 34 (NC NC NC), John T. 10 (NC), James 8 (T), David J. 6, Isaac 4, Henry L. 2
94. INGRAM?, David 24 (T NC T), Jane M. 27, Julia E. 7, Franklin 5, John L. 2
95. CARRIER, William 67, Vimae 54 (wife), Sarah C. 16, Sherman 2/12 (b. Apr)
96. LACY, John L. 25, Cellia D. 19, Callie M. 1, Lewie 3/12 (b. Feb) (dau)
97. COOPPERS, Thomas 25 (NC T T), Sarah 40 (wife) (NC T T), Jorden 18 (bro) (NC T T)
98. INGRIM, Thomas 68 (T NC T), Nancy 63, Emma 24, Mary 20, John 18, Hester A. 17, Rhoda 12, Mary 10 (g dau)
99. LACY, Alexander 30, Mary E. 27, Manda J. 9, Rhoda A. 8, John W. 7, Mary D. 5, David W. 4, Minna F. 3, Emley C. 1 (dau)

Page 12, Dist. 3

100. CARVER, George 36, Martha 36, Mary 13, Joseph 10, Jane 8, Susa 6, Sarah 4, Charles 3, Elizebeth 1
101. SIZEMORE, Nat 24 (T NC NC), Emley 20, Minney B. 9/12 (b. Sep)
102. ANGEL, Thomas 21 (rheumatism), Elen 21, Ann 45 (mother), Andrew 18 (bro in law)
103. BLEVINS, Willy 40, Eviline 25 (wife), William 13, James 10, John 6, Bidia 5, Swinfild 1, Wishy 40 (m) (servant)
104. TEAGUE, James 23 (NC NC NC), Eliza E. 19, John H. 1
105. INGRAM, Nancy A. 40 (widow), Martha 24 (dau), Mary 22, William 17, Jane N. 14, Charles 9, Minnia 7, Daniel 7 (g son), Elizabeth 3 (g dau), Dosho 1 (g dau), Eviline 1 (g dau)
106. WARD, William 23, Elizebeth 24
107. BLACKWELL, William 53 (NC VA NC), Emiline 40 (T T NC), James L. 17
108. MILLER, William H. 36 (T T NC), Carline 28, Samuel C. 7, Sarah A. 11/12 (b. Jul)

Page 13, Dist. 3

109. WHITHEAD, James C. 32, Elizebeth A. 42 (wife) (NC NC NC), William C. 9
110. MORGAN, Elizebeth 58 (widow) (T NC T), Martha 22 (T NC T), Hannah 19, Andrew 17
111. GUIN, Amos 24 (T NC NC), Sarah 21 (T NC T), William 6, Elan 55 (mother) (NC NC NC)
112. ARNETT, Timothy 22 (NC NC NC), Mary A. 16
113. GODFREY, William 27 (NC NC NC), Anna 24 (NC NC NC), Joseph 1 (NC)
114. ARNETT, Sarah 61 (widow) (NC NC NC), Rachiel 35 (NC NC NC), Mary 17 (NC), Martha 19 (NC), William 9 (g son) (T T NC), James 4 (g son) (T T NC), Andrew 1 (g son) (T NC T); MILSAPS, Maniel (m) 60 (servant) (NC NC NC)
115. NELSON, William H. 45; SMITH, Matha 40 (servant) (NC NC NC), Jerinireta (m) 5 (relationship omitted) (T NC NC); MILLER, William A. 20 (servant)
116. STAPHINA, Mikiel 33 (T NC NC), Fanna J. 34 (T T NC), Julia A. 13, William W. 10, Mary M. 7, Eolgah 5, Jacob D. 2
117. ROBERTS, John 62 (NC NC NC), Nancy 63 (NC NC NC), Robert L. 21 (NC), Isaac 20 (NC), Elizebeth R. 12 (g dau) (NC NC NC), Alford R. 9 (g son) (NC NC NC)
118. ROBERTS, Alen H. 24 (NC NC NC), Nancy 26 (T NC T), Marilda 5, John H. 2; MYRES, William 28 (servant) (NC NC NC)
119. WHISHUNT, Noah 49 (NC NC NC), Lousinda 33 (wife) (NC NC NC), Nancy 7, Matilda 5, Milia 3 (dau)

Page 14, Dist. 3

120. FAUBUS, David 20 (NC NC NC), Mary J. 27, John H. 1, James 1/31 (b. May)
121. HILS, Henry 30 (NC NC NC), Sarah 36, Mary 10 (dau) (T T T), Aden A. 1 (son) (T NC T)

Hh#   Page 14 (cont'd)

122. MILERUN?, Calvin 46 (NC NC NC), Mary 49 (NC NC NC), William 11, Jane E. 9
124. HOPSON, Isaac 29 (NC NC NC), Susa 25 (T NC T), Sarah 8, William W. 6, James N. 4
125. HOPSON, Sarah 48 (widow) (NC NC NC), Jason N. 25 (NC NC NC), Nancy 21 (dau in law) (NC NC NC)
126. CHAMBERS, John 54, Mary 58, Sarah 18, Nancy A. 13, Roda 12, Mary 7 (g dau)
127. HORVEL, William M. 36 (VA NC NC), Mary 33 (NC NC NC), Sarah E. 9 (NC NC NC), Mary 7 (NC NC NC), Perriler 5 (dau) (NC NC NC), Watisel 2 (son) (NC NC NC)
128. BLEVINS, Elisha 22 (T NC T), John 21 (bro) (T NC T), Mary 13 (sis in law) (NC NC NC); FAUBUS, Fannia 30 (servant) (NC NC NC), Charles 2 (son) (NC NC NC)
129. BLEVINS, David 25 (T NC T), Nancy 16 (NC NC NC), Elizebeth 2 (NC)
130. WHITEHEAD, James 60, Sarah 69 (wife)
131. WRIGHT, Wesly 46 (NC NC NC), Mary 33 (wife) (NC NC NC), Charles T. 6 (NC), Martha C. 4 (NC)

Page 15, Dist. 3

132. CHAMBERS, William 46, Cathrin 39, Jacob 11, Dealia 9, James W. 7, Mary 3, Eligah S. 2; GREENLEE, Miles (B) 30 (servant) (NC NC NC), Rufus 15 (servant) (NC NC NC)
133. ELISON, John 40 (NC NC NC), Nancy 29 (NC NC NC), William T. 12, Samuel 7, Mary 4, Jacob 1
134. SIMERLEY, James 29, Nancy 30 (T NC T)
135. GAUGE, Ruben T. 33 (NC NC NC), Hannah 35, Elizabeth J. 8, Mauriae 6 (dau), John J. 4, Mary S. 2
136. POTTER, Daniel W. 33, Mary J. 39, Cealia C. 8, Rebecca J. 7, Alice F. 5, Taylor T. 5, James J. 8/12 (b. Oct)
137. MILLER, William 50 (NC NC NC), Sarah 45 (T NC NC), John B. 19, Francis 17, Samuel 15, Jane H. 13, Bronlow 10, Jacob 8, Elicana H. 6 (son)
138. SIMERLEY, William 26, Elen 20 (NC NC NC), Rebecca J. 4, David 1
139. MOORE, John 47 (T VA T), Mary 43 (T NC NC), Miria 19 (T T NC), Emline 18 (T T NC), David 17 (T T NC), Elizebeth 14 (T T NC), James 11 (T T NC), Sarah 9 (T T NC), Roda 7 (T T NC), John 5 (T T NC), Docter 1 (T T NC)

Page 16, Dist. 3

140. CARVER, Benjaman 23, Eliza 21, John H. 3, James C. 1
141. COOK, Alexander 27, Sarah J. 24, Mary E. 5, Hannah 2
142. GUIN, Isaac 40 (NC T NC), Elizebeth 39 (NC NC NC), Adam 13 (T), James 10 (NC), Susa A. 7 (NC), Jacob 3 (NC), Nancy E. 4/12 (b. Feb) (T)
143. HIX, Sarah 60 (widow) (NC NC NC), William L. 9 (g son) (T NC T)
144. HIX, Daniel 35 (NC NC NC), Nancy 31 (T T NC), Tunna? J. 7 (dau) (VA), Robert C. 5 (VA), Mikiel 4 (T), Emiline 1
145. MOORE, Mary 60 (widow) (T NC T), Delia 23 (doughouse), George 22 (son), John 19, Levi 16, Mary 13, Susa 12, Mary 1 (g dau); MOORE, Luvania 18 (dau in law)
146. HIX, William 60 (NC T T), Selealee? 50 (wife) (NC NC NC), Willis 29 (NC), David 19 (NC), John 17 (NC), Hannah 22 (dau in law), Susa A. 6 (g dau), Liue 1 (g dau)
147. COCHREN, Whit 32 (VA VA VA), Dorthania 30, Hannah 13, Clersey 11, James 8, William 7, Kairit 4 (dau), Robert 2

Page 17, Dist. 3

148. GAUGE, Calvin 26 (NC NC NC), Cathren 30 (T T NC), Martha 8, Mary 6, John W. 4, Elin L. 1

Hh#   Page 17 (cont'd)

149. TRICE, Jackson 30 (NC NC NC), Mary 32 (NC NC NC), John L. 8 (NC), Thomas R. 6 (NC), Manda J. 3 (T)
150. HYDER, Nathaniel K. 36, Olley J. 36 (wife) (T NC NC), James C. 17, Godfrey B. 15, Carline S. 13, Judy C. 11, Sarah E. 8, David S. 3, William H. 10/30 (b. May)
151. MORTON, Merieth Y. 28 (T T NC), Carline R. 25 (T NC NC), David S. 8, William H. 6, Debia B. 4, John S. 1
152. ELIETT, David 36, Mary 26, Peter 10, James 5, John 2, Sarah 4/12 (b. Feb)
153. McKINNEY, Samuel 35 (T NC NC), Lusinda 16 (wife) (T T NC), John B. 17 (son), Julia A. 14 (dau)
154. STREET, Samuel 42 (NC NC NC), Emly 42, Jane 22 (dau) (T T T), Rebecca 14 (dau (T NC T), Sarah E. 13, Henry M. 11, Bidia E. 8, John S. 5, Emna 1, Thomas C. 5 (g son) (T NC T), Charles C. 4 (g son) (T NC T), Julia A. 1 (g dau) (T NC T)

Page 18, Dist. 3

155. LEWIS, Hampton H. 43 (T NC T), Lorina 43, Mary E. 19, Bengamen G. 18, Eliza J. 16, David 13, Anna 11, Marget E. 8, Charlotta 6, Samuel H. 3, Julia 1
156. McKINNEY, Wilson 66 (NC NC T), Rebecca 56 (NC NC NC), Thomas C. 21, Hester 19
157. BAY, Marshel 30, Marget 28 (T NC NC), Charles 7, Matison 5, Edmon 2
158. KENT, James 64 (NC NC NC), Sarah A. 61, Abigill 23, Lewis 24, Talbert 13 (g son), Edward 2 (g son), William 7/12 (b. Nov) (g son)
159. GILBERT, John 71 (NC NC NC), Mary 53 (wife), Marget E. 10, Julia A. 5
160. STREET, Johnathan 25 (NC NC NC), Eviline 23, Charles H. 2, Taylor 1
161. HYDER, John W. 71, Luvina 68, Matha 46, Nathaniel 36, Emma 27, David F. 22
162. ROWE, William H. 40, Lydia 39, Samuel 14, Lola J. 11, William 7, Robert 4, Albert 4/12 (b. Feb)
163. CLARK, Willborn 60 (NC NC NC), Mary 45 (wife) (NC NC NC), William 20 (NC), James 18 (NC), John 15 (NC), Sarah 12 (NC), Susa 9 (NC), Leuvania 7 (NC), Samuel 5 (NC), Willis 3 (NC), Elizebeth 1 (NC)

Page 19, Dist. 3

164. HELFEL, Daniel 39, Marget 35, Rackasa 14, Mielia 9, Mima 5
165. MILLER, Hily 44 (widow), Bida A. 16, James C. 4
166. PRICE, Thomas 37 (NC NC NC), Marget L. 39 (NC NC NC), Mary A. 16 (NC), William C. 12 (T), John H. 9 (NC), Thomas C. 7 (NC), James B. 5 (NC), Joseph 4 (T), Eliza J. 3, Samuel H. 1
167. PRICE, Redman 73 (NC NC NC), Cathrine 70 (NC NC NC)
168. McKINNY, William 28 (T NC NC), Cealia 28, John S. 11, Hannah E. 8, Delia? C. 5, Jacob H. 4, David A. 2
169. SIMERLEY, William 18, Marget 18 (T NC T)
170. STEPHENS, Joshua 70 (NC NC NC), Marget 70 (NC NC NC), Eligah 25, Sarah A. 18 (dau in law)
171. STEPHENS, Charles 52 (NC NC NC), Susa A. 46 (NC NC NC), Ervin 21, Hester 18, Cealia 13, William L. 11
172. STEPHENS, John 40 (NC NC NC), Elizebeth 40 (NC NC NC), Eligah 13, Jane 11, Bida 9, Juda 7, Charles 5, John 2

Page 20, Dist. 3

173. MORTON, David N. 57 (T VA VA), Lydia M. 32 (wife) (NC NC NC), Edward E. 8, Merian M. 7 (son)
174. MORTON, Jacob S. 24, Mamdealia 18, Mary J. 2, Bidia E. 3/12 (b. Mar); McKINNEY, William 21 (bro in law)

Hh#	Page 20 (cont'd)

175. SHEWMAKE, Mary 60 (widow) (NC NC NC), Carline 30 (NC NC NC), Mary E. 9 (g dau) (T T NC)
176. GAUGE, David 26 (T NC T), Mary J. 25, John H. 7, Sarah A. 6, Elizebeth S. 4
177. SIMERLEY, Jacob 66 (miler), May 70 (NC VA VA), David 21 (g son), John 18 (g son), Susa 15 (g dau)
178. SIMERLEY, David 42 (T T NC), Judah 39 (wife) (T NC NC), Butler R. 14, John H. 11, Lafayett T. 9, Samuel H. 7, Jacob E. 5, Mary E. 2
179. WITEHEAD, Marget 42 (widow) (T T NC), Dealia E. 23, Matilda 15, Nathaniel 14, Eligah 12, Elen 9, William L. 7, James A. 1 (g son)
180. ALLEN, John F. 32 (T T VA), Nancy A. E. 34, Malia T. 7 (dau), Lura K. 3, May 4/12 (b. Feb)
181. CROW, James C. 27, Theodocia 19, John W. 2/12 (b. Apr)

Page 21, Dist. 3

182. HALL, Oliver 51 (NC NC NC), Elizebeth 49, Dealia C. 23, Mary E. 21, Samuel P. 14, Eligah S. 11, John M. 8; GRINDSTAFF, Franky 23 (nephew) (school teacher)

Page 1, Dist. 5

1. SCOTT, William T. L. 43 (typoid fever) (T T VA), Rachal Ann 45; WILLIAMS, May C. T. 24 (dau), John P. 22 (stepson), Samuel L. 14 (stepson)
2. SWAMER, Amon 50 (house carpenter), Loucinda J. 39
3. ANDERSON, Wade 46 (NC NC NC)
4. SWAMER, George W. 43, Amanda J. 46 (T T VA), Mary E. 23, Analiga L. 21, Samuel C. 17, James F. 13, Joshua 11, Nancy C. 10, Margaret A. 8, John 4, Loucinda H. 3/12 (b. Feb)
5. PEOPLES, Andrew J. 51 (T T VA), Clerrissa E. 39 (NC NC NC), Usury M. 21, Henry M. 21, George L. 18, William L. 16 (NC), Margaret E. 14 (NC), Julia A. 12 (NC), John W. 10 (NC)
6. GLASS, Smith S. 30 (NC NC NC), Emaline 21, Daniel 4, Eliza 1
7. BOWMAN, Lee 30, Nancy 30, Mary S. 7, Emma J. 4 (asthma)
8. BUCK, Isaac G. W. 47 (T PA T), Mary J. 43, Julie A. 22, John B. 20, Zernah I. 18, Thomas N. 15, Isaac G. W. 13, Mary J. 11, Susan E. 9, Sarah A. 7, Harriet L. E. 5, Daniel M. 2
9. CLARK, William J. 24, Julia A. 22
10. McINTURFF, John 31, Sarah E. 19 (married within yr), Julia A. 6, Elizabeth J. 4

Page 2, Dist. 5

11. BOWMAN, Sarah 40 (widow), Louvena E. 11 (idiotic), Susan E. 4 (idiotic), Nancy J. 18 (sis), Ann E. 25 (sis), William M. 4 (nephew)
12. BUCK, Nathaniel L. 52 (T PA T), Clemma J. 33 (wife), Nancy A. 87 (mother), Isabelah M. T. 63 (sis) (rheumatism) (T PA T); WHISENHUNT, Mary 18 (servant)
13. BOWMAN, Isaac 34, Margaret L. 24, Samule T. 10, Martha E. 6, Julia A. 3, John P. 10/12 (b. Aug)
14. BOWMAN, Harris 27, Elvina 24, Gardner L. 8, Madison 6, David 4, Thomas 69 (father) (rheumatism), Mary C. 68 (mother)
15. BRITT, Ellen 24, William 20 (bro) (idiotic), Barbra A. 45 (mother)
16. WHISENHUNT, Loucinda 50 (widow), Isaac 21 (idiotic), Nathaniel 17 (idiotic), Abner 15 (idiotic)
17. WATSON, Eliazor 75, Martha 74; COMBS, Mary 40, James T. 15 (g son), Martha P. 11 (g dau), Julie E. 7 (g dau), John M. 1 (g son)

Hh#	Page 2 (cont'd)

18. McCRAW, Napoleon B. 76 (blacksmith) (flux) (T Ire NC), Martha 75 (T VA VA)
19. PRICE, James P. 42, Manerva J. 42, Martha J. 11, Charles L. 8
20. TAYLOR, Issac N. 50 (T T Ger), Catharine A. 42 (T Ire NC), George W. 20, Mary E. 17, Margaret E. 15, Emaline 13, John W. 10, Hannah E. 6, Robert 3

Page 3, Dist. 5

21. CARROLL, William C. 43 (T T NC), Ann E. 47
22. HAMMET, George D. 24, Julia A. 21, Harriet E. 3, Mary E. 7/12 (b. Nov), Joshua 22 (bro)
23. PUGH, Hester A. 43 (widow), Emma 21, Rachal F. 45 (step dau), Nannie C. 25 (step dau) (rheumatism), William 12 (g son), Dora 9 (g dau)
24. PUGH, Zachariah T. 32 (blacksmith), Caroline S. 34, Mary A. 6, Elner L. 5 (son), Preston T. 4, William L. 2, Nora C. 2
25. KEEN, Mary 62 (widow), James M. 30; DANIELS, James 22 (son in law), Sarah F. 27 (dau), Mary A. 1 (g dau); JOHNSON, Enoch L. 18 (g son), Mary A. 15 (g dau); PUGH, David W. 7 (g son)
26. KEEN, John V. 31 (wagon maker), Hannah 24, Julia A. 8, Enoch C. 4
27. JOHNSON, Carter 35 (blacksmith), Martha J. 38, Enoch F. 6, Charles J. 11/12 (b. Jul)
28. TAYLOR, Rufus (B) 60, Sarah 30; MILLER, Alexander 17 (stepson), Adie 13 (stepdau)
29. RANGE, James C. 59, Sarah A. 48, Charles E. 14, Nora L. 12

Page 4, Dist. 5

30. WILLIAMS, Alphonzo 63 (hernia), Eliza 64 (neralgia)
31. CAGLE, Benjamin 35, Eliza M. 19 (wife), Jimmie 10/12 (b. Jul) (dau)
32. JOHNSON, Charles 32, Elizabeth 31, Mary J. 9, Bertha 4, Margaret 2, John 2/12 (b. Mar)
33. WRIGHT, Thomas 56, Margaret H. 52 (T MD SC), William A. 28 (teacher), Sarah E. 24, Thomas M. 21, Mary B. 18, Henry C. 14
34. WILLIAMS, Thomas E. 27, Charlotte 32, John F. 5
35. WILLIAMS, George E. 52, Sarah J. 48, Nathaniel E. 24, Julia A. 20, Samuel W. 6, Edmond 84 (father)
36. MILLER, Robert 58 (house carpenter), Elizabeth 60, Mark B. 29 (house carpenter), Edmond 27 (mill wright), Alfred (B) 15 (relationship omitted)
37. GOURLEY, William 26 (wagon maker), Jane 20, Nancy 3/12 (b. Mar)
38. TATE, Andrew (B) 45 (VA VA VA), Nancy 33, GORMAN, Ritchard 13 (stepson), James 10 (stepson), Amanda 6 (step dau), Mary E. 5 (step dau), Jane 2 (step dau)
39. KLINE, Sarah (Mu) 35 (widow), Ida 11, George 4, Laura 10/12 (b. Jul)
40. SMITH, Ellen 64 (widow); COX, Robert 21 (son), Hugh 3 (g son)

Page 5, Dist. 5

41. HUGHES, Albert 47, Laura 21 (wife), David W. 2
42. HUGHES, James 56, Jane 46, George R. 17, Isaac D. 15, Albert 10, Martha E. 4, Frank W. 3/12 (b. Mar) (dau); GLOVER, Belle 23 (servant)
43. SMALLING, Duke W. 69 (peddling), Nancy 69 (VA PA PA), Virginia A. 22, Robert W. 20, Margaret 17
44. SNODGRASS, William 30, Loucilla 33, John F. 5, Carrie D. 3, Hassie 1/12 (b. May)
45. SNODGRASS, Thomas 25, Martha C. 25, Charles 8, Nora A. 6, William C. 2
46. HAMMET, Samule 42, Nancy C. 28 (wife), Ann E. 10, John N. 8, Martha N. 3

12

Hh#   Page 5 (cont'd)

47. SMALLING, William 35, Mary A. 44 (wife),
    John F. 12, Amanda 10, Caswell W. 4;
    BLEVEN, Agnes 66 (mother in law)
48. BOYD, William 73, Elizabeth 47 (wife),
    Emma 8, Albert 5. Bula 8 (g dau)
49. PAYNE, William 25 (teacher) (VA VA VA),
    Hassie 19
50. WILLIAMS, Nathaniel 44, Martha 44, Isaac L.
    20, Thomas J. 18, Mary E. 13, Samuel
    A. 11, Nathaniel M. 8, Martha A. 5

           Page 6, Dist. 5

51. TAYLOR, James M. 42 (miller), Mary A. 40,
    John B. 20, Martha W. 18, Andrew K.
    14, William P. 12, Elizabeth C. 9,
    James F. 7, Noah D. 5, Emma E. 3,
    Charles E. 1
52. BIRDWELL, Nannie 42 (widow merchant) (VA
    VA VA); LYONS, Mary J. 18 (dau) (T VA
    VA), James B. 15 (clerk in store),
    George E. 13, David S. 10; KIRK, Eliza-
    beth 41 (servant)
53. SNODGRASS, John 52 (doctor), Tibetha 29
    (wife) (NC NC VA), Nathaniel 15 (son),
    Ida S. 13, George S. 4, Sarah E. 1;
    HOOPER, Mary 39 (sis in law) (NC NC VA)
54. WILLIAMS, George D. 77, Loucinda 67, George
    T. 27 (g son), Lavance 17 (g dau) (NC
    NC NC), Emma E. 18 (niece), Robert 16
    (nephew); MOSLEY, Margaret 24 (servant)
    (T T NC); WISSENHUNT, Rhoda 12 (ser-
    vant)
55. WILLIAMS, Joshua 71 (paralysis) (T NC T),
    Elizabeth 70; CROCKETT, Loucretia A.
    20 (g dau), Rorda L. 18 (g dau);
    CARROLL, John (Mu) 21 (servant)
56. WYETT, Elizabeth 57 (widow) (T NC T), Mary
    A. 33, Ida A. 17
57. WILLIAMS, Samule 36, Angeline 37 (T NC T),
    Robert C. 10, Mary E. 9, Archibald E. 7,
    Rhoda J. 5
58. PEOPLES, John W. 27, Cornelie 22, Hattie 1;
    SWANNER, William 13 (servant)

           Page 7, Dist. 5

59. HAMMET, Newton 79, Milla 70 (wife) (in
    poor house), Nancy 35, Fannie 33,
    William 11 (g son), James 11 (g son),
    Andrew 8 (g son), Hannah 5 (g dau)
60. WILLIAMS, Pinkney P. 66 (widower), SArah A.
    34, Cordelia M. 32, Mary L. 26, Nancy
    E. 24, Madison L. 21, Rebecca B. 20,
    Emma 18
61. JESTUS, Harvy 39 (NC NC T), Martha M. 43
    (NC NC NC), Isaac R. 9, Mary A. 5,
    Steven 72 (father) (NC NC NC); NAVY,
    Elias 23 (stepson) (NC NC NC), William
    E. 19 (stepson) (NC NC NC)
62. WILLIAMS, Archibald 46 (lumber dealer),
    Sarah 38, Maggie E. 19, Nathaniel R.
    17, Rhoda A. 16, John L. E. 7, Joseph
    A. 3
63. ANDERSON, James M. 41 (trader) (catarh of
    throat) (GA NC T), Sarah L. 35, Addie
    L. 16 (GA), Mary J. 13 (GA), William
    E. 8 (T), Joe H. 6, Ida L. 21 (niece)
    (GA GA T), Ernest W. 19 (nephew) (GA
    GA T)
64. SWANNER, Joseph 70 (T MD MD), Susanah 60;
    DOUHARTY, James 10 (g son)
65. HAMBRICK, David 20, Susanah 21 (NC NC NC)
66. MASTEN, George W. 48 (house carpenter),
    Mary 35 (wife), Mary E. 18; PAYNE,
    Aubra 8 (servant); MASTON, James 17
    (son) (apprentice carpenter)

           Page 8, Dist. 5

67. JACKSON, Andrew (Mu) 29 (VA VA VA), Annah
    (B) 31 (VA VA VA); SHERFFORY, Annah 9
    (g dau) (VA VA VA)

Hh#   Page 8 (cont'd)

68. ANDERSON, John A. 56, Mary A. 43, George A.
    30 (son), Soloman J. 20, Florence J.
    14, John R. 8, Frank H. 2, Annie A. 3
    (g dau); TAYLOR, John (B) 25 (servant);
    McELRATH, Elizabeth 23 (servant) (SC SC
    SC)
69. WRIGHT, James (B) 24 (VA VA VA), Elizabeth
    16 (wife), George 3, Ellen 6/12 (b. Jan)
70. PERSON, Alexander 35 (widower), Rhoda 13,
    Jane 8, Walter 4
71. BOWMAN, John W. 34, Martha A. 31; GOURLEY,
    Dora 2 (niece)
72. BOWMAN, William 74, Nancy 73, Loratta 32
73. KEEN, William M. 42 (wagon maker), Martha A.
    41, Mary E. 18, Julia A. 16, John W. 15,
    Nancy E. 12, George F. 10, Martha 8,
    William E. 5, Laura A. 1
74. PEOPLES, Nathaniel T. 37, Harriot 17 (wife),
    Loucinda E. 2, Elizabeth 76 (mother);
    LANDRETH, Henry 17 (relationship
    omitted) (apprentice carpenter)
75. BOREN, Wiley B. 48, Arzilla 38, George E.
    19, William G. 12, Rhoda A. 69 (mother)
76. HAUN, George A. 47, Mary E. 36, Jinnie M.
    10, Walter E. 5, Jane 87 (mother) (old
    age)

           Page 9, Dist. 5

77. BRITT, Franklin 58 (T VA NC), Emily 49 (T
    NC NC), John W. 17, Hester A. 14, James
    R. 12, George W. 8
78. SHOEMAKER, George (Mu) 51 (T Ire Irc), Ellen
    L. (B) 35 (wife) (T Africa VA), Habakkuk
    17, George W. 16, Mary E. 13, Joseph A.
    7; WILLIAMS, Harriet 75 (widow) (rela-
    tionship omitted) (VA VA VA); GAITER,
    David 14 (step son) (T NC T)
79. McINTOSH, David 47 (T NC T), Harriet 47 (T
    NC NC), Samule 17, Elizabeth 15, Thomas
    12, James 10, Sarah 8, Laura 11/12 (b.
    Jul); WHITEHOOD, Mary 21 (dau)
80. BRITT, Melvina 48 (widow) (T Ire T), Alfred
    M. 21, Anderson 18; BLEVENS, Melvina 3
    (g dau)
81. SIMMONS, Flavious J. 44 (cabinet workman)
    (VA VA VA), Susanah 30 (wife), Edgar
    18 (son) (VA VA VA), George C. 16 (VA VA
    VA), James M. 14 (VA VA VA), Margaret M.
    12 (VA VA VA), Ann M. 10 (T VA VA),
    Emery H. 7 (T VA VA), Mary 65 (mother)
    (VA VA VA)
82. SIMMONS, Lewis A. 28 (VA VA VA), Alice C. 29
    (T T NC), Magnola 5 (adopted dau);
    BRITT, Mary 11 (servant)
83. WILSON, Elijah 62 (diarrhea) (NC NC NC);
    Pheba F. 40 (wife); SMITH, William 12
    (stepson)
84. ROWE, Thomas Y. 39, Elizabeth 22 (wife) (VA
    VA VA), John 6, Vance L. 5, Landon P.
    3, Pinkney P. 41 (bro), Emaline B. 39
    (sis)

           Page 10, Dist. 5

85. MARTIN, James H. 57 (NC NC NC), Loucinda 53,
    Fenettie L. 27 (dau), George L. 25,
    James M. 21, Rebecca E. 18, Mary A. 15,
    Martha E. 13
86. PATTON, Drury M. 40, Joanna L. 45, Nora J.
    17, James C. 10, Charles H. 8, Erastus E.
    6, Luther B. 2
87. YOUNG, John W. 47 (house carpenter), Alice
    E. 38, Samuel P. 18, Laura A. 16, Mary
    E. 13, Hettie L. 10, Joseph R. 7, Cora
    S. 4
88. DICKSON, John (B) 35 (SC SC SC), Elizabeth
    19 (wife), William 10/12 (b. Aug)
89. BUTLER, William 44 (T NC T), Margaret 40
    (VA VA T), Mary E. 13, Sarah M. 10,
    William B. 8, Frazier S. 5
90. BOWMAN, Jacob 55 (NC PA NC), Angeline A. 46
    (NC NC NC), David N. 24, Nancy C. 22,
    Hester E. 20, Daniel A. 18, William F.
    15, George D. 13, Henry M. 8, Mary A. 6,
    John S. 4

Hh#   Page 10 (cont'd)

91. BRITT, Samule W. 38 (T VA T), Sarah L. 34
    (T NC T), William A. 10, Jerry D. 7,
    Mary C. 4

                Page 11, Dist. 5

92. LINSEY, George (B) 30 (GA GA GA), Mariah 35
    (NC NC NC), William 17 (NC NC NC),
    Charles 15 (NC NC NC), Hattie A. 13
    (NC NC NC), John 6 (T NC NC)
93. GEISLER, George W. 24, Edney M. 23, Mary M.
    2
94. HOOPWOOD, (first name omitted) 37 (teacher)
    (KY KY KY), Sarah E. 33 (wife)
    (teacher) (KY KY KY); LaRUE, Jesse V.
    69 (father in law) (KY VA VA), Latia
    71 (mother in law) (KY VA VA), CORN-
    FORTH, Rosa 40 (sis in law) (teacher)
    (KY KY KY), Lettie 10 (niece) (MO KY
    KY), Charles W. 7 (nephew); SNYDER,
    Henry 26 (student--relationship
    omitted); LATY, james A. 20 (student--
    relationship omitted); ELLIS, William
    21 (student--relationship omitted);
    NETHERLY, John 17 (servant), Hiram 15
    (servant)
95. WILLIAMS, George T. 32 (county court clerk),
    Susan N. 26, James R. 9, Ollie E. 6
    (dau), Oscar 1; TUCKER, Emma 18 (ser-
    vant)
96. GILES, William H. 39 (shoe maker) (T NC T),
    Margaret E. 39, Virginia A. 12,
    Charles C. 8, William R. 6
97. GEISLER, William D. 26, Elizabeth J. 28,
    David A. 10/12 (b. Aug)
98. GOURLEY, Mary A. 55 (widow), George W. 31
    (son) (fits), Martha 20, Elizabeth A.
    16; CROW, Daniel 26 (son in law)
    (tanner), Mary L. 22 (dau), Bessie H.
    10/12 (b. Jul) (g dau)
99. GOURLY, William 34 (house carpenter),
    Mahala 26, Alfred 13, Ann 10, Robert
    8, Emma 6, Lucy 3, Samule 10/12 (b.
    Aug)

                Page 12, Dist. 5

100. COLLINS, Theadotia 47 (widow) (T KY T),
     George L. 20, Isaac M. 18, John N. 12,
     Tolbert 10, Walter B. 8
101. OWENS, Hamilton 45 (T NC NC), Matilda 48
     (T NC NC), James 18, John W. 13, David
     S. 11, Samule T. 8; McKEEHEN, Cinthia
     65 (mother)
102. STEPP, Silas H. 55 (fruit grower) (VA VA
     VA), Saphina J. 40 (wife), Virginia T.
     22 (dau) (T VA VA), Susan I. 18 (dau)
     (T VA VA), Zora E. 16 (dau) (T VA VA),
     Robert N. 8 (son) (T VA T), Emma J. 6
     (dau) (T VA T), Edward E. 5 (son) (T
     VA T), Henry P. 3 (son) (T VA T)
103. SHELL, Aron 48, Abba J. 51, William H. 26,
     Louvena 22 (dau in law), Alexander
     2/12 (b. Mar) (g son), Lucretia? E. 19,
     Archibald 17, Lucinda 13, Robert W. 12,
     John L. 7
104. SHELL, Andrew 23, Lidda 22, David H. 1
     (fever)
105. MILLER, Moses A. 63 (SC NC NC), Mary 45,
     Stokes 21, William 15, Mary E. 11
106. PATTON, Joshua M. 40 (T T NC), Julie 40
     (NC NC N), Temperance 18, Samule B.
     16, Robert P. 5; McKEEHAN, Elizabeth
     16 (servant)
107. PATTON, Thomas Y. 37 (T T NC), Mary J. 35
     (NC NC NC), Sarah A. 17, Mary S. 16,
     Hattie D. 14, Annie E. 12, Loulie L.
     10, Irena B. 7, David B. 3, John M. 2,
     Hugh 1/12 (b. May)

                Page 13, Dist. 5

108. BURMMET, John 34, Mary 21 (wife) (NC NC NC),
     Susan B. 2; BRANCH, Emma 59 (mother in
     law) (NC NC NC), Sidney D. 19 (bro in
     law)

                Page 13 (cont'd)

109. MOSLEY, John D. 24, Julie A. 20; CATES,
     Sarah J. 56 (mother in law)
110. CATES, Franklin 31, Matilda 31, John 8
111. BRITT, David P. 51, Jane 48 (VA VA VA),
     Thomas 23, Evy C. 18 (dau in law), Roda
     J. 10/12 (b. Jul) (g dau)
112. MILLER, John 58 (widower), Sarah A. 29,
     Daniel K. 26 (asthma); GILLAM, Matilda
     13 (servant)
113. PRICE, Joseph D. 65 (brick mason) (T MD VA),
     Emaline E. 56, Elizabeth 28, Martha J.
     21, Sabrina 18, Michael 18, Florence 14,
     Charles 12
114. McKERSEY, Eliza 60 (widow); SANDERS, Susan
     A. 22 (servant) (SC SC SC); HOSS,
     Walter (B) 11 (servant)
115. HAYES, Robert 47 (NC NC NC), Rebecca L. 45
     (NC NC NC), Monroe 19 (NC), Joseph S. 9
     (T)
116. McKEEHAN, Landon 52
117. BENNET, David 19, Nancy E. 17 (wife)
118. SMALLING, Martin 26, Evie 29, Cora N. 8
119. TAYLOR, Edmond 50 (widower), Samule 17,
     Mary 16, Landon 13, Ida 11

                Page 14, Dist. 5

120. NAVE, Abraham 46, Abigail 49, Barbra 20,
     Joseph 13, James S. 11, Andrew J. 7
121. NAVE, Henry 24, Sabina J. 25, Walter E. 3,
     Beatrice 2/12 (b. Mar); TUCKER, Addie 6
     (servant)
122. HYDER, Andrew F.? 34 (supt. of public ____),
     Margaret A. 27; ALDRIDGE, George 13
     (servant); TUCKER, Mary 12 (servant)
123. PAYNE, James I. 35 (widower), Margaret 5,
     Henry 2
124. GRINDSTAFF, John H. 22, Sally 23, Mary K.
     7/12 (b. Oct)
125. HYDER, Rosanah 57; McKEEHAN, Arzilla 42
     (sis); WILLIAMS, Margaret 30 (cousin);
     McKEEHAN, Rosa 21 (niece), Thomas 18
     (nephew), Martha 17 (niece)
126. HYDER, Caswell T. 51, Vallura 50, Thomas
     R. 19, James 15
127. BRYANT, Jasper N. 26 (NC NC NC), Caroline
     33; TUCKER, Edmon 20 (stepson), Sarah
     12 (stepdau), Annie 6 (stepdau)
128. WALKER, Benjamine 70 (NC NC NC), Becca 65,
     Joseph 21, Jane 41 (dau in law)
128. SNYDER, Alexander 29, Celie M. 27, Norman
     8, Mary C. 6, Noah H. 2
129. GIBBS, Frank (B) 34 (NC NC NC), Sarah 24,
     John 10, Robert 6, Julie 4, James 3,
     Franklin 2

                Page 15, Dist. 5

130. SANDERS, Richard 35 (works at lumber mill)
     (NC NC NC), Mary C. 25, Sarah E. 16,
     Alexander 7 (stepson)
131. HYDER, Micheal E. 35 (house carpenter),
     Jula 20 (wife), Manta 11/12 (b. Jul)
     (son); TREADWAY, Julie 17 (servant);
     HODGE, Rowe 18 (servant); HYDER,
     Samule 14 (nephew)
132. HANN, Martha 55 (widow), Mary 24, Edmond
     20, Ann 15
133. HYDER, Samule W. 62 (merchant) (T VA VA),
     Sarah 40 (wife) (T NC T), David 17,
     Samule 15, Julia 14, Chester 11;
     LIVINGSTON, Murray 30 (servant);
     McKEEHAN, Addie 16 (servant)
134. HYDER, Henry 33, Mary I. 27, Frank M. 8,
     William 2
135. WATSON, Wiley (B) 40 (NC NC NC), Rhoda 45
     (NC NC NC), John W. 21 (NC), William 19
     (NC), Polly 17 (NC), Malinda 15 (NC),
     Wiley 13 (NC), Thomas 11 (NC), Martha
     9 (NC), Therba 7 (dau) (NC)
136. McKEEHAN, Wiley W. 61, Nancy 60, William C.
     17, Elijah B. 26; SILUS, Elizabeth 21
     (dau) (widow), Margaret 2 (g dau);
     DOUGLASS, John 13 (nephew)
137. SNODGRASS, Cornelia 27 (m), Sabina E. 24,
     John W. 4, Robert 2, Sarah 1

14

Hh#	Page 16, Dist. 5

138. KUHN, Andrew J. 50, Nannie E. 35 (wife)
139. HYDER, Joseph 24, Sarah 21
140. McKEEHAN, William 53, Jula F. 33 (wife),
James S. 18 (son), David F. 12, Minnie
10, Sarah I. 8, John M. 6, Nora J. 4,
Martha 2
141. SMITH, Jacob 61, Mary 45 (wife)
142. LANDY, Thaddius 35, Emaline 29, Frank 19
(son), Samule 15, Edmond 12, Melvin 10
143. DUGLASS, William 41, Mary R. 44, Mary C. 14,
Jacob 9, Julie E. 4; CAMPBELL, William
12 (stepson), Emma 8 (stepdau)
144. McKEEHAN, Samule 47, Hannah 44, John F.
19, Samule R. 17, Thomas 15, Augustus
10, Lucy B. 8, Margarett 6
145. MURRAY, William 41 (widower) (KY T T),
Andrew 17, Madison 13, James E.? 11,
Thomas G. 9, John 7, Joseph F. 5,
William 6/12 (b. Dec); HENDERICK,
Emaline 28 (servant), Elizabeth 8
(nurse)

Page 17, Dist. 5

146. SIMERLY, John M. 30 (sheriff of county),
Alice L. 27, Loucretia A. 8; LONY,
William 20 (servant)
147. HYDER, John W. 59, Martha J. 51, Micheal
28, Nathaniel 26 (boot & shoe maker),
Emma 24 (house carpenter), William 21
Samule 18; SNODGRASS, Lucy B. 10
(cousin)
148. PAYNE, Nathaniel 23, Eva 32 (wife), Jane
48 (sis), Alfred 26 (bro)
149. TAYLOR, Caswell C. 35, Frances T. 32,
Lucinda A. 11, Margaret E. 8, George
C. 6, Caswell C. sr. 85 (father)
(doctor) (T VA MD); SNODGRASS, James
18 (servant)
150. ENSOR, John K. 75 (T MD T), Alexander 44
(son) (engineer), Edny 35 (dau),
Triphosa 28 (dau)
151. ENSOR, Preston 39, Margaret 30, Jula 9
152. WILLIAMS, Samuel W. 45 (deaf & dumb),
Edney 33 (wife), Sarah T. 17, John W.
14, George D. 12, Amy L. 10, Charles
C. 6, William 4, Ida E. 1
153. WILLIAMS, James M. 35, Nancy H. 25, John J.
J. 8, Samule R. 6, William P. 4, Hugh
M. 2, Lucinda 5/12 (b. Jan); HYDER,
Martha (Mu) 16 (servant)
154. SWANNER, Joseph 37, Elizabeth 33, Henry
13, Nora E. 10, Mary 8, Julie E. 6,
Iela? J. 4 (dau), Charles T. 2

Page 18, Dist. 5

155. TREADWAY, William 35, Sarah 36, Mary E.
13, John H. 11, William 8, George 6,
James 4, Randolf 4/12 (b. Feb)
156. TAYLOR, Andrew (B) 38, Hannah 55 (wife),
George 8 (son); LACY, Sarah 18 (step
dau), Mary A. 4 (g dau), Lou 2 (g dau),
Sarah 1/12 (b. May) (g dau)
157. HODGES, Waitsel 37 (shoe maker) (NC NC NC),
Loventia 34, William 9, James 8, Ida
4, Mary 2, Nancy 56 (mother) (T NC T)
158. CAMPBELL, David P. 53 (blacksmith) (VA VA
VA), Eliza J. 54 (T VA T), Mary A. 20,
Alfred J. 18, Winnie E. 17, Elizabeth
13, Margaret 12, David P. 10, Loulie V.
2 (g dau); KITE, Andrew 18 (son in
law), Nancy 16 (dau)
159. LINVILLE, John 35, Emily 32, William 12,
Mary E. 10, David 8, Loucinda 6, Isaac
J. 3, Jula A. 1, Martha 76 (mother) (T
NC NC)
160. GUY, Elizabeth 50 (NC NC NC)
161. MOSLEY, Samule 35 (T NC NC), Elizabeth 28
(NC NC NC), Mary J. 10, William 8,
John M. 6, Margaret 4, Eliza A. 2

Page 19, Dist. 5

162. WALKER, Emaline 52 (widow), Kanada D. 21
(son), Rabecca 17

Hh#	Page 19 (cont'd)

163. LYONS, Joseph 39, Rachal E. 37, James M.
19, Montgomery 16, William 13, Elizabeth
J. 12, John A. 10, Nancy A. 7, Susan E.
5, Mary A. 2, Samule 1/12 (b. May)
164. FINE, Alfred 46, Julia 35, Vinons 13 (son),
Alice 11, Susan 9, Mary 5

Page 20, Dist. 6

164. SMITH, Andrew 20, Mary 30 (wife), Samule 1
165. DUGLAS, James 31, Mary 43 (wife); HOLLY,
Julia A. 20 (step dau), David 15 (step
son); DUGLASS, John 2 (nepew)
166. BRADSHAW, Albert 29 (NC NC NC), Hester 23
(NC NC NC), Gracy 5, Emma 3, Mary 1/12
(b. May)
167. DIAL, Pleasant 50 (blacksmith) (T NC NC),
Mary 56, Mary 17, John 15, Alfred 13
168. PRICE, Charles 30, Susan 30, Hulda 11,
Hugh 9, Minnie 6, Crook 4 (son), Rabecca
1
169. DUGLASS, Alexander 45, Eliza 41, Hannah 1,
Harriat 9, James 7, Debbie 5, Pheoba 2
170. FRITTS, George 30, Sarah 41 (wife), James 4,
Mary 1
171. BRYANT, Peter 52 (NC NC NC), Elizabeth 40
(NC NC NC), William 14 (NC), Robert 11
(NC), Charles 9 (T), Mary 7, John 6
172. HYDER, Jesse 47, Susan 44, Leroy 18, George
16, Stacy J. 14 (dau), Joseph 12,
Nancy 8, Micheal 6, Samule 4

Page 21, Dist. 6

173. HYDER, Nathaniel 31 (doctor), William 56
(father), Margaret 51, Laura 4; TREAD_
WAY, Eliza 21 (cousin)
174. CONSTABLE, John 35 (blacksmith), Caroline
44 (wife), William 13, Amner 10 (dau),
Sarah 8, Ida 7, Emma 4, Robert 1
175. HYDER, Nelson (B) 62 (widower), Grant 12
(son)
176. McKINNEY, Thomas 28, Martha 22, Mary 6,
Charles 3; HYDER, Ann 48 (mother in
law)
177. HYDER, William 25, Mary 18 (wife), Robert 1
178. SMITH, Nathaniel 40, Margaret 33, Mary S.
13, John 10, Victory 8, Joseph 6, William 1
179. WHOSHORN, Frank 30, Louvena 30, James 5,
Lenard 6/12 (b. Dec)
180. HYDER, Jacob 38, Rabecca 38, Clarrissa 9,
Joseph 6, James 4, Martha 3, Micheal
1/12 (b. May); SIMMS, Mary 24 (niece),
James 2 (nepew)
181. GLOVER, Richard 40, Mary 35, James 19,
Delia 13, Tibitha 11, Amanda 9, Ann 7,
Alfred 6, Dora 4, Hampton 2, Susan 71
(mother)

Page 22, Dist. 6

182. GOURLEY, George F. 23, Mary 24, Amanda 2
183. HYDER, Frances U. 42, Martha 39, Louisa F.
3, Augustus 2, Roscoe 4/12 (b. Mar)
184. HYDER, William 34, Jane 35, John 13, Nancy
7, James 4, Mary 2, Harriat 1, Micheal
67 (father) (T T SC); DOUGLASS, Mary 21
(niece); CAMPBELL, Nat 18 (nephew)
185. DAVENTPORT, Patsey 76 (widow); TREADWAY,
Letta 80 (sis); LOVELESS, Letta 57
(dau) (widow)
186. HYDER, Joseph (B) 70
187. GOURLEY, William 25, Vina 19 (wife), Nathaniel 2, Jasa 3/12 (b. Feb) (dau)
188. SIMMS, Henry 30, Eliza 25, James 13 (son),
Eliza 11, Chrilley 6, Lillie 1
189. KITE, Catherine 36 (widow), Robert 13,
Charles 10, Franklin 8, Hamilton 6,
Nathaniel 1
190. MERRIT, James 41 (T ___), Mary 41 (NC NC
NC), Hester 17 (T NC NC), Mary 14 (T T
NC), James 11, John E. 5, Rosa K. 3

Hh# — Page 23, Dist. 6

191. SIMMS, John 45 (no occupation) (blind), Rachel 30 (wife), William 19 (son), John 13, Andrew 10, Mary 7, Sabina 4, Charles 2, Alice 4/12 (b. Feb)
192. RODGERS, Joseph 26. Sarah 25, Pearly 5, Mary 1 (diarrhea), Charles 6/12 (b. Dec)
193. HUMPHREYS, Curly 20, Martha 19, Eliza 6/12 (b. Dec)
194. HYDER, John W. 56, Susan 38 (wife), Edmon 16, William 14, Minton 12, Julia 10, Franklin 9, Calvin 8, John W. 5, Sarah 5/12 (b. Jan)
195. HYDER, Henry 38, Rhoda 29, Ann 10, Josie 6
196. TAYLOR, David 45, Joannah 40, Julia E. 17, Margaret 14, Isabelle 12, Clema 10, William 8, Thomas 4, Johnathan 3/12 (b. Mar)
197. LEWIS, Sarah 40, William 17 (son)
198. KITE, Alvin 36 (name omitted) 42 (wife), Mattie A. 16 (consumption), Samule 14 (diarrhea), Mandy J. 12 (diarrhea), William 10, Henry T. 8 (diarrhea), Mary S. 7, Dora E. 4

Page 24, Dist. 6

199. KITE, Mary 57 (widow), Nancy 27, James 10 (g son), William 9 (g son), Harriat 6 (g dau), James 2 (g son); SIMMS, Charles 19 (g son)
200. GOURLEY, Adam 49, Mary A. 42, Margaret L. 17, William A. 6, Evaline C. 4
201. RANGE, Sarah F. 40 (widow), Robert 11, Peter G. 10, William A. 8, Eliza 5; LUSK, Tennessee jr. 19 (son)
202. DAVENPORT, Elizabeth 44 (widow), Susan 17; GOURLEY, Mary A. 34 (sis); SIMMS, Milburn 1 (adopted)
203. GLOVER, Peter G. 24, Martha 19, Lucy B. 2/12 (b. Mar)
204. RANGE, Johnathan 54, Nancy 31 (wife), Martha 12, Nathaniel K. 11, Barsha A. 9 (dau), Faitha? J. 7 (dau), George W. 6, Mary L. 4, Emma S. 2, Ulyssis S. C. 6/12 (b. Dec)
205. WILLIAMS, Pleasant 72 (T NJ VA), Sarah 62, Sarafina 23, TUCKER, Martha 16 (servant), GOURLY, Alford 22 (servant)
206. DELOACH, Kanada 25, Margaret 20 (wife), William 5 (son), Charles 1

Page 25, Dist. 6

207. TAYLOR, Starling (B) 70, Mary 45 (wife) (rheumatism) (NC NC NC)
208. STOVER, Robert (B) 30, Letia 22 (wife), John 10, Joseph 8, Andrew 6, James 2
209. BREWER, James E. (B) 46, Rachal 55 (wife); TIPTON, Harriat 16 (step dau); SMITH-PETERS, William 75 (father in law)
210. LOVE, Henry (B) 50, Julia 35 (wife), George 13, William 8, Mandy 4, Charles 2
211. CLARK, Thomas J. 52, Louisa D. 35 (wife), William 17, George W. 15, Sarah A. 13, Nora E. 9, Edney R. 7, Leanner C. 4 (dau) (fever)
212. LOVE, Alexander (B) 70 (forgeman), Elizabeth 56 (consumption), Fanny 25, Mary 20; HAYNES, Dicy 6 (adopted dau); LOVE, Georgianna 1 (g dau); TAYLOR, Deliah 75 (aunt) (VA VA VA)
213. YOUNG, Henry (B) 57 (VA VA VA), Diannah 56
214. RITCHARDSON, Spin? 28 (NC NC NC), Caroline 44 (wife), Margaret 2; MOORE, Mary 23 (step dau), Clayton 18 (step son)
215. TAYLOR, John (B) 38, Laura 24 (wife), Mariah 13
216. TAYLOR, Tener (B) 50 (widow), Roda 26, Josaphine 19, John 11 (g son), Alfred 5 (g son), Laura 3 (g dau), Julia 1, Thomas 2/12 (b. Mar)

Hh# — Page 26, Dist. 6

217. SCOTT, William (B) 60 (NC NC NC), Harriat 48, Robert 13, Nathaniel 11, David 6; DUFFIELD, Nelson 23 (stepson); TAYLOR, Henrietta 7 (g dau)
218. BLAIR, Alfred (B) 36, Malinda 47 (wife)
219. TAYLOR, William (B) 41, Mariah 40, David 20, Rufus 13, Jane 11, Evie 9, Elizabeth 7, John 4, William 2, Contango J. 1/12 (b. May) (son)
220. LOVE, Alexander (B) 34, Eliza 35, James 4; TAYLOR, Julia 13 (step dau)
221. RUSSEL, Thomas 61 (miller) (VA VA VA), Louisa 50 (NC NC NC), Mary 26, Archbald 22, John A. 19, Evaline 24; TOUCHPOINT, Nat 4 (g son) (T VA T)
222. FAIR, James N. 56 (T NC NC), Stacy 60 (wife) (VA VA VA), Margaret 20, John 17, Samuel 14
223. ADAMS, James 25, Sarahfina 24 (T T VA), William 4, Nathaniel 2, Minnie L. 1/12 (b. May)
224. JONES, Ambros 25, Elizabeth 59; EDENS, Matilda 18 (step dau), Samule 20 (step son)
225. JONES, Wesly 30, Mary 26, Martha A. 10, Liddie J. 8 (dau), Sarah E. 5, Margaret 2, James 4/12 (b. Feb)

Page 27, Dist. 6

226. TILSON, Nathaniel 30, Rhoda 30, Mary 9, Loretta J. 1/12 (b. Apr)
227. LUSK, Tennessee H. 53, Mary F. 24 (wife), Sarah J. 6, John R. 4, Mary E. 2, Jane 74 (mother), Mary E. 50 (sis)
228. LUSK, John A. C. 49, Mary J. 36 (wife), Robert A. 16, Samule L. 13, Julia C. 11, John L. 9, Mary E. 7, Andrew J. 5, William 3, Rhoda E. 1; HIGGINS, Gilbert 30 (servant) (NC NC NC)
229. THOMAS, John O. 47 (T T VA), Josia 25 (wife), Sue 2, Charles 1; LOVE, Kittie (B) 18 (servant); HALE, James (Mu) 30 (servant) (VA VA VA); HYDER, Samule 19 (servant), Nathaniel 18 (servant)
230. TAYLOR, Nathaniel 60 (minister), Emaline 58, Alford A. 32 (politician), Robert L. 30 (lawyer), Sarah 23 (dau in law) (NC NC NC), David H. 23 (clerk in US Treas) Hugh L. 21 (teacher), Sanna R. 18 (dau), McINTURFF, Mary 15 (servant); GORDON, Doma (B) (f) (servant); STRALY, Josaphine (B) 14 (servant); McINTURFF, William (W) 25 (servant); STUART, Burten (B) 14 (servant)
231. JOBE, Ethelbert K. 31 (manufacture), Mary E. 25, Alford T. 2, Ethelbert 1; OBRIEN, Julia 16 (servant)

Page 28, Dist. 6

232. ROBISON, John 52 (NC NC NC), Rosa 52 (VA VA VA), Susan 10 (VA), Susan 10 (VA), Matilda 6 (VA)
233. LOUDERMILK, James 41, Mary 44, George 13, William 11, Alford 9, John 8, Barbra 7, Noah 4; LITTLE, Rebecca 18 (step dau)
234. TAYLOR, William 55, George D. 47 (bro); LOVE, Franklin 10 (cousin); BOON, Margaret 40 (servant) (NC NC NC), Birdie 4 (T NC NC)
235. MASTON, Joseph 24, Julia 24, William 1/12 (b. May); SPENCER, Elizabeth 40 (mother in law)
236. KEYS, William 26, Eliza J. 26, Henry A. 13, Richard 11, Lillie C. 8, John A. 6, Margaret 4, Nannie 1
237. WILLIAMS, John Q. 60 (blacksmith) (T MD T), Elizabeth 60, Frank E. 30 (blacksmith), Lizzie 22 (dau in law), John L. 4 (g son), Alfred 1 (g son)
238. FAIR, James D. 69 (NC NC NC), Joannah 55, Millard 28; MOODY, Martha 18 (g dau)
239. BOREN, Montgomery 60 (widower) (T T MD); COOPER, Sarah 83 (mother) (T T T--sic)

Hh#	Page 28 (cont'd)

240. BOREN, David 33, Nancy 30 (T NC NC), Charles 13 (T T NC), Mary 1/12 (b. May) (T T NC)
241. COOPER, William 46 (widower), James T. 21, Joel 19, John 14

Page 29, Dist. 6

242. RANGE, Harrison 41, Harriot 35, Liddia E. 13, George P. 9, Ida 7, James T. 5, Samule 2
243. HENDRIX, William 52, Mary 47, Henry 19, James 18, William 16, Mary D. 12, Noah D. 9, Calaway 7, Nathaniel 6
244. HUMPHREYS, Jessie 71, Eliza 68, John 41, William 37 (teacher), Elizabeth 29 (dau in law), Lemual 6 (g son), William 3 (g son); ALDRIDGE, Sarah 21 (servant)
245. LENARD, John 45 (T VA VA), Martha 38 (T VA VA), Sarah 21, Elizabeth 19, Jacob 16, Isaac 14, John W. 12, Vollay 10 (son), Edney 4, Martha 3
246. HUGHES, John 60, Ellen 33 (wife), Albert 6, Mary A. 3; MORRISON, Rosa 75 (boarder) (Ire Ire Ire)
247. WILLIAMS, Mandy (B) 55 (widow), Franklin 22, John T. 21, Jane 19, Ruben 17
248. HUGHES, David (B) 25, Ellen 22, Dora 1
249. CRAWFORD, Thomas (B) 33, Phenett 26 (wife), Mack 9, Martha 7, Hussie 1/12 (b. May)

Page 30, Dist. 6

250. OFLARITY, Patrick 55 (stone mason) (Ire Ire Ire), Mary 33 (wife), Eliza 5, Sarah 3, John 3/12 (b. Mar)
251. KING, John 38 (miller), Saraphina 38; BOWMAN, John 8 (nepew)
252. DUNCAN, Thomas 24 (miller) (VA VA VA), Lillian 22 (VA VA VA), Henry 4 (VA), Edward 2 (NC NC NC)
253. SHORTS, David 64 (NC NC NC), Margaret 48 (wife) (NC NC NC), Henry 20 (NC) (works in lumber mill), William 19 (works in lumber mill) (NC), Alexander 17 (NC)
254. PEOPLES, Kenada 44 (cabinet workman), Mary 41, John H. 20 (works in shop), William 18 (works in shop), Martha 16, Gallatin 14, Samule 12, Arzilla 10, Alice 8, Mary 6, King 3
255. COOPER, Montgomery 25 (painter), Rhoda 18, Robert M. 5/12 (b. Jan)
255. WHITLOW, James 55 (painter) (VA VA VA), Deba 36 (wife), Virginia 14, Emma 12, John 11, James 7, Martha 4
255. SMITH, James 50 (T NC NC), Martha 45, William 14, John 12
256. CROCKETT, Pleasant 55 (T Ire T), Jane 45, Robert 11, James 9, Charles 6

Page 31, Dist. 6

258. HUMPHREYS, John 49, Nancy 49 (T KY VA), Vicey 18, Henry 17, Mary 13 (dau in law) John 11
259. HUMPHREYS, George 21, Delcena 21, Ann 1
260. TAYLOR, James P. 52, Mary 50, Robert 13, William 11
261. ESTEPP, John 21, Martha 20, James 1
262. HUMPHREYS, William 22, Sarah 19, George 2, Lucy 7/12 (b. Dec)
263. TAYLOR, Martin 27, Mary 25, James 4, John 2
264. LANE, Joseph 25, Mary 25, Susan 2, Margaret 1
265. TAYLOR, Barsha 55 (widow), Alfred 38, Nancy 17 (dau in law), Charles 10 (g son); FULLER, John 13 (servant)
266. TAYLOR, Scott 27 (widower), Samule 4, Joseph 2
267. TAYLOR, Isaac 34, Mary 33, Ellen 16, Alice 13, Andrew 11, William 9, Julia 7, Ida 2
268. HUGHES, Joseph 33, Susan 30, John 10, Mary 9, Loulie 7 (dau)

Hh#	Page 31 (cont'd)

269. BUCK, Osborn 45, Evaline 38, Landon 10, Charles 8, David 3; TAYLOR, Nathaniel 88 (father in law)

Page 32, Dist. 6

270. McDANIELS, Alford 43, Elizabeth 30, Lucy 9, Julia 6, Minnie 2, Elvira 48 (sis)
271. RANGE, Landon 39, Oakey 35 (wife) (fever), William 10, Ann 7, Anthony 1
272. RANGE, Elizabeth 50 (widow), Louisa 15, Lizzie 13; MURRAY, Simon 63 (servant)
273. LOUDERMILK, Noah 24, Elizabeth 34 (wife), Henry 2
274. JOHNSON, George 44 (T NC NC), Mary 47 (T T VA), Alice 20, Richard 17, William 12
275. MARSHAL, Landon (B) 35 (fever) (VA VA T), Alice 25 (T VA T), Lucy 15, Federick 7, Julia 1
276. ORENS, Nancy 48 (widow) (NC NC NC), James 25 (T NC NC), Jacob 19, William 17, Mary 14, Eliza 11, Charlotte 7
277. DANIELS, Sylva (B) 40 (widow), Hannah 26, Martha 12
278. GRIFFIN, Hages (B) 30 (widow) (NC NC NC), Isaac 7 (T NC NC), Jane 5
279. LOUDERMILK, Vina 66 (NC NC NC), Martha 33, John 26, Magdaline 14 (g dau), Eliza 6 (g dau), Collumbus 3 (g son), Robert 18 (g son), Peter 17 (g son)

Page 33, Dist. 6

280. DANIELS, Green (B) 48, Nancy 30 (wife), Julia 12, Rutha 10, William 8, Nathaniel 6, Isaac 4, Landon 3, Nora 2, Walter 1/12 (b. May)
281. LOUDY, Catherine 47 (widow) (NC NC NC), Dora B. 6 (T NC NC)
282. SAYLOR, Henry 23, Nancy 33 (wife), Charles 11/12 (b. Jul); McFALL, John 13 (stepson)
283. MULL, Manual (B) 58 (NC NC NC), Malinda (Mu) 40 (NC NC NC), Sarah 14 (NC)
284. SAYLOR, Noah 48 (T VA T), Rachal 25 (wife), Mary 19, Alice 13, Martha 10
285. LYLE, George 33, Jane 27, Sanna 13 (dau)
286. HINKLE, Micheal 33, Victory 33 (VA VA VA), Mary 13, Nancy 10, George 10, Ida 8, Minnie 6, Carrie 4, James 64 (father) (father) (shoe & boot maker); LYLE, Daniel 17 (boarder)

Elizabethtown, District 7

1. BRADLY, Robert 29, Hester 25, Charles 1
2. BAKER, Sally (B) 60 (widow) (T VA VA); NAVE, Julia 30 (boarder) (VA VA T); TAYLOR, Sally 8 (boarder) (T T VA); NAVE, Britty (f) 3 (boarder)
3. COOPER, Elizabeth 76 (widow) (VA VA VA), Ann 45 (dau) (T T T--sic), William 25 (g son), Margaret 18 (g dau), David 15 (g son), Mary 5 (g dau), Adda 3 (g dau), Saml. 5/12 (b. Dec) (g son)
4. TUMER?, Rutha 63 (widow) (NC NC NC), Louretta 7 (g dau)
5. STOUT, Saml. 25, Adaline 21, Mary 5, Henry 3, Delcena 1
6. WILLIAMS, Elizabeth 47 (widow) (T NC T), Christly 17 (works in woolen mill) Laura 12, Dilla 9, Harrison 7, Butler 5, Thomas 3
7. CRUMLY, George 45 (shoemaker), Emma 34 (wife) (T PA T), Nanny 18, Martha 15, Loyett 12 (dau), William 10, Dudly 5, Robert 1
8. BOYD, James O. R. 60 (teacher), Rhoda 55, Mary 30 (dau), John 18, Ellis 16; HODGE, Dusky 17 (f) (servant) (NC T NC)
9. TIPTON, Nancy 41 (widow), Joseph 22, Mary 19; FAIR, George 5 (boarder) (NC NC NC)
10. LOVE, Jacob (B) 37 (NC NC NC), Mary (Mu) 27 (NC NC NC), Roy (B) 5 (T NC T), Fanny 5 (T NC T); TAYLOR, Henry 9 (boarder)

Hh#	Page 2, Dist. 7

11. WILBOURN, Maggie (Mu) 29 (widow), Dora 8, Charles 6
12. HOWARD, Maria? (B) 30 (widow) (VA VA VA), Mary 12 (T T T--sic), Florence 6, William 5, Laura 1
13. ROBERTS, John 37 (wagon maker) (T NC NC), Sarah 26, Orvel 8 (son), Fletcher 3
14. FLETCHER, James 30 (teacher), Jennie 26, Ada 9, Lilly 7, William 5, Carl 3, Carry 2, Eamert 1/12 (b. May); SMITH, Safrona 28 (servant)
15. MILLER, Jerry B. 45, Emma 35 (T T NC), Edgar 15, Abraham 11, Duddly 9, Lilly 7, Hatty 4
16. STEFFEY, John 48 (house carpenter) (VA VA VA), Margaret 30 (wife) (T NC NC), Eugene 7, Mary 5; FONDRON, Susan 10 (niece)
17. BEASLY, Henry 48 (saddler) (VA VA VA), Susan 41, Henry 21 (saddler), Sally 15, Charles 12, Hatty 1; CRIMLY?, John 82 (boarder) (T VA VA)
18. ANGEL, Landon 26, Mattie 21, Emma 4, Gaines 2
19. HENNIGER, George 29 (minister of the gospel) (VA VA VA), Minny 24 (VA VA NC), Berty 1 (NC)

Page 3, Dist. 7

20. HILTON, David 57 (wagon maker), Jennie 31 (wife), Truman 18, Betty 15, George 10, Ally 8 (dau), Mariemen? 3 (dau)
21. CRUMLY, William 50 (shemaker), Nancy 46, Eliza 23, Alice 20, George 18 (shoe-maker), John 16, William 14, Lizzie 12, David 8, Simpson 3
22. ROBERTS, William 27 (wagon maker), Rebecca 27
23. TURNER, John W. 35 (brick Mason) (T T NC), Mary 34 (T VA T), Ruth 12, Saml. 10, Eliza 8, Alice 6, Cany 1 (dau)
24. ANGEL, George 35, Leticia 34, Maggie 6, Laura 4, Frank 1
25. ANGEL, James 63 (jailer) (T VA VA), Mary 62 (T NC T), Alice 31, Robert 21 (clerk in store) (MO); BOWERS, Butler 18 (prisoner)
26. CAMERON, William 24 (dry goods merchant), Mary 26 (T T SC), Bessie 9/12 (b. Aug); GIPSON, Mary 17 (servant) (OH OH OH)
27. PERRY, George M. 33 (house carpenter), Cathrine 22 (wife) (T NC T), Charles 6, Harvey 4, Clifton 1

Page 4, Dist. 7

28. ALENSTER?, Sarah 39 (widow) (music teach-er) (CT CT CT), Fanny 10 (CT CT CT)
29. BURROW, John 55 (blacksmith) (T NC T), Matilda 53 (T NC NC), Saml. 29, William 27 (blacksmith), James 16 (black-smith), Laura 14
30. ROBERTS, Nancy 64 (widow) (T MD T), Angess 29 (T NC T), Bascum 24 (T NC T)
31. FOLSOM, Henderson 47 (atty at law) (T NC NC), Sarah 40 (T VA MD), John 23 (artist), Ida 16, Minny 13
32. CARTER, William 59 (T T VA), Elizabeth 50 (PA T MD), William E. 24 (druggist?), Mary B. 20, Cany C. 13 (dau); BLAIR, Dicy (Mu) (f) 24 (servant)
33. BOYD, H. Clay 31 (post master), Buna 30 (wife) (T VA T), Frederick 6, Henry 3
34. WILCOX, John 32 (landlord) (T VA __), Maggie 32 (T VA NC), Charles 13, Mary 10, Sally 6, Frank 5/12 (b. Jan); BARKER, Nancy 57 (servant) (cook in hotel) (NC NC NC)
35. HEADRICK, Chas. 33 (carpenter) (T VA SC), Elizabeth 28 (T NC T), Mary 7, Frank-lin 5, Sarah 3, Henderson 7/12 (b. Nov)
36. LEE, Alexander 40 (works in woolen mill) (VA Ire Ire), Julia 41 (VA VA VA), Sarah 13 (VA), Alexander 11 (VA), Julia 10 (VA), Robert 8 (VA), John 7 (VA)

Hh#	Page 4 (cont'd)

37. FITZSIMMONS, Eliz. 49 (widow), William 26 (son) (editor) (T VA T), Charles 21 (works in printing office), Jas. 17 (works in printing office) (T T T), Sally (B) 22 (servant), William 10 (servant); McLEOD, Rutha 79 (aunt), GIBBS, Edgar 16 (boarder) (printer) (NC NC NC)

Page 5, Dist. 7

38. ROBERTS, George 34 (dry goods merchant), Emma 32, Ella 12, Dora 8, Lilly 5, Bell 2
39. CAMERON, James 46 (physician), Eliza 46, Jennie 16, Nola 11, Josephine 10
40. ALEXANDER, James 34 (physician), Cinoretta? 28 (VA VA VA), Henry 5 (T T T), Maggie 3 (T T T), Edmund 1 (T T T); COOPER, Rhoda 17 (servant)
41. PERRY, James 66, Sarah 27 (wife), Dolly 19 (dau), James 17, Emma 10, Nathaniel 9
42. TONCRAY, Alexander 34 (dry goods merchant) (VA VA VA), Sally 23, Charles 3, Nelly 3/12 (b. Feb); COX, Cany (Mu) (f) 10 (servant)
43. EMMERT, Caleb 37 (physician), Hester 29, John 27 (bro) (clerk in store), Mary 25 (sis), Eva 3 (dau)
44. PEREGRY?, John 50 (miller) (VA MD MD), Lucinda 46 (VA VA VA), George 17 (VA), White 15 (VA), Chara 10 (dau) (VA)
45. COLLINS, Christopher 30 (atty at law) (T VA T), Sarah 28 (T VA VA), Emiline 4 (deaf & dumb), Inez 2 (deaf & dumb), Maggie 11 (sis) (T VA T), Sally 9 (sis) (T VA T); RUSSELL, Emma 22 (servant)

Page 6, Dist. 7

46. TONCRAY, William 41 (dept US marshal) (VA VA VA), Caroline 30 (wife), James 9 (adopted son); COLLINS, Rebecca 23 (servant) (T VA T)
47. WILCOX, David 49 (minister of gospel), Lucy 46 (VA VA VA), Nancy 9, Sally 7; CROW, Lucy 6 (g dau); HOUN, Flonune (f) 18 (boarder) (music teacher)
48. WILCOX, James 25, Jennie 24 (T VA T), John 1
49. SNYDER, Henry 52 (dry goods merchant) (VA VA VA), Betty 42 (VA VA VA), Nanny 10 (adopted dau), Kate 45 (boarder) (WI WI WI), Frank 10 (boarder) (WI WI WI); LOVE, Molly 18 (boarder); MATSON, Thomas 32 (boarder) (engineer) (IN IN IN), Frances 26 (boarder) (IN IN IN); COX, Ann (Mu) 40 (cook in hotel); RANGE, Ann (B) 40 (cook in hotel)
50. McFARLAND, Nat 31 (cabinet maker), Mary 39 (T VA T), Cally 9 (dau), Eliza 4, Russell 1; JENKINS, David 24 (cabinet maker) (boarder); HENRY, Russell 23 (boarder) (cabinet maker)
51. McFARLAND, Elizabeth 66 (widow), Lydia 33 (works in woolen mill)
52. SHELL, John 39 (butcher), Susan 34; JORDEN, Cany 21 (nephew); HINKLE, Edgar 3 (nephew)
53. WELCH, John 39 (Mu) (blacksmith) (VA VA VA), Sarah 38 (VA VA VA), Bettie 23, Milla 21, Sally 15, William 13, Joseph 11, George 9, Lucy 7, Anna 5
54. SHELL, William 62 (carpenter), Ann 58, William 26, Andrew 24, Alfred 22, Thom-as 19, Mary 16, James 13; HINKLE, William 6 (g son), Lotta 4 (g dau)

Page 7, Dist. 7

55. EMMERT, George 52 (clerk cir court), Kate 34 (wife), Manny 1 (dau)
56. RYON, Elizabeth 42 (widow) (T NC NC), John 19 (T VA T), Mary 14, William 10, George 7; SINGLETARY, Maryann 72 (mother) (NC NC NC)

Hh#   Page 7 (cont'd)

57. MARKLAND, Susan 45 (married), Kily 18 (dau),
    John 17, Nancy 15, Elizabeth 10, Pheby
    8, Alice 6
58. HAMS, John (B) 50 (FL FL FL), Nancy 40 (VA
    VA VA), Rosa 6, Cany 3 (dau); TAYLOR,
    Vonnie? 9 (boarder); CAMPBELL, William
    (Mu) 34 (boarder) (barber) (VA VA VA)
59. MILLER, Rachel 75 (widow); DENNY, Myrtle 12
    (g dau) (OH OH OH), Saml. F. 10 (g son)
    (T OH T), Mary R. 8 (g dau) (T OH T),
    Georgia 6 (g dau) (T OH T)
60. CAMERON, John 44 (hotelkeeper) (T T VA),
    Mary 42? (deaf & dumb), Jane 79
    (mother) (genl debility) (VA VA VA);
    WELCH, Angess (Mu) 37 (servant--cook
    hotel) (VA VA VA), Mat 2 (child of
    servant) (T T VA); COLLINS, Katy (W)
    56 (servant) (VA VA VA); BAMES,
    Milliara? (m) 22 (boarder--shoemaker)
61. SMITH, Robert 34 (atty at law) (T NC T),
    Elvina 29, Clinton 5, Lena 2
62. OLLIVER, Mary 82 (widow) (genl debility) (VA
    VA VA), Jane 37 (dau) (VA VA VA)
63. TAYLOR, Mary 37 (seamstress), Rosa 77
    (mother) (genl debility)

                     Page 8, Dist. 7

64. EDMONDSON, William (Mu) 30 (VA VA VA), Sally
    21, Mary 2, George 8/12 (b. Sep)
65. CHANDLER, William (B) 38 (shoemaker) (SC SC
    SC), Chara (Mu) 30 (NC NC NC), Eliza-
    beth 12 (step dau) (NC NC NC)
66. TIPTON, John W. 31 (atty at law), Mary 30
    (VA VA VA), Berty 7, Kate 6, John 4,
    Milla (Mu) 17 (servant) (VA VA VA)
67. BURROW, William 58 (tailor) (T NC T),
    Rebecca 53, Mary 30, James R. 26 (dept
    Co Court Clerk), Eliza 19, William 17
    (clerk in store)
 8. (addition from page 1 per enumerator)
    PERRY, Saml. 19 (boarder)
25. (addition from page 2 per enumerator)
    ORR, Brownlow 19 (boarder)

        End of Elizabethtown, Dist. 7

                     Page 9, Dist. 7

 1. RUSSELL, Theopolus 27 (widower) (T VA VA),
    Samuel 6, James 3, Charles (less than
    1 yr old--figures obliterated)
 2. DOUGLESS, Susan 48 (widow), Harriett 25
 3. MERRITT, Edgecomb 55, Elizabeth 52 (T NC VA),
    William 18, Elizabeth 7?
 4. SIMS, Susan 86 (widow) (gen disability (VA
    PA PA), Lucinda 37 (T NC VA), Hannah
    35 (T NC VA), Sabina 17 (g dau), Martha
    13 (Mu) (g dau), Harriett (Mu) 11 (g
    dau), Mary 7 (g dau), Fanny (W) 4 (g
    dau) (T NC VA), Sarah 2 (g dau) (T NC
    T)
 5. MATHERLY, Jane 40 (widow) (genl disability),
    John 18, Susan 16, James 13, Thomas 6
 6. HENRY, John 25, Julia 22, James 2, William
    3/12 (b. Feb), Mary 20 (sis)
 7. HYDER, Joseph 46 (paralysis), Martha 41;
    SIMS, William 12 (boarder)
 8. HYDER, Daniel 25 (consumption), Martha 19,
    Mary 2
 9. GOURLY, Thomas 25, Sarah 19, Mary 2, Susan-
    na 2/12 (b. Mar)
10. HYDER, James E. 61?, Eliza J. 40 (wife),
    Byron 21, Samuel 19, Jonathan 17,
    Nicholas 16, Saloma 13, Margaret 11,
    Lilly 9, Joseph 6, James M. 3

                     Page 10, Dist. 7

11. JENKINS, Martha 28, Clarinda 25 (sis),
    Lydia 9 (dau), James 9 (nephew), Lucy
    7 (dau), Ellen 9/12 (b. Aug) (niece)
12. JENKINS, William 22, Josephine 30 (wife)
13. JENKINS, William 53, Margaret 52
14. ANGEL, James R. 45, Elizabeth 45, Saml. 15
15. WILSON?, James 26, Florence 24, Elizabeth 4,
    Robert 2

Hh#   Page 10 (cont'd)

16. JENKINS, ABe 25, Rebecca 26, Sarah? 5,
    Rhoda 2
17. GRINDSTAFF?, David 29?, Eliza 29, Daniel 2
18. LIVINGSTONE, Saml 33, Mary 26, John H. 4,
    William 3, Lula 1, George 2/12 (b. Mar)
19. SIMERLY, Ellen 35, Robert 18 (son), Mary T.
    11 (dau), Husser? 7 (dau), lllice? 4
    (dau), __les 3/12 (b. Mar (son), _____,
    Susan 17 (servant)
20. MERRITT, Leonard 37, Martha 35, Margaret 17
21. TREADWAY, John 24, Mary 22
22. WILLIAMS, Elijah 30, Atha 30 (wife) (T SC
    VA), William 7, Mary 62 (mother)
    (diarhea)
23. MERRITT, John 50 (T VA T), Susan 46, James
    22, Rebecca 10, Benjamin 9, Mary 7,
    Margarett 3, John 2

                     Page 11, Dist. 7

24. LIVINGSTONE, Eliza 42 (NC NC NC), Sally 27
    (sis) (T NC NC), Saml.? 14 (son) (T T
    NC), John 11 (son) (T T NC), James 10
    (nephew) (T T NC), Nathaniel 9 (son) (T
    NC NC), George 4 (nephew) (T T NC)
25. _____, Leonard 68 (NC NC NC), Rebecca 51
    (T NC T), Sally 10, Martha 9, Eliza 6
26. WISHON?, David 25 (T NC T), Mary 17, Henry
    10/12 (b. Aug)
27. McKINNEY, John 38 (T NC NC), Vina 41 (T VA
    T); MERRITT, Rebecca 75 (mother in law)
28. CHAMBERS, David 45 (T NC T), Nancy 32 (wife),
    William 11, John N. 9, Sally 7, Manerva
    5, Lilly B. 2
29. CHAMBERS, Mary 58 (widow) (T NC T), Sarah 33
    (T NC T), Saml. 21, William 19, Daniel
    E. 17, Martha 13
30. WILLIAMS, Pleasant 26, Amy 25, Mary 8, Roxa
    J. 6, Charles 4, Rhoda 1
31. ELLIS, Radford 21, Permelia 27, Charles 7
    (son), Ida 4
32. WILLIAMS, Matt? 57, Mary 42 (wife), John 21,
    Nathaniel 18, William 13

                     Page 12, Dist. 7

33. ELLIS, Daniel sen. 53 (T NC VA), Martha (VA
    VA VA), William 24 (VA), Wily 20 (VA),
    Elizabeth 19 (T), Hooker 16, Grant 14
34. TREADWAY, Jacob 49, Catherine 34, Monroe
    13, Mary 12, Onany 11 (dau), William 8,
    James 6, Lilly B. 4, Louisa 2
35. GLOVER, Elbert 25, Amy 27 (VA VA VA), Betty
    7, Oscer? 5, Emily 2, Lena 1; COLLINS,
    Saml. 21 (boarder) (T VA T), Cordia 12
    (boarder) (T VA T)
36. CAMPBELL, William 31, Elva 21 (wife), Winny
    5, John P. 4, James 5/12 (b. Dec), Saml.
    11, Nancy 9
37. TREADWAY, Benj. 62, Evalina 61, James 29,
    Rebecca 26, Robert 20, Henry 18
38. TREADWAY, John 50, Mima? 50, William 33,
    Andy 19, Martha 11; SHEETS, Ellen 22
    (servant)
39. REYNOLDS, Pompy (B) 37 (T VA VA), Amanda
    34 (VA VA VA), Walter 14, Harriett 11,
    Mary 7, Warster 4, Dilliard 1

                     Page 13, Dist. 7

40. ROGGERS, Hugh (B) 29 (NC NC NC), Emma 23
    (NC VA VA), Berry M. 2 (dau) (NC),
    Edgar 10/12 (b. Aug) (T)
41. ERVIN, Charles (B) 65 (widower) (NC NC NC),
    Thomas 43 (NC NC NC), Jane 43 (dau in
    law) (NC NC NC), Julia 25 (dau) (NC NC
    NC), William (Mu) 7 (g son) (NC NC NC),
    Harriett (B) 6 (g dau) (T NC NC), Cany
    2 (g dau) (T T NC), Thomas (Mu) 1 (g
    son) (T T NC), Lucy (B) 5/12 (b. Dec)
    (g dau) (T T NC)
42. CAMPBELL, James 24, Sarah 44 (sis), Gourly
    17 (nephew)
43. BRADLY, Nathaniel 27, Sarah 30, James 6,
    Elizabeth 6, Geo. T. 4, Saml. T. 3,
    William 1

Hh#	Page 13 (cont'd)

44. BRANCH, Hannah 50 (widow) (T VA VA), Eva-lina 30 (T NC T), Jackson 28 (T NC T), Laura 8 (g dau)
45. FAIR, James 21 (NC NC NC), Fairy? 22 (wife), Walter 2/12 (b. Mar), Charles 9 (nep-hew) (NC NC NC)
46. SMITH, G. H. M. 21, Nany 23 (wife), Louisa 40 (mother)
47. SMITHPETERS, Eliza (B) 40 (widow), Peggy 70 (mother), Grant 8 (son)
48. BROOKS, David (B) 35, Angeline 30, Elben 8 (son), William 7, James 6, George 4, Andy 2, Elizabeth 4/12 (b. Feb)
49. BOWERS, Henry (B) 35 (NC NC NC), Eliza 30 (NC NC NC), Elizabeth 6, Charles 4, Sally 3, Lucinda 51 (mother) (GA GA GA), Lodena 54 (aunt) (NC NC NC), Josephine 14 (niece) (T NC NC), Buton 10 (niece) (T NC NC)

Page 14, Dist. 7

50. MORGAN, Giles (B) 55 (VA VA VA), Betty 50 (VA VA VA); STRATHER, Daniel 35 (boarder) (VA VA VA), Margaret 24 (boarder) (VA VA VA), Eliza 1/12 (b. May) (boarder) (T VA VA)
51. GOURLY, Charles 45, Adaline 39, Ona 14, Elbridge 12, Robert 9, Elfleau 6 (dau), William 1
52. MOONY, Eliza (B) 60 (widow); WELCH, Mary 6 (adopted dau)
53. SHELL, Saml. 37, Jane 37, Nathaniel 12, Jane 10, Charles 7, Margaret 6, William 3, Robert 1; GOURLY, Nathaniel 16 (boarder)
54. HOLLY, David 45, Mary 42 (T NC T), Winfield 20, James 19, Carrie 16, Julia 14, David 10, Hugh 8, Jackson 5
55. MOTHORN?, John 24, Margaret 22, Authur 1
56. McKINNEY, Wilson 33, Ann 37 (T VA T), William 17, John 10, Minny 3, George 1
57. DUFFIELD, William (Mu) 35, Laura 24 (NC NC NC), Lottie 1, George sr. 70 (father), Charlotta 70 (mother), George jr. 9 (nephew)

Page 15, Dist. 7

58. CRAIG, Hiram (Mu) 34 (VA VA VA), Harriett 28, James 9, William 7, George 4, John 2
59. DELOACH, Pheby 50 (T SC T), Matilda 60 (sis) (T SC T), Mary 36 (sis) (T SC T), James 16 (son), Angeline 13 (dau)
60. DELOACH, William 34 (T T VA), Elizabeth 26, Eliza 7, Robert 5, Saml. 2, Elizabeth 26 (servant)
61. DELOACH, James 38, Matilda 27, John 8, Mary 8, John 8 (stepson), Maggie 3, Martha 5/12 (b. Dec)
62. DELOACH, Thomas 65 (T SC T), Pulina 50 (wife) (T NC NC), Jaen 26, William 24, Saml. 20, Nellia 17, Emiline 17
63. DELOACH, John 30, Elizabeth 29 (NC NC NC)
64. DELOACH, Nathan 63 (T SC T), Elizabeth 34 (wife) (T T NC), Mary 14, Pheby 12, Henry 10, David 6, Malind 2 (dau)
65. GRINDSTAFF, John 52, Sabina 51, William 14
66. JENKINS, Hugh 53, Clainda (sic) 44 (T IN VA), Axy 16 (dau), Henry 13, John 11, Charly 10, Mary 5

Page 16, Dist. 7

67. MORRIS, Virgie 42, Amanda 42 (VA SC VA), William 18, James 17, Chatherine 16, Rena 7
68. McCATHRINE, James 66 (wagon maker) (SC SC SC), Marina 66 (VA VA VA), Rebecca 32, Sabina 30, James 26, Elizabeth 25 (dau in law) (T SC VA)
69. HEADRICK, Chas. 57 (T T VA), Rosanna 51 (SC SC SC), Charles 18, George 13, Cornelia 10

Hh#	Page 16 (cont'd)

70. LEWIS, Alfred 24 (T T NC), Delia 23, Bertha 2, Spense 7/12 (b. Oct) (son)
71. HATHAWAY, John 31, Julia 20 (wife), Edgar 6 (son), Osker 5, Caleb 4
72. LIVINGSTONE, John 42 (NC NC NC), Martha 38 (T NC NC); GRACE, Elijah 21 (relation-ship omitted), Margaret 22 (wife) (T T NC), Rhoda 2 (dau)
73. HUMPHREY, Eliza 61 (widow); CALAWAY, Columbus 26 (son in law) (NC NC NC), Mary 19 (dau), Francis 8/12 (b. Sep) (g son) (dead) (T NC T)
74. ALLEN, Sarah 62 (widow) (VA VA VA)
75. TIPTON, Isaac 70 (paralysis) (T VA T), Ann P. 66 (MD MD MD), Ellen 30 (T T T), Josephine 28 (T T MD), Cornelius 21 (T T MD)
76. TIPTON, Thomas 24 (T T MD), Alice 24 (VA VA VA), Lorlee 2 (dau)
77. STOVER, Lamarr? (Mu) 47, Mary 38, Nathaniel 22, Ellen 21 (sis), Gen? 11/12 (b. Jun) (nephew)

Page 17, Dist. 7

78. HOLLY, James 70 (shoemaker) (T NC NC), Mary 71 (T VA VA), John 37, Mary 26, Madison 32 (works in woolen mill), Margaret 27 (dau in law) (works in woolen mill)
79. MURRAY, Andy (B) 34, Eliza 23 (T Africa T), Walter 2, Mima 10/12 (b. Aug), James 8 (nephew); CROW, Mima 52 (mother in law), MURAY?, David 23 (boarder); RUSH, Benjamine (Mu) 25 (boarder)
80. LOGAN, Joseph (Mu) 42 (VA VA VA), Betty 35 (NC NC NC), Lula 7 (T VA VA), William 4 (T VA NC), Mary 3 (T VA NC), Cameron 3/12 (b. Feb) (T VA NC)
81. WEBB, Rod 42, Mary 42, Joseph 18, William 15, Charles 11, Susan 8, Lucinda 6, Mary 1/12 (b. May)
82. CROW, John 28, Eva 30, Jennie 12, George 10, Jessee 8, Mary 6, Lilly 2
83. COLBOUGH, William 68, Elizabeth 70, George 28
84. SMITH, W. B. C. 31 (Co Register), Lydia 29 (T VA NC); POWELL, Nathan (Mu) 56 (servant)
85. JENKINS, David 50 (manufacturer), Eva 27 (wife), James 9, Minny 7, Stover 6, Mary B. 2, Wily 2/12 (b. Apr); PEOPLES, Emma 31 (servant)

Page 18, Dist. 7

86. SONGER, George 45 (miller grist mill) (VA VA VA), Martha 40 (VA VA VA), Mary 18 (VA), Mavon 14 (VA), Nora 5 (VA), Minny 2 (VA)
87. SCOTT, James 45 (manufacturer), Emma 35, Fletcher 9, Raiman 8, Buneece 6 (dau); HESTER, Mary 18 (servant); LEWIS, Nancy 25 (boarder--works in woolen mill); COLLINS, Ally (m) 15 (boarder--works in woolen mill); BURNNETT, Abe 25 (boarder--works in wool mill)
88. MARKLAND, William 26 (works in wool mill), Frances 19 (works in wool mill), Alice 1
89. HENSELY, Thomas 22 (works in wool mill) (NC NC NC), Elizabeth 22, Rutha 2, Hariett 4/12 (b. Feb), James 17 (bro) (works in wool mill) (NC NC NC); JENKINS, Eliza 17 (sis in law) (works in wool mill); EFFLER, Sarah 47 (boarder) (works in wool mill) (NC NC NC)
90. BAKER, James 24 (works in wool mill) (T NC T), Maggie 28, Charles 18 (bro) (works in wool mill) (T NC T); CLOUSE, Sally 18 (boarder) (works in woolen mill)
91. HUNLET, Eugene 33 (manufacturer), Mary 28 (T T NC), Walter E. 6, Frederick 5, Earl 2, Charles 1; SNYDER, Henry 21 (boarder) (machinist) (WI NY NY); HAMMER, Laina? 18 (f) (servant)

Hh# Page 18 (cont'd)

92. CARRIGER, Niol 38, Kate 27, Elizabeth 6,
    Saml. 3; SMITHPETERS, Ann (B) 14
    (servant); COLLINS, Gilson O. 52 (VA
    VA VA)
93. HATCHER, William 23 (blacksmith), Mary 18
94. CAMPBELL, William 25, Delia 17, John
    7/12 (b. Nov)

Page 19, Dist. 7

95. GLOVER, John 46, Margaret 40, Mary 20,
    Celia 14, George 11, Vista 9, Louisa 7,
    Ella 3, Robert E. 1/12 (b. May) (g
    son)
96. HATCHER, Martha 54 (widow), Louisa E. 19,
    Saml. 16
97. TAYLOR, David 44 (blacksmith) (T NC T),
    Caroline 40, Mary 13, Ella 11, Ena 9,
    Rosa 7, Lurana 5, Edmond 1; HUMPHREY,
    Pinkney 25 (servant) (NC NC NC)
98. NAVE, Mark W. 62, Maryann 50, William 29,
    Elizabeth 17, Lafayett 16, Susan 15;
    PATTER, Sarah 30 (dau) (widow), Saml.
    17 (g son)
99. HUMPHREY, John 82 (T VA VA), Celia 74
100. HYDER, J. H. 68 (minister of the gospel),
    Elizabeth 56, William 17, Daniel 15,
    Emma 13; COLLINS, James 26 (servant),
    Jane 16 (servant); HENRY, James 24
    (servant)
101. HYDER, Loss F. (m) 36 (physician), Maggie
    33, Charles 9, Reuben 7, Permelia 5
102. BAYLESS, John 46, Sarah 43, Elizabeth 20,
    Sarah 19, Margaret 17, Celia 16,
    Cardid? 14 (dau), Gilbert H. 13, Jos-
    ephine 11, James C. 10, Nola C. 8,
    Henry 7, Augusta 4 (son), Eugene 1;
    CAMPBELL, Hamp 22 (m) (servant)

Page 20, Dist. 7

103. HUMPHREY, France 25, Rhoda 24 (wife);
    CAMPBELL, Eda 16 (sis in law), Michael
    9 (bro in law)
104. WILLIAMS, Alfred 44, Norah 44, Mary 18,
    Joannah 17, Eliza 14, Charles 13,
    James 10, Robert 8, Hammy 6 (son),
    Maggie 4
105. TADLOCK, Robert 25, Emily 24 (VA VA VA),
    Maggie 5, Howard 3; FOLSOM, Ellen (Mu)
    19 (servant)
106. MORRELL, Edlet 25, Alice 24 (VA VA VA),
    John 6/12 (b. Dec)
107. SMITH, James 59 (T NC T), Mary 54, Daniel
    29, George 27, James 25, Texanna 24
    (dau in law), Eva 19 (dau in law),
    Daniel 9 (g son), Minny 6 (g dau),
    Davidson 4 (g son), Cameron 2 (g son),
    Clay 2 (g son), James (Mu) 21 (servant)
    (NC NC NC)
108. EDENS, John 48, Edna 51, Forence 23 (dau),
    Joseph 18, Charles 16, Ella 13, Eddy 7
    (son)

Page 21, Dist. 7

109. EDENS, David 26 (blacksmith), Mary 26,
    Wilkie 4, Ella 1; TAYLOR, William 22
    (servant)
110. TAYLOR, William (B) 31, Mary 39, George (Mu)
    16 (stepson), Maggie (B) 6, Saml. 4,
    Andrew 2; CAMERON, Jane 64 (mother in
    law) (Mu), Malisy 24 (sis in law);
    TAYLOR, Lucinda (B) 29 (boarder)
111. HAMPTON, Thomas 24 (cabinetmaker) (T NC NC),
    Sally 22, Saml. 3, William 1; FAIR,
    Joseph 31 (boarder--house carpenter)
112. ANGEL, Thomas 31, Emma 24, George 4
113. BRITT, Mat 34, Flora 33, William 4/12 (b.
    Feb); MOLLER, Lear (B) (f) 25 (servant)
114. STOVER, Nathaniel (B) 49 (T VA T), Ama 35
    (NC NC NC), Eliza 16, Burtha 14, Gillam
    12, John 10, Isaac 8, Jacob 3, Landon
    2/12 (b. Apr)
115. OVERHULSER, William 41, Elizabeth 39, Wilson
    13, Thomas 11, Mary 10, Lucinda 8, Otta
    6 (dau), William 2

Hh# Page 21 (cont'd)

116. JOHNSON, Nancy 61 (widow), Abraham 27, Wil-
    liam 24, Robert 21, Minny 21 (dau in
    law) (NC VA VA)

Page 22, Dist. 7

117. JOBE, Abraham 62 (physician), Salvona 54
    (NC NC NC), Rutha 15, Sally 12
118. SMITH, Hamilton 60 (state judge) (T VA VA),
    Sarah 36 (wife), James H. 25 (teacher)
    (son), Jos. H. 13, Sarah 10, John A. 5,
    Adam 3, Rebecca 6/12 (b. Dec)
119. GARRISON, John 24 (T NC T), Mary 16, Hannah
    45 (mother)
120. SMITH, James G. 66 (co. surveyor) (NC VA
    VA), Rosannah 61 (T NC VA), Margaret
    35 (NC), Hamilton 24 (NC), Byron 21
    (NC), Lucy 18 (NC)
121. ELLIS, Daniel jr. 26 (teacher), Eliza 21,
    Lilburn 3 (son), Amy 1
122. BLEVINS, Charles 57 (NC NC NC), Sarah 50,
    Brownlow 13, Charles 8 (stepson)
123. ALLEN, Daniel jr. 41 (miller G & SM), Mary
    40 (T T NC), William 12, Wilbourn 11
124. MERIDITH, William 46, Elizabeth 40, Mary 13,
    James 11, Joseph 7, Lilly 4, William 1
125. OBRION, B. M. G. 64 (T T Ire), Elizabeth 28
    (wife) (NC NC NC), Mary 6, William 4,
    Margaret 3, Joseph 1, Henry 35
    (servant); MOSELY, Julia 37 (servant)
126. YOUNG, Alfred (B) 48 (NC NC NC), Vina 50
    (SC SC SC), Sarah 9 (dau), Sheurman 7;
    GREENLEE, James 4 (adopted son) (T NC T)

Page 23, Dist. 7

127. HART, Cam R. 45, Sarah 39, Alice 23
    (teacher), Thomas 21, Mary C. 17, Jobe
    15, Columbus 13, Lilly 11, Charles 6
128. BRADLY, Elizabeth 64 (widow) (T NC T),
    James 23, Eva 21, William 18; HELTON,
    Robert 7 (g son)
129. TIPTON, Albert 62 (insane), Catherine 55
130. LEFTWICH, Horace (B) 30 (VA VA VA), Char-
    lotta (Mu) 25, Mary 8, George 6, Saml.
    3, Rosa 5/12 (b. Dec)
131. STOVER, Thomas (B) 56, Lucy 56, Emma 20,
    CARRIGER, Thomas (Mu) 88 (father)
132. BECK, John 28 (NC NC NC), Mary 27, Lilly 6,
    Cany 4 (dau), James 1
133. PRESTON, Pleasant (Mu) 54 (VA VA VA),
    Nancy? 52 (VA VA VA); COLWELL, Sarah
    (B) 30 (boarder) (idiotic) (NC NC NC),
    Thomas 2 (boarder) (NC NC NC); DAVIS,
    Ann 27 (boarder) (NC NC NC)
134. CARTER, William 26 (T T GA), Cordelia 30,
    Lula 4, Mary 2, Anna 1
135. COLLIT, Tolbert (Mu) 57 (NC NC NC), Eliza
    22 (wife) (SC SC SC), Frank 7 (son),
    Vina 5, Alfred 3, Virgil 1

Page 24, Dist. 7

136. COLLIT, Stia (Mu) 56 (T NC NC), Mary (B)
    22 (wife), Butler (Mu) 4, Grant 1
137. SUTHERLAND, Kisy 40 (widow), Charles 10,
    Anna 8, James 6, Winny 5, Lilly 1
138. CAMPBELL, Eliza (Mu) 40 (widow), Tecumpsy
    16, Duddly 14, Daniel 11, George 9,
    Zannah 5 (dau), Mary 3, James 1;
    WALLICE, Elizabeth (B) 22 (boarder) (NC
    NC NC), William 7 (boarder) (NC NC NC)
139. FELLERS, John G. 60 (T VA T), Susan 51 (VA
    VA VA); MILLHOM, Alice 18 (servant);
    CAMPBELL, Henry 22 (boarder) (cabinet
    maker)
140. TONCHAY, Charles 43 (dry goods merchant)
    (VA VA VA), Maggie 40 (deaf & dumb),
    Saml. 20 (married within yr), Connie 17,
    Mary 14, Rachael 14, Hester 22 (dau in
    law) (married within yr); CROCKETT, John
    27 (boarder) (clerk in store); PEARCE,
    Mary 22 (servant); FONDREN, Nancy 42
    (servant), Saml. 3 (boarder)
141. SMITH, John C. 35 (clerk in court) (T NC T),
    Eva 34 (T T MD), Mena 10, Calby 9 (dau),
    Otter 7 (son), Hubert 4, Cecil 1;
    EDENS, Matilda 20 (servant)

Hh#	Page 1, Dist. 13

1. ROBERTSON, John C. 36 (railroad agent) (widower), J. Frank 13, Sarah M. 12, N. Cordie 10 (dau), Stella M. 2, Mary 38 (sis)

2. BUNCH, R. J. 53 (carpenter) (VA VA VA), Rhoda 51 (wife) (T NC T), Wm. W. 6 (g son)

3. KING, Vina 30 (married), Charles 7 (son), Emma 6, John T. 5

4. THOMPSON, E. M. 21 (T __ __), Winnie 22 (wife)

5. ANGEL, Albert G. 48 (boot and shoe maker) (VA VA VA), Mary 46 (VA VA VA)

6. FAIR, Bethul 31, Eliza 33, Isaac 9, William 6, Elizabeth 4, Maggie F. 5/12

7. HESS, John B. 52 (boot & shoe maker) (VA VA VA), Mary C. 28 (wife), Alice D. 6, John W. 3

8. ROBERTSON, William (B) 29 (NC NC NC), Margaret 21 (NC NC NC)

9. PENIX, Miles 44 (blacksmith) (NC VA NC), Catherine 37, Emma 8

10. ELLIS, John 46 (T NC T), Sallie J. 27 (wife) (T VA T), Rhoda 20 (dau) (T T VA), Maggie 11, Sena M. 9, John M. 7, Anna S. 5, Charles 2, Minnie L. 7/12 (b. Oct)

11. HOUSTON, H. Basher? 28, Robt. S. 3, Victor H. 2, Ella 9 (adopted dau) (T __ __)

12. FOUST, Daniel 45 (cooper) (T NC NC), Marth A. 46 (T AL T), S. Harrison 21 (cooper), Catherine 21, William 16, Samuel 14, Daniel 11, Mary Jane 9, Warren 6, Charles H. C. 3

Page 2, Dist. 13

13. HENDRIX, Jacob R. 31 (miller), Mary C. 34, Wm. Brownlow 16, James A. 12, Adetha E. 10, John H. 8, Mary E. L. 4, George Gurly? 2

14. HENDRIX, Solom H. 39 (postmaster), Emma J. 27 (T VA T), James B. 14, William J. 12, Charles M. 10, Robt. E. 8, Lillie P. 4, Fred A. L. 3/12 (b. Feb); GLOVER, Rutha A. 22 (cook)

15. KIDWELL, Richard 47 (merchant--dry goods) (VA VA VA), Lou B. 31 (wife), Nancy 19 (dau) (T VA VA), Elizabeth 13 (T VA VA), Ida 11 (T VA VA), Virginia 8 (T VA VA), Birdie 4 (T VA T), MONROE, John 84 (father in law) (VA VA VA); SMITH, Alice 19 (cook)

16. DANIEL, Greene B. 59 (grocer) (NC VA VA), Elizabeth 58 (T T NC), Jane 31 (T SC T), Ben Frank 29 (T NC T), Alice 22, Margret 21, Riley B. 18, Amanda 15, Robt. A. 6 (g son) (crippled), James 4 (g son), Nora 4 (g dau)

17. PINN, George (B) 45 (widower) (cooperer) (VA VA VA)

18. LILLEY, John S. 43, Elizabeth 40, George T. 15, Caleb V. 14, David 12, Farris C. 10, Laura J. 8, Rhoda Ann 6, Rebecca E. 5, John 3, Blair 1/12 (b. Jun)

Page 3, Dist. 13

19. REESE, D. N. 40 (dry goods merchant) (KY KY KY), Anna 35, Minnie L. 14, Thomas T. 12, George A. 10, William 2

20. DANIEL, Mary F. 35 (NC T NC); TAYLOR, William B. 39 (cousin) (carpenter) (T T PA)

21. HOUSTON, Finna 32 (f) (T T PA), Mary A. 45 (sis) (T T PA), John 15 (nephew) (T __ T)

22. LACY, Andrew J. 39 (T T NC), Elizabeth 36 (T T NC), William J. 17, Mary E. 14, Julia A. 8, George T. 6, Corneleas S. 3, Robt. T. 8/12 (b. Sep), John 50 (bro) (T T NC)

23. BOWMAN, Henry K. 38 (widower), Ida E. 12, Callie E. 12 (dau), Robt. L. 9, Joseph A. 7; KING, Callie 35 (sis in law)

24. GARLAND, William W. 28 (miller), Margret A. 27

Hh#	Page 3 (cont'd)

25. GIBSON, William B. 24, Letticia 25 (VA VA VA), Albert H. J. 2, Charles C. 7/12 (b. Oct)

26. SNAPP, Alfred (B) 33 (blacksmith) (widower), Laura 5; DEBOSE, Rebecca 19 (cook) (VA VA VA)

27. LACY, Sarah 79 (widow) (SC SC SC), Hannah 44 (T T SC), Alice 15 (g dau); HUTSON, Miles 77 (bro) (SC SC SC) (crippled)

28. LACY, Albert K. 33 (T T SC), Mary 32, Thomas 5, Charles 4, Robt. E. 2, Julia E. 7/12 (b. Nov)

Page 4, Dist. 13

29. LACY, Samul 28 (T T SC), Mary A. 26 (SC NC NC)

30. BURK, Elizabeth 52 (widow) (T T SC); WHALEN, Julie E. 25 (T Ire T)

31. SCOTT, Sarah 52 (widow), John 28, Robt. 25, Benj. F. 22, Andrew J. 14, Francis M. 12, Martin L. 7

32. SCOTT, William M. 32, Hannah 28, Lafayette 10, Charles M. 8, Ida D. 4, Prascora G. 1

33. HUMPHREYS, William 42 (T T NC), Elizabeth 40, Matilda A. 12, James A. 10, Melville 7, Fannie S. 3; HUMPHREYS, Lecy 66 (mother) (NC __ SC)

34. SMITH, Elizabeth 74 (widow) (VA VA VA), William 31 (T T VA); PERRY, Jane 50 (boarder)

35. FOUST, Back 25 (T T NC), Mary 22 (T NC NC)

36. FULKERSON, William 63 (widower); HYATT, Lucinda 60 (cook), Allen 17 (boarding), Sis 11 (boarding)

37. HUMPHREYS, David 45 (partially blind) (T T NC), Sarah 40, David jr. 17, Allen 16, Delcinia 13, Gordon 10, Elizabeth 9, Martin 6, Rhoda 5, Maude F. 1/12 (b. Jun)

38. HUMPHREYS, Marion 20, Martha 19, Edward W. 1, Oscor 3/12 (b. Feb)

39. GIBSON, Pleasant 64, Nancy A. 65

Page 5, Dist. 13

40. CONWAY, Stephen (B) 56 (practicioner of medicine) (T VA VA), Rosanna (Mu) 46 (T VA AL); BOYD, Eliza (B) 14 (niece)

41. GILES, James A. 51 (crippled) (VA VA VA), Caroline E. 42 (bronchitis) (VA VA VA), James T. 17 (VA), Susan E. 16 (VA), Martha C. 14 (VA), Ansey A. 12 (dau) (VA), William I. 11 (VA), Samuel E. 10 (VA)

42. GREENWAY, James K. 35 (T __ __), Mary J. 35, George 12, Susanah 10, Sarah E. 7, John W. 5; COX, Richard (B) 50 (boarder) (VA VA VA)

43. LITTLE, George W. 37 (works at sawmill), Charlotte A. 35, Oscar L. 12, David P. 9, Bascom L. 3

43. LITTLE, Henry 74, Matilda 61, James M. 24; KEPPLER, Christopher C. 61 (boarder--potter) (divorced) (Ger Ger Ger)

44. LITTLE, Andrew J. 23, Racheal 17

45. MOTTEM, William 51, Susanah 57, Eliza 28, James R. 18, Solomon 16

46. MOTTEM, George W. 32 (carpenter), Harriet 23, A. Milton 8

47. MORRELL, John S. 66 (divorced), Sarah A. 45 (dau)

48. MORRELL, Joseph P. 30 (pasterer), Nancy D. 23

49. MORRELL, William E. 27 (plasterer), Susan E. 23, Minnie E. 5; HENDRIX, John S. 14 (bro in law)

50. VEST, Archibald J. 35, Nancy 29, Solomon J. 11, John 9, Mary M. 8, Sophia 4, Sarah E. 1

Page 6, Dist. 13

51. THOMPSON, William 37 (Mu) (work on rail road) (NC NC NC), Emma 14 (dau) (VA VA NC), Rhoda 4 (T NC NC), Lucinda 2 (T NC NC)

Hh#   Page 6 (cont'd)

52. FAIR, James N. jr. 23 (boot & shoe maker) (T
    T VA), Alice 23, Henry P. 2, Nellie B.
    7/12 (b. Oct)
53. WILLIAMS, Redding (B) 55, Lucinda (Mu) 48
    (NC NC NC), Cora 21 (NC), Landon 13 (VA);
    DUFFIELD, Mary 16 (dau) (NC T NC),
    James W. 1 (g son) (T NC T); WILLIAMS,
    Mary Anna 1 (g dau) (T T NC)
54. BARR, David 43 (T ___), Nancy 38, William
    H. 21, Joseph J. 17, James 13, John 10,
    Mollie 6, Author 3, Martha 2
55. BRETT, Henderson 55, Deborah 44 (T T PA),
    Elizabeth 29, Anna 16, Susan 13, William
    10, Evaline 8, Emiline 8, Jane 5, John
    2; HINES, Christena 70 (mother in law)
    (PA PA PA)
56. BARBER, Tilman (Mu) 70 (VA VA VA), Mira 54
    (wife) (VA VA VA), Alice 12 (T VA VA)
57. SHELL, James 35 (crippled), Marth A. 33,
    Mary E. 15, Nancy A. 12, Elizabeth E. 9,
    Andrew C. 7, Isham N. 5, Milburn 3, Ida
    J. 1; COOPER, Mary 50 (mother in law)

Page 7, Dist. 13

58. SHELL, Emeline 60 (widow), Joseph 20 (son),
    John 16
59. DEMPSY, Melina? 56 (widow) (T SC T);
    SPEARS, Marion 4 (boarder)
60. CAGLE, Isaac 42 (laborer) (NC NC NC?), Sarah
    M. 27 (wife), Samuel 7, Martha 4, William
    1
61. MOTTEM, Henry D. 22, Rutha A. 20, Bessie A.
    1
62. VEST, William J. 41, Catherine 29 (wife),
    Mary 8, James H. 6, George D. 5, Maggie
    S. 3
63. VEST, Susanah 64 (widow), Elizabeth 16
    (adopted)
64. HENDRIX, John 57, Louisa 53, Sallie 27 (dau
    in law) (widow), Julia E. 8 (g dau),
    Joseph H. 6 (g son), Emily 3 (g dau)
65. RANGE, Jacob 58, Mary J. 33 (wife), George M.
    12, Jacob M. 2
66. DAVIS, Brownlow 33 (engineer), Louisa 33,
    Sarah E. 9, Alexander P. 7, Eliza E. 6,
    Charles E. 3, Hazel B. 69 (father)
    (widower) (boarder), Rosanna 23 (sis)
67. CARTER, Frazier 45 (VA VA VA), Julia E. 34
    (wife) (VA VA VA), Rosanna 8 (WV VA VA)
68. HAWLEY, John (B) 24 (works on rail road) (VA
    VA VA), Lucinda 22 (wife) (T KY T),
    Margrett 10, Julia 8, Frank 2, Samuel 2,
    Frank sen. 23 (brother) (boarder) (T VA
    VA); KINCHELOE, Harriet 15 (cook)
    (servant)

Page 8, Dist. 13

69. SMALLING, Alfred B. 30, Louisa 23, Clarance
    6, Robt. B. 1; PLOTT, Ellen (Mu) 16
    (cook) (VA VA VA)
70. CAREY, William 49 (Mu) (laborer) (VA VA VA),
    Alice (B) 50 (wife) (VA VA VA), John 14,
    Robt. 8, Mary 3 (Mu); ARRANTS, Charles
    (B) 4? (boarder); REYNOLDS, Mary 23
    (boarder) (cook); ROBERTS, George 22
    (boarder) (works on Rail Road) (GA GA
    GA)
71. SWINEY, Westley 44, Lucinda 45 (T T SC),
    Alice 17, Martha 14, Barrha 12 (dau),
    James 10, Thomas 8
72. CAMPBELL, William R. 50, Margarett 43, Mat-
    tilda 19, William G. 14, Nancy A. 11,
    Ann V. 9, Bertie L. 7 (dau), Samuel M. 3
73. PERSINGER, Lewis 30 (married within yr) (VA
    VA VA), Elizabeth 17 (wife), George 80
    (father) (widower) (VA PA PA)
74. PERSINGER, John H. 38 (VA VA VA), Sina 30,
    Julia 10, Charles 8, James 4, Robt. L. 1
75. RANGE, Elkanah D. 56, Barsha 50 (wife),
    Rutha A. 20, Andrew J. 17
76. THOMPSON, Samuel 44 (T SC T), Sarah 36,
    Mary 13, Larkin F. 11, William 10,
    Sufroney E. 7, Cordelia R. 2; DEMPSY,
    James 19 (boarder) (laborer) (VA SC VA)

Hh#   Page 9, Dist. 13

77. MOTTEM, William 37 (widower), Jerremiah 12
    (son), James H. 8, Matilda E. 5
78. CAMPBELL, John J. 37 (widower), Nancy E. 10
    (T T NC), Neoma C. 8 (T T T--sic),
    Melvin 4 (T T T)
79. FEATHERS, Andrew J. 27, Adiline 28, Lillie
    Bell 4, Mirtle V. 3, Ida M. 1
80. HUGHES, John 19 (works at sawmill) (T T VA),
    Mary V. 20
81. FOUST, Samuel J. 25 (T T NC), Mary 68
    (mother) (NC NC NC), John 10 (cousin)
82. TAYLOR, James 29, Charity 62 (mother) (T
    NC NC), Elizabeth 36 (sis), Mary 32
    (sis), William 27 (bro), Barsha A. 20
    (sis)
83. SHELL, Elkanah 47 (T NC T), Hannah 48 (T SC
    T), Mary E. 19, Barsha A. 17, Nathaniel
    T. 13, Robert P. 11, Larkin T. 9,
    George S. 8, Alexander E. 5
84. HENDRIX, Harrison 67, Lavina 47 (wife) (VA
    VA VA), Samul C. 16, Mary E. 12;
    GLENN, James S. 18 (stepson) (VA VA VA)
85. SHELL, Alvin P. 41, Barsha 39, Isaac T. 16,
    Samuel 13, Rhoda 11, Mary E. 8, Lidia
    5, William H. 1
86. FAIR, William C. 51 (T NC NC), Emiline 45,
    Henry 2; FLOYD, Rosencrans 17 (stepson)
    (huckster)

Page 10, Dist. 13

87. HAWLEY, Frank (B) 46, Nancy (Mu) 40, Robert
    19, Mary 15, George 14 (pneumonia), John
    6 (g son), Phillip 4 (g son), Henry R.
    1 (g son); REEVES?, Elizabeth (B) 30
    (cook) (NC SC SC)
88. GIBSON, Elbert 27, Mary J. 21, Robert L. 5,
    Sophia E. 2, William J. 5/12 (b. Dec)
89. HIGGINS, Isaac (Mu) 26 (NC NC NC), Sarah (B)
    39 (wife) (T T NC), William (Mu) 10;
    YOUNG, Jackson (B) 70 (father in law);
    LOVE, Eva 18 (niece) (T T NC), Samuel
    H. (Mu) 1 (boarder)
90. BOOKER, Runa (B) (m) 30 (T Africa T),
    Sarah (Mu) 25, Elizabeth 8, Franklin 5,
    Nora 2, Margret 1
91. RANGE, Henry 62, Elizabeth 48 (wife), Mary
    31, Sarah E. 16, Louisa A. 13, Rutha
    C. 4; WATSON, John 13 (boarder)
92. RANGE, Alfred 50, Lydia 29 (AR T T), Mary J.
    6, Lula A. 4, James H. 2, Margret E.
    4/12 (b. Feb); CALDWELL, Taylor 19 (laborer)
    (T VA VA); CLAIMEN?, Martha 30 (sis
    in law)
93. RANGE, Jerimiah B. 43, Sarah E. 35, Nancy S.
    13, Fatha E. 12, Julia C. 10, Sarah A.
    8, Robert Andrew 6, Margrett E. 4, Ida
    Jane 1, Fatha 78 (mother), Juilus? H.
    46 (bro)

Page 11, Dist. 13

94. LACY, John M. 25, Mary 24, Ella 1/12 (b.
    Apr)
95. RIGGS, James 33 (plasterer) (NC NC NC),
    Sabra 24, J. Elbert 4, William C. 3,
    Samul J. 1, Nancy 65 (mother) (NC NC NC)
96. EMMERT, Jeremiah 53 (divorced), John 21,
    Harriet 18, Sarah 15, Jeremiah 13,
    Fannie 13, Lydia 11
97. SCALF, William 43 (T T NC), Mary E. 40 (T
    NC NC), Modina 10, Molissa 5, Rhoda A. 2
98. EMMERT, George W. 20, Mary 16 (wife), James
    L. 6/12 (b. Nov)
99. CRUMLEY, William 41, Susan E. 39, William
    M. 15, John A. 12, James M. 11, Arty A.
    7, Elizabeth A. 4, Delia M. 2
100. EMMERT, Fannie 50 (divorced) (T NC T),
    William 11
101. TAYLOR, Levi 81 (wheelwright) (VA T T),
    Sarah 63 (wife) (NC NC T); SCALF,
    Adlaide 21 (niece) (T T VA), Jessie 1
    (boarder)
102. READY, John 23 (blacksmith) (VA VA VA),
    REbecca 20 (T T NC), Charles E. 1/12
    (b. May)

Hh#	Page 11 (cont'd)

103. SMALLING, Robert 56, Harrett 56, James H. 25 (bridge carpenter), Andrew T. 22, David R. 17, George P. 14; SHELL, Virgina A. 11 (niece); SMITH, Alfred (B) 16 (servant); BENNET, Lucinda 20 (W) (cook)

Page 12, Dist. 13

104. CROW, Martin (B) 54 (widower) (T Africa T), Solomon 23, Lewis 21, Martha 18, Samuel 13, Tenna 23 (dau in law), Ellen 1 (g dau), Ida 2/12 (b. Apr) (g dau)
105. HUGHES, Sandy (B) 76, Lucinda (Mu) 56 (wife) (T Africa T); LOVE, Richard 17 (g son) (T T NC), Eliza 13 (g dau?) (T T NC)
106. GREENE, Timothy (B) 40 (VA VA VA), Lena (Mu) 22 (wife), Sarah (B) 13 (dau) (VA VA VA), George 11 (VA), John 10 (VA), Kincaid (Mu) 3 (T VA T); LOVE, Margret (B) 20 (niece) (T NC T), Henry A. (Mu) 5/12 (b. Dec) (boarder) (T NC T)
107. HYDER, Hannah (B) 56 (divorced), Alice (Mu) 15 (dau?)
108. TAYLOR, Nathaniel L. 62, Malinda 63, Alfred 26, Sarah 23, Elizabeth 21
109. TAYLOR, Danul W. 27, Nancy 27, Nathaniel L. 9/12 (b. Aug)
110. TAYLOR, James P. 35, Mary S. 35 (T T VA), Nathaniel F. 13 (Washington DC), James P. 11 (MD), Napoleon 9 (T), Shakspeare 8, Gertrude 5, Baxter 3, Emma J. 1, Maria (B) 12 (servant); GLOVER, Vinnie (W) 24 (cook)
111. HARRIS, William (B) 25, Lyllie 20, William 2, Hester L. 1/12 (b. May); DUNCAN, Alfred 10 (nephew)
112. HUGHES, Margret 40 (widow) (VA T T), Charles 17 (T T VA), James L. 14, Robert L. 11, Eugene M. 9, Samul T. 3, Julia M. 1

Page 13, Dist. 13

113. DANIEL, Ryley B. 46 (wagon maker) (T VA NC), Abigal 44, Cornelia E. 22, William 19, Mary E. 16, Flora J. 13, Samul J. 8, Hugh T. 4
114. HART, Leonora 44, Eliza 47, William R. 23, Mary E. 20, Nathaniel T. 12, John S. 8
115. HART, George 26 (plasterer), Margret 25, Rhoda A. 3
116. BUCK, Barzina 50 (divorced); FAIR, Cordelia 27 (dau), Mary 9, Louisa 6 (g dau), Lafayette 4 (g son)
117. GIBSON, John 32, Rossanna 29, William H. 10, Ida Bell 8, Andrew 5, Jennie 4, Bertie? 2, Jefferson 1, Rhoda 3/12 (b. Mar)
118. TROXWALL, Mary 66 (widow), Nancy J. 40, Rutha A. 30, David J. 21, Clemmie J. 10 (g dau), Alcey 9 (g dau); GIBSON, Catherine 43 (dau)
119. SHELL, Robert P. 37 (works on railroad), Mary J. 32 (T SC T), Ella 10, Thomas G. 7, Callie 4, J. Ettie 2
120. CROY, Z. Jordon 47 (plasterer) (VA VA VA), Elizabeth 47, Jordon M. 14, James D. 13, J. Thomas 13, Anna Bell 11, Cornelios G. 11; COOPER, Anna 77 (mother in law) (T VA VA), Sarah J. 35 (sis in law); CROY, Laura 24 (dau) (VA VA VA)

Page 14, Dist. 13

121. TREADWAY, J. Hampton 24, Anna 22, Stetta F. 1; GOURLEY, Joseph 18 (bro in law); HEWITT, Anna 16 (cook)
122. MOTTEM, John H. 28, Emma 26, Edwin 6
123. HART, Christly 35, Julia 30, James L. 10, Caswell 8, Magret 6, Delcima 5, Eliza 3; CAMPBELL, Delia 20 (cook)
124. HART, Thomas C. 42 (carpenter), Eliza 36, James N. 18, Ferdenando 14, David 11, Mary J. 9, Isaac E. 7, Minnie B. 5, Elizabeth 2, Eva K. 5/12 (b. Jan)

Hh#	Page 14 (cont'd)

125. HART, Solomon 72, Elizabeth 70, James G. 20 (g son)
126. DUNBAR, George 31, Jane 27, Callie L. 6, Anna N. 4, James H. 11/12 (b. Jun)
127. HART, Abraham 69, Mary 68, Tennesan 26, Fronis 23 (dau in law); CROW, Mary 39 (niece), Robert 17 (nephew); STOVER, Elizabeth 12 (g dau), William 10 (g son), Damil 6 (g son), John 4 (g son), Maynard 2 (g son); HART, William H. 5/12 (b. Feb) (g son)

Page 15, Dist. 13

128. BISHOP, Samuel 46 (T Ire Ire), Alice 26 (wife), Wheeler 3, Gertrude 8/12
129. STEPP, George O. 30 (VA VA VA), Mary 30 (T T VA), Lucinda 3, Ellen 7/12 (b. Oct), Anne 14 (sis) (T VA VA)
130. SLAGLE, Levi 49, Margret 48, Mary 24, Samual 20, Henry 14, Robert 11, Carrie 8, Peter B. 4
131. MOTTEM, George 68, Adline 57, Samuel S. 27, George jr. 19; CAMPBELL, Elizabeth 19 (cook)
132. MOTTEM, Isaac H. 40 (widower), Lafayette 12, Samuel 5, Worley 3
133. HODGE, Nathan L. 27 (physician), Margrett 23

Page 16, Dist. 8

134. ERWIN, Charles (B) 28 (NC NC NC), Martha 17 (wife) (NC NC NC), William 5, Samel 3, Mary 2
135. CAMPBELL, Calvin 48, Phebe 46, James 23, Nancy 17, Julia 15, Sarah 13, Emma 11, Samuel 11, George 9, David T. 6
136. LAWRENCE, William 39 (US storekeeper) (Ire Ire Ire), Frances 25 (wife), Kellie C. 3 (dau)
137. ORENT, Lewis 33 (NC NC NC), Sarah 32 (NC NC NC), Mary 6, Charles 3, Robert 2
138. RENFRO, Henry M. 54 (T VA T), Marth J. 39 (wife) (T VA VA), Samuel 7, Stewart 5, Annis? 2 (dau); DUFFIELD, Eliza 60 (mother in law), Nannie 30 (sis in law) (seamstress)
139. COLE, Joanna 46 (widow) (VA VA VA), Harriet 20 (T T VA), William 18, James H. 16, Elizabeth 14, Nancy 12, Nora 10, George 8, John 5, Charles 3, Cameron 8/12 (b. Sep)
140. LACY, Ann 65, Adelia 41 (niece), Mary 11 (niece)
141. LACY, Joseph 22, Sarah 20, William B. 3; MOTTEN, George 6/12 (b. Jan)
142. KELLY, Nancy 48 (divorced); CARRIER, Rhoda 24 (dau) (widow); KELLY, Harriet 18 (dau); POLAND, Catherine 15 (dau); CARRIER, John 5 (g son)

Page 17, Dist. 8

143. MARLER, David (B) 30 (NC NC NC), Mary 24 (NC NC NC), Samuel 6, Vinna 4, Delia E. 1
144. ELLIS, Haynes 37 (T NC NC), Sarah 41, Clifton 15, Eva 13, U. S. Grant 10, Lorina 9, Charles E. 6, George 2
145. SWINEY, Martha 33 (married) (T NC NC); PENIX, Susan L. 16 (T VA VA), Sherman 13 (T T T), Sarah 10 (T T T), Elizabeth 6 (T T T); SWINEY, John B. 1 (T ___ T)
146. CAMPBELL, John 36, Eliza 29 (T ME NC), Sarah 10, Harriet 8, Bell 6, Bessie 6/12 (b. Dec)
147. THOMAS, Licy (B) 30 (NC NC NC), Jane 35 (NC NC NC), Ellen 14
148. WILSON, Emanuel 35, Ellen 32, Henry S. 11, Leona 9, Joseph M. 7, Emma 5, Clifton 1
149. JENKINS, Catherine 75 (widow) (T VA T), Matilda 44, William 16 (g son)
150. SLAGLE, John 39, Nancy A. 33, Nettie 13, Mary J. 8, Charles W. 1
151. PHARR, Joseph 79 (NC NC NC), Tempie 65 (NC NC NC), William? 8 (g son)

Hh#	Page 17 (cont'd)

152. STOVER, William B. 21 (T T SC), Amelia L. 22 (sis) (T T SC), Charles D. 14 (bro) (T T SC), Henry T. 9 (bro) (T T SC), Emma B. 6 (sis) (T T SC)

Page 18, Dist. 8

153. VAUGHN, William 33, Lottie 32 (VA VA VA)
154. DRAKE, David (Mu) 68
155. PHARR, Jackson C. 30 (T NC NC), Ellen 30, David 11, Joe 10, James 4, John H. 2, Mittie 6/12 (b. Dec) (dau)
156. STOVER, George (B) 70, Ellen 40 (relationship omitted) (SC SC SC)
157. CARTER, William J. 30, Jane 24
158. CARTER, Landon 53, Rebecca 27 (wife); FOUST, Eva 13 (boarder)
159. MORRIS, Henry 31, Lucilla 22, Lottie A. 3, Mary E. 1
160. PERRY, Andrew J. 28 (merchant), Margaret 27, Josie 8 (dau), Elizabeth 5, James T. 3, Lena Bell 1, Mary A. 52 (mother)
161. MILLER, Lafayette 52, Sarah 38 (wife) (T NC NC), Elizabeth 85 (mother) (widow)
162. SLAGLE, Peter jun. 44, Sarah J. 43, Margret E. 21, James P. 19, Henry R. 17, Andrew J. 15, Sabine 11 (son), George W. 9, Rethi C. 1 (dau)
163. MORRIS, Mary 59 (single), Amanda 28 (dau), Corda 8 (g dau)
164. CARRIER, John M. 50, Mary 28, Murphy 18, Elizabeth 16, Robert L. 9, Bailess 2

Page 19, Dist. 8

165. SLAGLE, Peter sen. 75 (T VA VA), Macy 74 (wife)
166. LYONS, John 26, Mary 22 (KY SC SC), Mary 22, Andrew A. 4, William H. 3, Elizabeth 1; LEE, Tabitha 13
167. SLAGLE, Abner 46 (widower), Macey 21 (dau), John H. 19, Mary S. 16, William 12, Carrie 9, Abner 5
168. OLIVER, John 35, Hannah 24, Mary E. 7, William 5, Elizabeth 4, Martha A. 3, Sarah C. 2, Joseph A. 1/12 (b. May)
169. SWINEY, John 41, Martha 30, Mary 13, James I. 11, Julia E. 7, William D. 4, Nellie C. 1
170. LEE, Louisa 50 (widow) (SC SC SC), Alice 19 (VA SC SC), David E. 10 (T T SC)
171. TROXWELL, James 24, Sarah 25, Mary E. 6
172. POLAND, William 24, Lausey J. 19
173. BRADLEY, Charles (Mu) 50 (T VA AL); ROCKHOLD, Mary 45 (sis) (widow) (T VA AL); BRADLY, Charles 23 &nephew), George 21 (nephew) (works on railroad); BOND, Mary 16; ROCKHOLD, Walter (B) 15 (nephew); BRADLY, Charles 9 (Mu), Grant 6
174. SPEARS, Franklin 20, Ann 19, Elizabeth 1

Page 20, Dist. 8

175. SWINEY, James sen. 70 (NC __ NC), Christina 64 (T VA VA), Mary 39? (dau); OLIVER, Marion 40 (nephew) (deaf & dumb)
176. SWINEY, James j4. 35 (T NC T), Ann 23 (wife), George W. 5/12 (b. Jan); VANDEVENTER, Mary 47 (mother in law) (widow) (boarder)
177. BARNETT, Henry 56 (cabinet maker) (crippled) (T NC NC), Cenith 55 (T VA VA), Susan 21
178. PERY, David 28, Sarah E. 32 (T VA T), James A. 10, Nancy H. 9, Eliza J. 7, Edline 5, Murry W. 4, Mary 1/12 (b. May)
179. PERRY, William 38, Emly 33 (T VA T), Eva 12, William 10, Jonas 9, George 6, John 4, Sarah J. 3, Jackson 7/12 (b. Nov)
180. LINDAMOOD, Susan 63 (widow)
181. DAVIS, George W. 66 (widower), Daniel 25 (son), Mary 22 (dau), Mary V. 1 (g dau)
182. GLOVER, Granville 22 (merchant), Harret 22

Hh#	Page 20 (cont'd)

183. LYON, Thomas 47, Leuvina 45, Alono M. 20, Sylvester S. 18, Rhoda A. 16, Hillsman 13, Samuel J. 11, Mary F. 7, Martha R. 3
184. CARR, William 47 (widower) (chairmaker), Julia 17, Susan 16, Elizabeth 13

Page 21, Dist. 8

185. CARR, Andrew J. 20, Nancy 16 (wife)
186. CARR, Elkanah 51, Margarett 45 (T __ __), Abraham 18, Samuel 15, William 13, Mary 11, Elkanah 8, Jackson 6, Isaac 3
187. REYNOLDS, Elizabeth 56 (widow) (VA VA VA), Susanna 29 (VA VA VA), James 24 (VA), Giles M. 22 (T), Samuel 17
188. ELLIS, Radford 74 (minister) (NC NC NC), Louisa 77 (T __)
189. ELLIS, Tipton 34 (T NC T), Harriett 33, Emma 11, James 8, Louisa 6, Radford 1
190. KEEN, Jonas H. 65 (T VA MD), Sarah 56; RODDIE, Eva 16 (boarder); WEST, Sarah 9 (boarder) (T NC NC)
191. LYON, Ezekiel 22, Ann 22, Andrew 1
192. POTTER, Margret 60 (widow) (NC NC NC), Joseph 24 (T T NC), Emily 19 (dau in law) (married within yr)
193. CARR, Alfred 55, Eliza 45 (T NC NC), Sarah 15, Nancy 12
194. LINDAMOOD, James 25, Mary 24, Thomas A. 11/12 (b. Jul)
195. LYON, William B. 39, Amanda 33, Andrew 13, Lovenia 11, Rutha 7, Susan A. 5, John W. 3, Alexander T. 5/12 (b. Dec)

Page 22, Dist. 8

196. PERRY, Nancy 66 (widow)
197. CARR, Mary 45 (widow), John 24, Susan 16, Samul 13, Joseph 12, Lafayette 8, Eva 7, TRUSLER, Margret 78 (relationship omitted)
198. STALLING, James 50 (NC NC NC), Margret 48 (NC NC NC), James Mc. 18 (NC), Joseph 15 (NC), Harret 15 (NC), Mary D. 11 (NC), Dona C. 9 (NC), George E. 7 (NC), John A. 4 (T)
199. PERRY, George 25, Martha 17, Porter 3, Owen 11/12 (b. Jul)
200. SAMS, Owen 37, Elzira 24, Washington 15 (son), Alfred 12, Edmond 10, Berry 5, Harrict 4, Rufus 2
201. LINDAMOOD, Thomas 55 (widower) (T __ __), Cyrus 16, Henry 10
202. MORRIS, John 33, Eveline 28; SMITH, Thomas 9 (stepson), Racheal 6 (stepdau)
203. MORRIS, Franklin 33, Ann 30, Martha 12, Henry J. 10, James A. 7, Magazine 2 (dau), Melinie E. 1/12 (b. May)
204. MORRIS, Henry 63, Elizabeth 63 (T T NC), Sarah 35, Luffie 25 (dau), Eliza 18, William H. L. 16, Rhoda 14, Lee 2 (g son)

Page 23, Dist. 8

205. RICHARDS, Benjamin 35, Mary J. 36, Mary E. 12
206. BISHOP, Micheal 49 (blacksmith) (T Ire Ire), Mary 45, Elizabeth 19, James 17, Sarah 13, David 11, John 8, Hattie J. 6, Ella 4, Mary 6/12 (b. Dec)
207. EMMERT, Delcenia 60
208. CROW, Isaac 25, Virginia 23, John H. 10/12 (b. Sep)
209. KUHN, Joseph 46 (T MD T), Lavina 48 (T KY NC)
210. KUHN, Millard 29 (T NC T), Margret 29 (T T NC), Joseph L. 6, William 4, Minnie B. 3, Myrtle 1
211. DAVIS, William 29, Margret 29, Elizabeth 8, Stacy J. 5 (dau), Sarah 2, Mary 6/12 (b. Dec)
212. LYON, Jerimiah 27, Martha 29, William 5, John 4
213. LYON, Martha 45 (widow), Tucker 18, Samuel 15

Hh#	Page 23 (cont'd)

214. MORRIS, Jefferson 30, Mary 27, Sarah 1
215. MORRIS, David 24, Elcy 17 (wife)
216. STOUT, Henry D. 65, Elizabeth 62, Josie 20
217. STOUT, Anderson 22, Julia 18, Wilkie 1

Page 24, Dist. 8

218. PATTERSON, Robert 36, Mary 33, William J.
     10 (IN), Sarah 7 (IN)
219. CASSADA, William 54 (T ___ ___), Mary 36
     (wife) (T VA T), William 17, Margrett 15,
     David R. 13, Mary L. 12, Peter 8, James
     A . 6, John H. 3, Elizabeth J. 1
220. LYON, Henry 36, Elizabeth 33 (T NC NC),
     Sarah 11, Emma 9, Peter 7, Charles 3,
     Massie 10/12 (b. Aug)
221. CHAMBERS, James 25 (T NC T), Julia 18 (T T
     NC)
222. C(H)AMBERS, John 23 (T NC T), Emma 24, An-
     drew 1
223. CHAMBERS, David T. 49 (SC SC SC), Mary A.
     53, Sarah J. 16, William 14, Mary 10,
     Elizabeth 8, David 6
224. SCALF, Elizabeth 32 (T NC T) (single),
     William 8 (son), Robert 4, Caldonia 1
225. SCALF, Nancy 36 (single) (T NC T), Rerne?
     8 (dau), Jerimih 5, Athie? 2/12 (b. Apr)
     (dau); HAMPTON, Lanon 66 (boarder)
     (farm laborer)

Page 25, Dist. 8

226. MILLER, Susan 66 (widow) (T T NC); SMITH,
     Anlisha 23 (dau) (widow), Edgard 8 (g
     son), John 5 (g son), Robert 1 (g son)
227. SMITH, John 38, Nancy 33, Jerimah 14, Wil-
     liam 13, George 10, Charles 9, Minnie 8,
     Nathaniel 6, James 3, Ella 8/12 (b. Nov)
228. McCORKLE, Joseph 34, Rutha 31, Porter 12,
     Luisa 10, Milton G. 8, Elmer S. 6,
     Bell B. 3, Samuel J. 1
229. ELLIS, Arnod 45 (T NC T), Margret 44 (T T
     NC), Lou 19 (dau), William 16, Daniel
     G. 14, Radford 13, David H. 11, Rhoda 6
230. KELLEY, Alfred 23, Emma 23 (wife)
231. PERRY, Isaac 23 (T NC T), Eliza 22, Joseph
     4
232. JOBE, Margret 61 (married) (T VA T); SMITH,
     Maggie 11 (g dau); JOBE, Robert 22
     (boarder)
233. LACY, William S. 47, Jane 43, Mattie 12
     (dau), George 10, Eliza 6, Porter 5,
     Laura 2, Iva 10/12 (b. Aug) (dau)

Page 26, Dist. 8

234. CROW, Levi 29, Margret, Martha E. 4,
     Alexander L. 3, Elizabeth 2, Hannah
     9/12 (b. Aug)
235. BLEVENS, Jerrimiah 51, Sarah F. 49, James
     19, Mary 17, Sarah E. 13, Margret 10,
     Charles 8, George M. 5
236. BLEVINS, William 27, Elizabeth 22, Robert
     11/12 (b. June?)
237. HAYES, James 45 (T NC NC), Rebeca 40, Eliza-
     beth 24, Hester 17, Elbert 17, Malissa
     11, Harriet 9, Sarafina 6, Carrie 3;
     ESTEPP, Samuel 20 (son in law) (VA T T),
     Eliza 22 (dau)
238. NEWTON, James68 (T Ire MD), Catherine 64,
     Elizabeth 38, Harriet 23; CALDWELL, Mary
     13 (g dau) (T VA T); NEWTON, David 29
     (son) (carpenter), Ella 20 (dau)
239. MINTON, Rufus 43 (NC NC NC), Ann 33 (wife)
     (NC NC NC), William 20 (NC), Rufus 15
     (T), Eldridge 13, Charles 11, John 9,
     Eliza J. 6, Mary C. 5, Rhudy 3
240. PEAKS, Eli 61 (cooperer) (NC NC NC), Martha
     63

Page 27, Dist. 8

241. STOUT, John 35, Sarah 33, Eliza 12, William
     R. 10, Millard F. 8, Andrew 6, Christy
     B. 4, Lillie 11/12 (b. Jul)

Hh#	Page 27 (cont'd)

242. ELLIS, Solomon 48, Sarah 40 (T T NC), Murry
     M. 18, Hari? L. 17 (son), Landen C. 14,
     Joseph W. 9, Charles H. 8, Mary A. 6,
     James E. 2
243. CARRIER, Washington 23, Mary 26, Martha 6,
     Jane 4, Ellen 2
244. LACY, James 35, Martha 37, Robert S. 9, Ida
     A. 7, Leonard 5, Carrie 3, John 1
245. CROW, Leonard 46, Nancy 56
246. ROYSTON, Mary 75 (widow), Mary 34, John R.
     13 (g son), Sarah 9 (g dau)
247. ROYSTON, Marion 22, Lucinda 20 (wife),
     Anderson 1
248. ESTEP, Andrew J. 49 (blacksmith), Mary J.
     50 (NC NC NC), James 21 (VA), Louisa 18
     (T), William 16 (g son) (VA VA T),
     Charles 12 (g son) (VA VA T), Cordelia
     10 (g dau) (VA VA T), Cratus 9 (g son)
     (VA VA T), Roderick B. 8 (g son) (VA VA
     T), Mollie 4 (g dau) (T VA T), Bell (g
     dau) (T KY T)

Page 28, Dist. 8

249. MAYES, Andrew 32, Sarah 36 (T NC T), Louisa
     12, Lillie 11, Martha 8, Sineritteo 6
     (dau), Laura 4, Lena 1
250. THOMAS, William S. 55, Jane 43, Andrew 15,
     Henderson 8, Addie 7

Page 1, Dist. 9

1. NAVE, Daniel L. 43, Elizabeth 40, Daniel L.
   jr. 16, John T. 13
2. BOWERS, Isaac N. 37, Emaline 42 (T KY T),
   Molly E. 13, Robert A. 19, Valentine 19
   (stepson)
3. BOWERS, John E. 29 (married within yr), Mary
   C. 21
4. GRINDSTAFF, A. S. 34, Susan 17, David G.?
   10, Edney E. 9, Marget E. 7, Andrew J. D.
   6, John S. 5, Sarah A. 3/12 (b. Feb),
   Caroline 3
5. HEATON, John W. 51, Catharine 56, Granville
   S. 24, John N. 21, Nancy L. 16, Rebecka
   11
6. BOWERS, Lilburn 23, Martha 21, Emeline E.
   4, Marget 1
7. BOWERS, Daniel E. 26, Abagail 26, Isaac M.
   6, Eliza C. 4
8. BOWERS, William C. 52, Rebecka 50, Julia Ann
   33, Reece? B. 21, Andrew J. 19; OBRIENT,
   Martha 21 (servant), Andrew 3 (boarder)
9. BOWERS, Valentine 30, Barbary 27, William 9,
   Rebecka 7, Martha 5, Anna 3, Robert T. 1
10. HEATON, Edward T. 33, Mary 26, Orah 5 (dau)

Page 2, Dist. 9

11. DELOACH, Susan 50 (widow), James 22, Jane 15
12. SMITH, Joseph 32 (T NC T), Nancy J. 31, Anna
    A. 4, Martha I. 1
13. WILLIAMS, Alexander 41, Diza Ann 42 (T NC
    NC), John D. 19, Lucinda 15, Pleasant
    13, Daniel M. 11, Delia 9, Marget 7,
    Charley 4, Henry 2
14. WILLIAMS, William 39, Pheby 35, David S. 13,
    Chrisley C. 12, Elijah 9, Thomas 6,
    Rhoda J. 6
15. DUGGER, John 23, Eliza A. 17, Thomas 1
16. GRINDSTAFF, George M. 49, Hanah M. 49,
    Sarah L. 26, Alcxander 18, Marget 17,
    George S. 13, Hanah A. 10, Leliah H. 7
17. LOVELESS, William H. 26, Catharine 21,
    Rebecka 7/12 (b. Oct)
18. MYERS, Elijah D. 24, Mary E. 23, William
    N. 2, Pheby E. 18/30 (b. May); GARRISON,
    Samuel 15 (boarder)
19. HARDEN, George 34, Adaliza 19 (wife), Isaac
    H. 7/12 (b. Oct)
20. BECK, Joel L. 59 (NC VA NC), Mary E. 58 (NC
    NC NC), James N. 26 (NC), Mary Ann 16
    (NC), Dove A. 12 (g dau) (T NC NC)

Hh#	Page 3, Dist. 9

21. LOVELESS, Elijah 27, Mary 23, William P. 6, Francis A. 3, Wiley M. 10/12 (b. Jul)
22. LOVELESS, Allen 24 (married within yr), Eliza J. 18
23. GARRISON, Jane 33 (T NC NC), Nancy C. 12 (dau), James 10, Sarah 6, John 1
24. HARDEN, Elijah D. 45, Eliza C. 43, Chrisley 19 (son), Joseph 17, Mary B. 15, William 13, Elijah D. 11, James 9, Daniel 7, John 5, Eliza 5
25. MYERS, Martha 56 (widow), Sarah 18, David 10/12 (b. Jul) (g son)
26. HEATON, Isaac M. 29, Catharine 24, Jemima 2
27. HARDEN, Isaac 64 (idiotic), Sarah 60 (T NC T), Elijah 29, Elizabeth 27 (idiotic), Thomas 25, Emaline 23
28. HARDEN, John H. 35, Mary 28, Tennessee 8, Robert B. 6, Eliza J. 3/12
29. McKINNEY, Martha 37 (T NC NC), Samuel 8 (son), Cordelia 5, Mary J. 4, Josephine 10/12 (b. Jul), Polly 28 (sis) (T NC NC), James M. 9 (nephew), Noly C. 6 (niece)

Page 4, Dist. 9

30. HARDEN, Elijah sr. 78 (T NC NC), Clary 31 (wife) (T T NC), Charley 10, Mark N. 8, Cameron 6, John N. 4, Mary J. A. 2
31. HARDEN, William 52, Ann J. 44, Hyter 23 (son), Pleasant 21 (neuralgia), Chrisley 19 (son), Jessee 16, Milison 13 (dau), Charley 10, Andrew 8; NAVE, Luvicy 73 (mother in law) (crippled)
32. HARDEN, John W. 37, Ellen 31, Hooker 8
33. JONES, Rebecka 44 (widow), Ellen E. 17, William 14
34. GRINDSTAFF, John 69, Elizabeth 68
35. NAVE, Levi 22, Martha 21
36. CARRIGER, Caleb 23, Marget 19, Joel 2 (paralysis), Martha 9/12 (b. Aug) (paralysis)
37. PIERCE, Chrisly A. 33, Martha 27 (wife), John T. 9, Eliza L. 7, Robert C. 5, Sarah C. 2
38. PIERCE, Henry C. 72, Elizabeth 72 (neuralgia)
39. DUGGER, Thomas 31, Elizabeth 27, Martha 7, William 4
40. BOWERS, Henry 25, Rosanah 27, Caleb E. 2
41. PIERCE, William A. 50, Lealy Ann 43 (T NC T), Thomas 22, Nancy L. 19, Elijah 17, Mary E. 15, Conelia J. 12, John Allen 10, Wilburn H. 8, Orley 8, Ety 6 (dau), William L. 2, Joel C. 3/12 (b. Mar)

Page 5, Dist. 9

42. WILLIAMS, Alfred M. 28, Evaline 28, John 10, Isabel 5, Marget J. 2
43. OLIVER, John 72 (widower) (rheumatism) (NC NC NC), Eliza 19 (T NC NC)
44. MORRELL, Isaac 24, Magie B. 2, Bretha A. 9/12 (b. Sep) (dau)
45. NAVE, Jemiah 52 (widow), Mary 35 (dau), Joel G. 15, Malisa 13
46. McKINNEY, Joseph 32 (T NC NC), Luvicy C. 33, William D. 13, Joel Alfred 11, Challey 9 (son), John 8, Elizabeth 5, Samuel C. 2
47. POWERS, John L. 49 (clergyman), Martha 22 (wife), Mary S. 12 (dau), Alexander 11, Elizabeth 9, Rhoda 7, Agnes 6, Joseph P. 4, Calvin F. 2, Charley V. 1
48. VANHUSS, Daniel S. 45, Elizabeth 50 (T PA VA), Thomas S. 10, John F. 7, Luvina 84 (mother) (T VA VA); WALTERS, Barby A. 21 (servant) (T VA VA)
49. VANHUSS, Thomas 56, Elvira 50, William M. L. 21, Rhoda 17, Eliza 14, Cordelia 8

Page 6, Dist. 9

50. ALLEN, Robert J. 62 (T VA VA), Mary 56 (VA VA VA), Nat. T. 22, Mifflin D. 19, William B. 16, Mary 13, William R. 16 (g son)

Hh#	Page 6 (cont'd)

51. CROW, Isaac 72, Elizabeth 64, Thomas 24; NIDIFFER, Jessee 21 (son in law), Permelia 18
52. ESTEP, Samuel M. 43 (T NC T), Nancy Ann 34, John W. 16, Isaac Jackson 14, James M. 12, Nancy E. 10, Martha E. 5, Mary C. 5/12 (b. Dec), Pheby 49 (sis)
53. DUGGER, David A. 26, Louisa E. 26 (T NC T) (wife), Hattie 3, David W. 1; PHARR, Sally S (step dau)
54. JONES, Robert 31, Analiza B. 25, Elizabeth 8, William A. 5, Carry Jane 3
55. NAVE, Henry T. 33, Pheby 25, Nancy J. 13, Sarah 9, William D. 7, Analiza 4, Campbell 1
56. NAVE, Samuel C. 31, Sally 42 (wife), William 10, Marget 7, Mary 4, Andrew 3; PIERCE, Rhoda J. 16 (niece)

Page 7, Dist. 9

57. NAVE, William H. 57, Jemiah 55, Rutha E. 16, Chrisley 19 (g son); PIERCE, Sarah E. 16 (g dau)
58. CARDEN, Ruben 25 (T NC NC), Mary C. 37 (wife), Marget 3, Martha E. 2; PIERCE, July A. 10 (step dau)
59. NAVE, Isaac N. 37, Elizabeth 26, John W. 4, William H. M. 1
60. VANHUSS, Joseph P. 47, Rebecka 46 (T MD VA), James M. B. 18, Daniel F. 16, Barbery E. 14, Florrinda J. J. 11, William L. M. 9, John D. H. 6; DUGGER, David 62 (uncle) (T NC T)
61. DUGGER, Martha 80 (T NC T), Resemond 76 (sis) (T NC T); PIERCE, Jenne U. 10 (servant)
62. CARRIGER, Allen T. 56 (T T NC), Caroline (T NC T), MAry 20, U. S. Grant 17 (dau); PETERS, Pleasant 17 (laborer)
63. MORRIS, Jefferson 64, Catharine 31 (wife) (T NC NC), Robert 13, Carry M. 11 (dau), George S. 9, Virgil 7, Eller 6 (dau), William A. 4, Milburn E. 2; SOUTH, Nella 71 (mother in law) (NC NC NC), Rahchel 34 (sis in law) (T NC NC)
64. HESS, David 72 (dropsy) (VA VA VA), Lealy 70 (T T PA); GOURLY, Ellen 21 (servant)
65. CARRIGER, Joel N. 38, Mary C. 37 (T VA); PETERS, Marget E. 19 (servant)
66. NAVE, Sary A. 53 (widow) (T T Eng), Mary 21, Andrew 19, Joel P. 17, Ulyssus G. 14

Page 8, Dist. 9

67. NAVE, Thomas 29 (crippled), Mary E. 23, Roderick 4, July Ida 3, Henry 1/12 (b. Apr)
68. NAVE, David F. 26, Manda 25, Joseph 7, Fredcy D. 5 (dau), Daniel N. 3, Sarah 1; MATHESON, Ella 16 (sis in law)
69. NAVE, James A. 28, Mary 25, Ulyses G. 7, Elizabeth 5, Mandy Jan 3/30 (b. May); GRINDSTAFF, Elvy 21 (servant)
70. CROW, Thomas C. 55, Elvy 50, Robert C. 25, William T. 15, Allice E. 12, Lena E. 9, Etta V. C. 6, Charley 3; MULL, Elleck 23 (laborer)
71. MORRELL, Caleb 62, Luvicy 57, Johnathan 20, Josep 18, Andrew 15; COMBS, Elizabeth 16 (g dau); CROW, Ebagail 71 (mother in law)
72. SUTTON, John 55 (NC NC NC), Mary 43 (VA VA VA), Nancy 23 (VA), John 20 (VA), Mary Ellen 18 (VA), Martha 15 (VA), Robert 13 (VA), Chesley 11 (VA), Charley 9 (VA), Shepey W. 7 (son) (T), Minney 4; CATES, Allen 14 (laborer)
73. PIPPEN, Westley 24 (VA VA VA), Bell I. 23, David C. 4, Andrew J. 1; TREDWAY, Lawson 10 (relationship omitted)

Hh#   Page 9, Dist. 9

74. WEST, John 29, Jane 27, William K. 8, James
    J. 5, Zack C. 1
75. BOWERS, Susan 28 (widow), Mary 10, Nancy 9,
    Marget 6, Rhoda 3, Rebecka 2; POTTER,
    Eliza 36 (sis) (divorced), Nathaniel 4
    (nephew)
76. PETERS, Chrisley 33, Eliza 33 (wife), Wil-
    liam T. 13. Mary C. 10, Alfred 6, Houston
    1; LEWIS, Lydia 57 (mother in law)
77. CASS, William 58 (NC NC VA), Rutha E. 50 (T
    MD T), Charles P. 23, Robert S. P. 21,
    Lucy A. 18, Josep W. 14, James M. 12,
    Edmund C. 10, Lewis W. 8, Henry M. 5;
    COX, Nancy Ann 77 (mother in law);
    JENKINS, Parele 15 (servant)
78. POWERS, Avery 23, Sarah F. 26, John A. 1;
    WILLIAMS, Caroline 6 (step dau)
79. WILLIAMS, William 30, Joanna W. 28, Abraham
    B. 10, John E. 8, Newjener? 6 (son),
    Daniel B. 5, William C. 3, Charley C. 1
80. STOVER, Cam. (B) 63, Easter 50 (wife) (NC
    NC NC)

                Page 10, Dist. 9

81. STOVER, Alexander (B) 25, Luvica 17 (wife)
    (NC NC NC), John A. 2
82. WHITAKER, Susan (B) 30 (widow) (SC NC NC),
    Mary 10 (T T SC), Minnie 4, John 1
83. LEWIS, Amy 55 (cholera mo) (T NC VA),
    Thisie 20 (dau), James 18
84. CARRIGER, David N. 33, Niga Jane 21, Jemima
    S. 3, Joel L. 1
85. TREDWAY, Robert 45, Eva 23 (wife), Minnie 7,
    Charley 5, Nany 3, Onijah 87 (mother),
    Samuel W. 18 (nephew)
86. POWERS, Isaac N. 24, Sally L. 17
87. BISHOP, Marget 33 (widow), John 16 (son);
    PERRY, Saryfine 17, Julia A. 9/12 (b.
    Aug) (g dau)
88. PHARR, David 33 (T NC T), Nancy J. 33,
    William 10, Charley 3, Henry P. 2,
    ESTEP, Martha 51 (mother in law)
89. WILLIAMS, John H. 35, Marget 32, George 13,
    Rhoda A. 10, William G. 9, Alfred 6,
    Thomas B. 4, Nancy 4/12 (b. Jan)
90. CARRIGER, William 24, Molly L. 22, George A.
    3
91. CARRIGER, Rebecka 67 (widow), Carrige S. 19
92. OLIVER, James 34, Mary Jane 35, Frances F.
    12, Lawson H. 10, Laura 7, Edney 6,
    Emma E. 4, Wiley C. 6/12 (b. Nov)

                Page 11, Dist. 9

93. BOWERS, David 32, Eliza 32, Caldonia 10,
    Reece B. 7, Hester 6, Elizabeth 3, Vir-
    ginia 1
94. BOWERS, David B. 59, Carolin C. 58 (T Ire
    PA), Elizabeth 39. Ann E. 24, John T. 25,
    Millard F. 22, William 16, Sally E. 19
    (dau in law), James 18 (g son), Josie
    9/12 (b. Aug) (g son)
95. BOWERS, David S. 62, Emeline 60
96. BOWERS, John M. 26, Malissie 23, Alfred
    Sten? 2, Martha E. 1
97. GARLAND, William 32, Vinna 30 (T ___ ___),
    Lilly M. 5, Mary Ann 3, Hily C. 9/12 (b.
    Aug)
98. ANDERSON, Susan 60 (widow), Marget 24
99. ANDERSON, James 32, Elizabeth C. 33, Rebecka
    3, Samuel 1, Alfred 4/12 (b. Feb)
100. BOWERS, Tetor U. 54, Mary 37 (wife), Lawson
     8, Rutha E. 7, Susan A. 4, Julia H. 2
101. WILLSON, Sarah 40, Samuel 14 (son), James G.
     10, Nicholas L. 6

                Page 12, Dist. 9

102. CROW, John 49, Luvica 48, Sary E. 21, Ten-
     nessee J. 19 (son), Marget J. 19, John R.
     16, Hester 17 (dau in law)
103. OLIVER, Elijah D. 36, Matild 29, Peter E.
     10, Eveline 7, Sophia A. 4, Nicholas J.
     B. 1

                Page 12 (cont'd)

104. OLIVER, James sr. 62 (T NC NC) (crippled),
     Mary A. 62, Joseph L. 21, Winfield S.
     18, James Thone 5 (g son)
105. OLIVER, Luvica 38 (divorced), Lillie 7
106. CARRIGER, John R. 74 (T PA PA), Sarah 72 (T
     NC NC), Marget 42; MORRELL, Alzenia 39
     (dau)
107. CROW, Daniel S. 29, Sarah 27, Lydia E. 7,
     Robert L. 6, Thomas 5, George A. 2
108. COLLINS, Jackson 20, Rhoda 17, Ulysis G.
     6/12 (b. Nov), Evaline 55 (mother)
109. CARDEN, Ancil C. 38 (NC NC NC), Jane 40 (NC
     NC NC), Mary L. 8, Alvin M. 3 (dau)
110. OLIVER, William 68 (T VA NC), Elizabeth 61,
     Levi 19
111. OLIVER, Chrisley 29, Winnie 27 (wife), John
     B. 6, Jane 4, Elizabeth M. 3, William
     jr. 7/12 (b. Oct)
112. OLIVER, Jackson 41, Elizabeth 36, William C.
     18, Moses L. 14, John N. 12, Thomas 10,
     Ellen E. 9, Richard 8, Andrew 5, Hettie
     2

                Page 13, Dist. 9

113. MOYERS, Samuel M. 23, Lorina V. 21, William
     A. 3, Doria Bell 1
114. LOVELACE, John 32, Mary J. 30, William T.
     12, Micheal J. 10, Marget C. 8, David K.
     6, Carry E. 4 (dau), Mary Allis 7/12 (b.
     Oct)
115. RICHIE, Jemima 61 (widow) (NC NC NC), Jane
     25 (T SC NC), Lauda G. 5 (g dau), Molly
     A. 17 (T NC NC)
116. FRASIER, Harry 19, Molly A. 17 (T NC NC)
117. JENKINS, Fannie 53 (widow) (T SC T), Rebecka
     20, Isaac 16, John 13, Mary 2 (g dau),
     Mand 2/12 (b. Mar) (g dau)
118. JENKINS, Martha 24, Richard 5 (son)
119. FAIR, Shadrack 72 (T VA NC), Martha C. 33
     (T __ T), Wily Dell 7 (dau), Alfred B.
     5, Wiley C. 2 (son), Marget C. 23/30
     (b. May)
120. LEWIS, James 24 (T NC NC), Rebecka E. 21,
     Rosand 1, Henry C. 3/12 (b. Feb)
121. GRIFFITH, James 73 (NC NC NC), Jane 63,
     William J. 18
122. BERRY, Elbert 30, Martha C. 24, James M. 4,
     William S. 3, John E. 7/12 (b. Oct);
     CROW, Jinna 7 (step dau)

                Page 14, Dist. 9

123. MYERS, Pheby 57 (widow), Joseph L. 19,
     Christian 16; HARDEN, Onijah J. 35 (dau)
124. HARDEN, John N. 72, Mary 69
125. CLEMENS, Benjamin 37 (T NC T), Sarah 33 (T
     NC T), William 17, Martha A. 13, James
     D. 11, Mary E. 8, Ida Bell 5, Charley
     F. 3, John F. 2
126. TONEY, Samuel 36, Rhoda 42, Mary 12, Lula 10,
     Maggie 9, Joseph P. 6, Lillie 3
127. MACKROY, Joseph 65 (miller) (crippled) (VA
     PA PA), Harriet 45 (wife) (T T NC);
     FOSTER, Nancy 87 (mother in law) (NC NC
     NC)
128. HINTOR, Thomas E. R. 51 (T NC T), Louisa J.
     45, Mary E. 19, William D. 17, BARNET,
     Laura B. 8 (servant); ALDRIDGE, Thomas
     E. 4 (boarder) (T VA T)
129. PETERS, Micheal S. 41, Elizabeth 39, Florra
     19, William 16, Co nny 12, Nancy 73
     (mother)
130. CARRIGER, Godfrey 51, Jane 45 (T NC NC)
131. BOWERS, Elizabeth 49 (widow) (NC NC NC),
     Henry 24 (T T NC), Eliza 17, Robert 14,
     John 11, Marget 8; WILLSON, Elbert 21
     (boarder)
132. RICHIE, Susan 72 (widow)
133. BOWERS, Tennessee L. 28 (m), Marget 20,
     Blaine 10/30 (b. May)

Hh#	Page 15, Dist. 9

134. OLIVER, Isaac 28, Mandy E. 21, John B. 1, Walter 1/12 (b. Apr)
135. BOWERS, Chrisley 29, Susan 24 (wife), Carry 4 (dau), Lawson 2, Garfield 1
136. WILLIAMS, Harvey 23, Catharine 22, Pleasant 1
137. PETERS, William 44, Elizabeth C. 45, James L. 18, Nancy 16, William 13, Everett 11, George W. 8, Minnie 6, Micheal 1
138. NIDIFFER, Calvin 26, Mary A. 36 (wife)
139. PETERS, David 34, Sarah C. 31, Lilly V. 9, Benjamine 14 (nephew)
140. WILLSON, Tenny 70 (widow), Isaac 22 (son), Sarrah 14 (dau)
141. HARDEN, Daniel 50, Jane 30 (wife), James 5, Charley 2
142. LEWIS, Joseph 25 (T NC NC), Evaline 20, Lurah M. 1 (dau)
143. CARRIGER, Isaac 32, Matha E. 31, Austin 10, Willis 8, Ettie Bell 7, Thurstin 3, Edgar 2, Gapha 1 (dau)
144. NAVE, Peter 26, Elizabeth 20
145. NIDIFFER, Thomas 27, Mary 22, Charley 4, George W. 2

Page 16, Dist. 9

146. BOWERS, David F. 42 (T T NC), Mary A. 43 (T NC NC), Sheridan S. 15, Loreta 6, Elizabeth F. 3
147. BOWERS, William 48, Mary 39, Francis F. 19, David 17, Rutha E. 13, Joana 10, Daniel 7, James M. 4, Mollie A. 2
148. CARRIGER, Jackson D. 59 (T NC NC), Edney G. 42 (wife), Godfrey 12, Elizabeth 9, Hannah 7, Eliza 4, Lula M. 1; STONE, Mary C. 17 (servant)
149. KITZMILLER, David 47 (clergyman), Elizabeth 46, Julia A. 19, Judson 18, Lillie? 16, Wakfall 13 (son), Emma 9, Maggie 8, John K. 5
150. MORRELL, William 34 (miller), Sarah E. 33, July A. M. 12, Louisa 8
151. SELLERS, John 50 (T NC T), Anna J. 42, James H. 12, Gaines W. 10, Oscar 19; HUNTER, John W. 29 (boarder) (drygoods m.), Robert 21 (boarder) (clerk in store)
152. RUTLEDGE, William 45, Evaline 50, John 17, Samuel 13, Elizabeth 10; WAGNER, Mollie 19

Page 17, Dist. 9

153. LEWIS, John 48 (boot maker) (NC NC NC), Nancy 40 (T NC T), Emily C. 6
154. LEWIS, Isaac 51 (gunsmith) (NC NC NC), Elizabeth 49 (NC NC NC), John 21 (son) (gunsmith), Anna L. 70 (mother) (NC NC NC)
155. CASS, James F. 72 (widower) (neuralgia) (NC NC NC), Robert M. 33 (clerk in store) (T NC T), Edward J. 23; RICHIE, Martha 42 (widow); GIBSON, Sharlot A. (B) (servant) (T NC SC)
156. BOWERS, Ann E. 45 (divorced) (T Ire T), Tennessee 23, Rhueda 5 (g son), Allice 3 (g dau), Elizabeth 73 (mother in law) (T NC NC)
157. NIDIFFER, Elizabeth 51 (widow) (T NC VA), Columbia 10 (dau); JENKINS, Ann E. 25 (dau), NIDIFFER, John 14 (son); COLLINS, John N. 22 (son in law); Permelia 20 (dau)
158. BOWERS, Christian 44 (carpenter), Martha 45, Jane 22, David 20 (idiotic), Permelia C. 15, Teter B. 10, Alfred 8, Murry 4
159. DUNGAN, William 65 (VA VA VA), Martha E. 62 (VA VA VA), Mary 22 (VA), Martha 24 (dau) (ovarian tu) (VA); WOLF, George 16 (boarder) (VA VA VA); NEATHERLY, William 18 (boarder) (KY VA VA)

Hh#	Page 17 (cont'd)

160. RHUDY, Levi H. 31 (VA VA VA), Carry D. 31 (VA VA VA), William P. D. 3; RANGE, Kelly 7 (boarder); JONES, Kate P. 60 (aunt) (VA VA VA)
161. ELLIS, Jane 49 (widow) (T VA T); MORRILL, Carry 14 (dau), John W. 27 (son in law) (married within yr)
162. DAVIS, Axey 60 (widow) (NC NC NC), Mattie 31 (T NC NC), Isaac 21, Virginia 15; HICKS, Jane 37 (dau) (widow), Willy 13 (g son)

Page 18, Dist. 9

163. DAVIS, David 26 (T NC NC), Matilda 21 (T NC NC), Bascum 1 (son)
164. FULKERSON, Abraham 56, Eliza 50, Green T. 21, Fatha D. 19 (dau), Johnathan S. 17, Robert G. 15, George A. 12, Ady E. M. 7
165. LYONS, George 26, Missouri 20 (wife), Sherman 3, Rutha A. 1
166. BROWN, Isaac H. 70 (T Prussia VA), Marget M. 51 (wife), Emma C. 13
167. BROWN, James 23, Mary 21, Mand 3/30 (b. May)
168. BROWN, Christian H. 42, Nancy A. 36 (T VA T), Leila I. 14, Laura E. 13, Charles H. 12, Eugine 9 (son), Lola 1; STROTTER, Daniel (B) 38 (laborer) (VA VA VA)
169. WOODY, Lenoir 50 (NC NC NC), Lida 47 (NC NC NC)
170. SHARP, James K. 29 (VA VA VA), Adelia G. 36, William F. 8 (VA), Nine A. 7 (T), James 7/12 (b. Oct)
171. NAVE, Allice 30, George (this name crossed out on schedule) 28 (sis?) (divorced), Linden T. 24 (sis)
172. CROW, William 53 (blacksmith) (T VA T), Ailcy 50, Abagail 16, William R. 14
173. CROW, Thomas 22 (blacksmith), Emma 22, Lula M. 10/12 (b. Aug)
174. STOVER, Solomon 68, Mary A. 56 (fever), Jinna 23 (neuralgia), David 21, Emma 18 (neuralgia)

Page 19, Dist. 9

175. LACY, John W. 64, Martha N. 61 (T VA T), William 15; SAULTS, Mary 19 (servant); BEARD, Frank 18 (boarder) (VA VA VA)
176. WHITESIDE, William 32 (Eng Eng Eng), Marget C. 30 (T T NC), Sarah L. 9, Laura E. 6, Ellen E. 5, John W. 4/12 (b. Jan); HAYES, Elbert 15 (boarder)
177. LYONS, Thomas 24, Samatha 20 (NC NC NC), Martha E. 6/12 (b. Nov)
178. PEACKS, Alfred C. 34 (T NC T), Selea C. 39, Newton 20, Alfred 17, Nancy J. 13, William 12, Elizabeth 10, Joseph 7, Andrew 3, Jeremiah 2
179. WILLSON, James 42 (T NC T), Mary J. 37, Landon 15, Henderson 11, Jackson 9, Delceny 7, Caleb E. 3, John 1/12 (b. Apr); FRIELDS, Esabel 30 (boarder) (SC SC SC)
180. BARRY, David 75 (NC Ire VA), Sarar 35 (wife); WIGHT, Landon 17 (stepson)
181. HART, Peter E. 34, Martha 28, Emma 11, Joseph 9, David L. 9, Charley D. 6, Carry E. 1, Ella M. 4
182. MINTON, Griffon 33 (NC NC NC), Elizabeth 34 (T T NC), Lilly O. 11, Wilburn G. 9, Robert Lee 5, Hattie L. 4, Isaac L. 1

Page 20, Dist. 9

183. BYERS, Frank 23 (NC NC NC), Clercy L. 21 (NC NC NC), Ider 1 (dau)
184. COLLINS, John 64 (brickmason) (VA VA VA), Susan 58 (VA VA VA), William 24, Virdia 14, Eliza 11
185. FRASIER, Marget (married) 42, Benjamin B. 18, Matilda 11, William A. 4
186. FRASIER, Alexander 44 (T NC T), Milison M. 37 (wife), Charley 16, Magie P. 13, Julia C. 12, John A. 6; TAYLOR, Eliza 23 (servant)

Hh#   Page 20 (cont'd)

187. CRUMLEY, James 28 (miller), Allice 21, Ida
     J. 3, Clandaz 2 (son)
188. McKINNEY, William 47 (T NC NC), Rebecka 54
     (wife), Robt. M. 24, Sallie A. 18,
     Harriet E. 16

               Page 1, Dist. 10

1. ROGERS, Nicholas 70 (blacksmith) (VA SC NC),
   Elizabeth 70 (T VA SC), Jane 44, Adaline
   30; DOLIN, Samul 25 (g son) (apprentice
   B.S.)
2. CANNON, Elbert 42 (NC NC NC), Isabell 41,
   Andrew 16, Julius? 13, David 11, Mary 8,
   Charles 4
3. BLEVINS, Ruben 48 (T NC NC), Sarahann 47
   (T T NC), William C. 22 (T T NC), Robert
   L. 18 (T T NC), James L. 15 (T T NC),
   Joseph G. 12 (T T NC), Alice 10 (T T T)
4. RASON, Rubin 24, Amanda 30, William 3, Wiley
   M. 1
5. CRUCK, Napoleon 26 (T NC T), Dillie 25
   (wife), William 4, George 2, Emma 3/12
   (b. Mar), Rebecca 65 (mother) (T SC NC)
6. RASOR, Vaught 55 (m)
7. CULBERT, James sr. 74 (NC Ire NC), Matilda
   62, Robert 25 (crippled), William 21,
   Mary 95 (mother) (NC NC Scot)
8. GRINDSTAFF, William 44 (T VA NC), Sarah 43,
   John H. 24, James 18, Joseph 16, George
   14, Pheby 12, Mahala 10, Rhodica 3
9. COLE, Winney 50 (widow), Luwesa 25, Minnie
   15, Benjamin 9, Joseph 2 (g son), Julia
   1 (g dau)

               Page 2, Dist. 10

10. RASOR, George W. 53, James 52, Mary 14,
    George W. jr. 7, Lauson 10
11. LOUR, George J. 34, Jemima 32, Henry 14,
    Mary 12, Rebecca R. 10, James N. 8,
    William J. 6, Eliza J. 4, John T. 1
12. BOUE, Joseph 36 (works in iron foundry)
    (VA VA VA), Alice 20 (wife), Emma 1
13. WILSON, John 23, Sarah 25, Eliza 10 (dau
    in law), Elizabeth 8 (dau in law)
14. RENFRO, Joseph 51 (T VA T), Permelia 44,
    James 22, William 21, Henry 2, Margret
    2 (twins), Joseph jr. 12
15. DAVIS, Samuel 35 (VA VA VA), Nancy 32,
    Elizabeth 2, Jennie 1; BROOKS, Elizabeth
    65 (mother in law) (T T NC)
16. BLEVINS, George 36 (NC NC NC), Rebecca 36
    (NC NC NC), James 18, John W. 14, William
    12, Alison 10 (son), Sarah 8, Estinza 6
    (dau), Charles 4, Maryann 2
17. FERGUSON, Andrew 51 (teamster) (T PA VA),
    Eveline 40, Robert 22, Jenner 13 (dau),
    Charles 10, Butter 9 (son), Daisy 1

               Page 3, Dist. 10

18. FERGUSON, Benjamin 43 (iron founder) (T PA
    VA), Julia 40, William 10, James L. 8,
    Nannie 7, Everett 4, John F. 1; CULBERT,
    Mary 21 (niece)
19. PEARCE, Tennessee 61 (not able to work)
    (heart disease) (T NC T), Delcema 55
    (wife), Levi 21, Nathaniel 19
20. HAMILTON, Joshua 43, Isibella 45 (VA IN VA),
    William 20 (crippled--not able to labor),
    Sarah 15, Josephine 13, John W. 8, Dora-
    bell 6, Lillie 4; PETERS, Thomas 30
    (son in law), Mollie 17 (dau)
21. CANNON, Nelson 48 (T NC NC), Jane 35, Mary
    14, Isaac 11, Granderson 8, Julia 5,
    Peter 2
22. LEWIS, Hasten J. 45 (miner), Mary 38 (T NC
    T), Elizabeth 19, Eliza 16, James L. 15,
    Matilda 12, Margret 8, Charles 7, Henry
    6, Benjamine 3, George 1, William 10
23. RICHARDSON, Eleana 55 (crippled), Mary 40
    (wife), Caroline 19, Isaac 18, Callie 16,
    Elcana 13, Martah 10, Florence 9, William
    4

Hh#   Page 4, Dist. 10

24. LEWIS, Frederick J. 38 (miner), Nancy 35,
    Stephen 16, Hester 14, Jannie 10
25. COLE, James 26 (works in iron foundry), Eliza
    29, Martha 4, George W. 2
26. ELLIS, Joseph 44 (carpenter), Margret 34,
    Andrew 17, Elizabeth 12, Thomas 2, Wiley
    M. 1/12 (b. May), Robert 4
27. RITCHIE, James 37 (T VA T), Maryann 36,
    Charles T. 14, Stacy C. 10 (dau),
    William B. 8, Wiley C. 4
28. NIDEFFER, William 35, Millie 32, Girtha 11,
    Marrion 9 (son), Jasper 7, Grant 4,
    Alice 1
29. PEARCE, Armstrong 52, Celina 52, Emilie 24,
    Samuel L. 22, Andrew B. 17, Julia 15,
    James L. 11
30. BROOKS, Jackson 36, Rhodica 27, Clerrie 6
    (dau); CULBERT, William 18 (nephew)
31. BERRY, Frances 58 (widow) (T SC NC), Margret
    30, Cary 21 (son), Alvin 17
32. CULBERT, James jr. 24, Barbary 30 (T NC T),
    Joseph 6, Robert 4, Eveline 1, William
    9/12 (b. Sep)

               Page 5, Dist. 10

33. LEWIS, Muny (m) 24, Eviline 24, William M. 3,
    Landon T. 1
34. STOUT, George 46, Eliza 44, Martha E. 2;
    CREED, William 18 (nephew); STOUT, Mary
    28 (cousin), Samuel 9 (cousin); LOVE,
    James 18 (servant) (T T NC); SMITH,
    James 19 (servant)
35. RITCHIE, Elbert 28 (apprentice black S.) (T
    VA T), Josephine 24 (T NC T), William
    6, Sanford 5, Washington 3, David 8/12
    (b. Oct)
36. NAVE, Pleasant 42 (blacksmith), Delila 31,
    Lauson 11 (T __ T), Emelia J. 9, James
    T. 7, Pleasant G. 4, John N. 3, Isibella
    1
37. ELLIOTT, Thomas P. 46 (blacksmith), Nancy A.
    36, Milburn 21 (blacksmith), Sarah 12,
    William 7, Peter B. 2, Susanah 8/12 (b.
    Oct)
38. PEARCE, Robert 24, Elizabeth 25
39. TAYLOR, Jacob V. 34, Beldora 32, Louisa? 15,
    Emmet 8, Daisy 4, William 1
40. HINKLE, William 26, Dillie C. 22 (wife),
    Luticia E. 6, John 2
41. BUCKLES, Andrew 27, Catharine 20, Mary 5
    (dau), Cora 3, William 1; HURLEY,
    Nicholas 19 (servant--teamster)

               Page 6, Dist. 10

42. BUCKELS, Robert 60, Matild 55, William 24,
    Luticia 15; WILSON, Eveline 30 (servant),
    CAMPBELL, Louise 23 (servant), Georg 19
    (servant--teamster)
43. NIDEFFER, James C. 28, Marthaann 29, Sarah
    Ann 7, Samuel T. 5, Mary C. 4, Nancy C.
    1
44. TRUSSEL, George 24, Sarah E. 16 (hurt by
    fall); PEARCE, Mary 20 (servant), Catha-
    rine 8/12 (b. Oct) (dau of Catharine?)
45. SHOUN, Frederick 39, Margret 25 (wife),
    Mary A. 8, Elijah D. 4, Lydia 1
46. PETERS, Alferd 27, Nancy 20, Charles 5, Conna
    3, Pheby 2, William 11/12 (b. Jun);
    NIDEFFER, Elizabeth 47 (mother in law),
    James 17 (bro in law)
47. HINKLE, Elizabeth 32, Florence 9; TAYLOR,
    Margret 77 (g mother) (blind) (NC NC NC)
48. ALFERD, James 30, Pheby 27 (T NC T), Napoleon
    8, George W. 7, John 5; HARDEN, Jacob
    19 (servant) (crippled)
49. TAYLOR, David 54 (miner), Jane 49, Allen 22
    (miner), Samuel 18 (teamster); BLEVINS,
    Riley 25 (border--miner); HURLEY, Irvin
    16 (servant); NIDEFFER, Luvica 15 (ser-
    vant)
50. ROBERTSON, David 20, Eliza 18?, Joseph 4/12
    (b. Feb)

Hh# Page 7, Dist. 10

51. HINKLE, Nancy 46 (widow), Jennie 10, Dillard 7; HARDEN, John 21 (son in law) (miner), Sallie 20 (dau)
52. PETERS, James 65 (T __ T) (attending mill), Elizabeth 46 (wife) (VA NC T), William 17, Mary C. 15, Nancy 11, Millie 8, Catharine 13
53. PETERS, Alerd 62 (T __ PA), Louisa 58, Micheal 19
54. COLBAUGH, Teter N. 34, Lorina 33, Daniel 12, Celia 10, Levica 8, Annie 6, Margret 4, Eliza 2
55. RASOR, William 30, Margret 32, John 4, Matilda 2; BOWERS, Powell 20 (servant--teamster); BRITT, Mary 15 (servant) (NC NC NC)
56. RITCHER, David J. 41 (blacksmith) (T VA T), Jane 36 (T NC T), Rebecca 17, Eliza C. 15, Thomas 14, Lafayett 12, Lillie 11, Roseabell 6, Lottie 3
57. HINKLE, George 23 (works in iron foundry), Amanda 20
58. VANDEVENTER, Joseph 36, Nancy 26, Marion 8, James C. 6, Cathaine 2
59. BUCKELS, Robert A. 53, Hincy E. 53 (wife), Jones A. 24, Ruben C. 23, Samuel L. 18, Nancy A. 22, Mary C. 15, Alice E. 12

Page 8, Dist. 10

60. PEARCE, Alferd 38 (works in iron foundry), Mary 24, Cashaim? 12 (dau), Nancy 6, Martha 1, Mary 1; WHITE, Robert 62 (boarder--works at foundry)
61. CAMPBELL, John 48 (T NC T), Elizajane 35, Martha 13, Mordica 11, Elizaann 8, Sarah 7, Isaac 3
62. STOUT, Kizey 67 (widow), Mary A. 28, Pheby 7 (g dau), Rebecca 6 (g dau)
63. OLLIVER, George 36, Sarahfino 32 (wife), Andrew 13
64. CAMPBELL, Daniel 45 (T NC T), Elizabeth A. 46, Samuel 22, Elender 18, Rogan 16, Marstia 14, Mordica 12 (son), George 10 (typhoid fever), Emelia 8, John 6, Mary 4; CAMPBELL, John 83 (father) (NC NC NC)
65. GENTRY, Sarah 58 (T T VA); VAUGHN, Lutiarn? 49 (sis) (T T VA)
66. NIDEFFIR, James 37 (consumption), Mary C. 43 (T NC VA), William S. 11, John F. 10, David K. 6, Eliza L. J. 2
67. LEWIS, Gideon 41 (works on public road) (T NC NC), Eveline 30, James I. 10, Andrew 8, Nancy H. 5, Mary E. 2

Page 9, Dist. 10

68. LEWIS, Ephraim 52, Sarah 52 (dropsy), Eliza 21
69. LEWIS, John 22, Elizabeth 24
70. MYERS, Henry 31 (works on public road), Rebecca 32, Eveline 9, Silas 6, Thomas 4, Benjamine 1; OLLIVER, Nancy 68 (mother in law) (midwife), Cary 16 (niece)
71. GRIFFITH, James 24 (T NC T), Dillie 21, Maryann 2; GENTRY, Mary 50 (mother in law)
72. LEWIS, Stephen 36, Manerva 22, Julia 3, Houston 1, Lillie 2/12 (b. Apr); FLETCHER, Lauson 19 (bro in law) (teamster)
73. WILLIAMS, Pleasant 59, Luvica 56 (T NC T), Nancy 27, Henry 19, Samuel 17, Everett 15, Ida 13, Elizabeth 82 (mother) (falling of womb) (T __ __)
74. FLETCHER, John 28, Nancy 28, Andrew 3, Margret 2
75. WILLIAMS, Arthur 36, Sarah J. 35, Alferd 14, Isaac 12, Eli 10, Mary 7, Robert 5, Allen 2
76. PEMER?, Samuel 35 (T NC T), Sarah 33, Andrew 13, Jacob V. 12, James C. 10, Thomas 8, William A. 5, Jonathan 4, Samuel E. 2

Hh# Page 10, Dist. 10

77. FORBES, Robert 31, Margret 25, Matilda 7, Elijah 3 (piles), Daisy 1
78. BOWERS, Murry 38, Eliza J. 38 (T NC T), Louisa 15, Daniel 14, John 10, Charles 6, Kelley 4 (son), Granvill 2, Amanda 1
79. PEARCE, William 58 (T NC T), Martha J. 48, Pleasant 18
80. LEWIS, James L. 27 (gunsmith) (NC NC NC), Elizabeth 25 (T Ire T), Idama 6 (dau), Samuel 4, Thomas 2; MORRATTA, Eliza 42 (mother in law) (T Ire Ire), Margret 20 (sis in law)
81. GEAVER, Jackson 21, Nancy J. 22, Nathaniel 1
82. WEAVER, Russel 23, Susanah 23
83. OLLIVER, George W. 38, Eliza 31, Mahala 20, Lyddia 18 (dropsy), Mary 14, Josophine 4
84. VANDEVENTER, Jacob 68 (T T MD), Lorina 66 (T VA SC), Samuel C. 35, Catharine 30, Jennie 7 (g dau)
85. TAYLOR, Daniel 26, Elizabeth 29, John W. 2, Alexander 8/12 (b. Sep)
86. TAYLOR, John W. jr. 22, Elender 18, David 2, Alferd 2/12 (b. Apr)

Page 11, Dist. 10

87. TAYLOR, John W. sr. 53, Jane 49 (consumption), Elbert 18, General B. 16, Sarah 14, James C. 13, Matilda 8
88. TAYLOR, Thomas F. 45, Angeline 42, William G. 22, Jacob A. 4, Nancy 78 (mother)
89. FULLER, Elizabeth 35 (widow) (NC NC NC), Mary J. 13 (NC GA NC), John C. 12 (T), James M. 11 (GA), Mahaly 9 (GA), Hiram E. 5 (AR), Alter V. 4 (son) (AR), Hettaann 3 (dropsy) (T)
90. TAYLOR, General 25, Amanda 22, Pheby J. 4, Nancy E. 2
91. WILSON, Solomon 27, Sarahfine 35 (wife), Stephen 12, Lawson E. 4 (dau)
92. STEPHENS, John 50 (NC NC NC), Caroline 34 (wife) (T VA NC), Margret 9, John Lazrus 7, William E. 5, Thomas 2
93. TAYLOR, William 26, Elizabeth J. 33 (wife) (T NC T), Sarah J. 10, James 9, William 9, Margret 6, Levi 1
94. TAYLOR, William B. 60, Susanah 53, Abraham L. 20, Eliza E. 19, Jacob G. 17, Nancy C. 12, Susanah 9; CAMPBELL, Sarah 27 (dau) (widow), Margret 7 (g dau)

Page 12, Dist. 10

95. MYERS, Harmon (carpenter), Maryann 21, Sarah E. 3, Willie E. 11/12 (b. Jul) (dau); TAYLOR, Elizabeth 72 (g mother) (NC NC NC)
96. TAYLOR, Levi 35 (boot & shoe maker) (crippled), Eveline 35; PETERS, Daniel 17 (stepson) (appretice boot maker)
97. GENTRY, Andrew 29 (color), Nancy ann 31, Mary E. 12, James R. 8
98. GENTRY, John 31, Susanah 33, Mary E. 7
99. LOWE?, Martha 39 (widow), Andrew 17, George 13, Hiram 11, Jacob 8, William 5
100. PEARCE, Richard 65 (miller) (T T NC), Rebecca 58
101. FAIR, George W. 31 (blacksmith), Luwesa 31, John 10, Martha 13, Amanda 8, Mary E. 6 (crippled), Sarah A. 3
102. TAYLOR, Thomas H. 49 (rheumatism), Margret 55, Joseph 29 (boot & shoe maker), Malinda 20
103. TAYLOR, William T. 27, Martha 20, Sarah 64 (mother)
104. BUCKELS, James 39, Sarah A. 36, William 16, Daniel 14, Isaac 12, David 8, Martha 7, Grant 6, Eveline 1
105. BERRY, Thomas 27, Margret 27 (cholerah morbas), Sarah 4, Samuel 1

Hh#	Page 13, Dist. 10

106. LEWIS, James F. M. 46, Mary A. E. 35, William H. 12, Stanford J. 10/12 (b. Aug), Stephen 80 (father); NIDEFFER, Martha 14 (servant)
107. NIDEFFER, Elihu 34, Eveline 34; BLEVINS, James 14 (nephew); WILLIAMS, Levi 22 (servant--teamster)
108. McKEE, Smith 29 (works in iron foundry), Larua 27 (wife), William 7, Ginter 4 (dau), Robert 5/12 (b. Jan)
109. HOUSLEY, Harison 51 (iron manufacturer), Eliza 48 (T NC T); LEWIS, Ell-a 10 (g dau)
110. RICHARDSON, John 42 (boot & shoe maker) (NC NC NC), Annie S. 42 (NC NC NC), Alexander 14 (NC), Christopher 12 (T), William P. 10, James N. 7, John N. 4, Maryann 1/12 (b. May)
111. GRINDSTAFF, Michel 40, Hily S. 35 (wife) (T T NC), William H. 16, Hanah K. 11, Thomas J. 5, David R. 3
112. GRINDSTAFF, David 29, Jane 23, Jacob H. 6, Charley L. 2, Juliaann 3/12 (b. Mar)
113. HODG, John M. 23, Nancyann 17 (wife)
114. WILLIAMS, John 26, Mary 24, Samuel 5, Elizabeth 4, William 1
115. CROMLEY, Frederick 33, Arazilla 30, Elihu J. 13
116. PEARCE, Nathaniel 47 (carpenter), Rebecca 62 (wife) (afflicted with rheumatism), William 19 (carpenter)

Page 14, Dist. 10

117. JENKINS, Samuel 23, Eliza 20, Callie 3 (dau), Elizabeth 2
118. WILLIAMS, Lorenzo 49 (miner), Elizabeth 48, James 17, Ruben 14
119. BOWERS, Landon 26, Barbary 32 (neuralgia)
120. WILLIAMS, Elihu 33, Mary 31, Martha 10, Cameron 4, Armstrong 1
121. BUCKELS, Thomas 28, Celia 26, Margret 10, Eliza J. 8, Mary C. 6, Addeline 4, Franklin 1
122. BUCKELS, William 72, Catharine 68
123. PEARCE, Lilburn 79, Eliza 77
124. LOVELACE, John 31 (colier) (T NC T), Eveline 30, Thomas 9, Joseph 6, Dorabell 2, Mary 1
125. CROUCH, George 40 (commercial tourest?), Mary 40, William 16 (blind & idiotic), Elizabeth 11, Sanford 9, John 7, Dorabell 5, Julia 2
126. RITCHIE, William 23, Rebecca 20, Jane L. 2, Matilda 5/12, Jane 65 (mother)
127. GARLAND, Voluntine 35, Rodicey 40 (wife), Noah A. 7, Godfrey D. 2

Page 15, Dist. 10

128. CAMPBELL, Nicholas 51, Susanah 51, Adaline 18, Loretta 16, Emelie 14, Sarah E. 12, Nicholas 9
129. ANDERSON, James 34, Jane 30, Lewis 13, Mary 11, Littie 1, Samuel 78 (father)
130. RICHARDSON, Andrew 25, Cary 24 (wife), James A. 2
131. DUGLAS, Landon 22 (teamster), Rebecca 22, Nancy E. 1
132. FRASIER, Jacob 38, Martha 34, James 10, Austin 8, Cordarell 6 (dau), Eldorador 4 (dau), Peter 2
133. LEWIS, Samuel 33, Matilda 30, Nancy L. 9, Margret E. 7, William J. 6, Eliza A. 4, John D. 2
134. PETERS, Ruben B. 35, Nancy 36, Teter 16, Millie 15, Christian 13, John 10, Alferd 9, Lorina 7, Wiley M. 4, Isaac 1
135. HARDEN, Andrew 30, Pheiby? 29, Michel 10, James 8, Mary 6, Margret J. 4, Alexander 1

Page 16, Dist. 10

136. NIDEFFER, Samuel 27, Margret 18
137. PETERS, Henry T. 22, Mary 21

Hh#	Page 16 (cont'd)

138. LOWE, Stephen 28, Elva 20 (wife), James M. 7 (son), Nancy J. 5, Rebecca L. 4 (cholera infantum), Noah B. 2
139. NIDEFFER, William 24, Mary E. 19, Margret 8/12 (b. Oct)
140. NIDEFFER, Mark 69, Eliza 50 (T __ __) (wife), Jane 36 (dau), Eliza Jane 19, Isaac 17; WOODS, Elizabeth 34 (dau), Alphatine 3 (g dau), Henry 2 (g son)
141. COLBOUGH, William 24, Elizabeth 26, Lilibell 4, John K. 3, Julia E. 1
142. HARDEN, Alvin 38, Eveline 37, Eliza 14, Lorina 12, Margret 9, John N. 8, Martha 6, Corado 4 (dau), Lilabell 1
143. HARDEN, Lydia 44 (widow), Ponel (Powel?) 17, Eli 13, Robert 11, Emelie 8, Maryann 5
144. BLEVINS, Adaline 38 (widow), Margret 12, Carie 9, Elihu 6, George 5, Sarah M. 2
145. RITCHIE, Carerick 26, Martiaora 25, Lottie 3

Page 17, Dist. 10

146. FRASIER, John W. 40 (T NC T), Annie 40 (T NC T), Orpha 18, Martha 14, Sarah 9, Rachel 7, William 5, Johister 3/12 (b. Mar) (g dau)
147. HAMPTON, Samuel 25 (cabinet maker), Martha 21
148. TAYLOR, Robert 27 (boot & shoe maker), Margret 23, Catharine 5, Jane 2, John 22 (bro)
149. BUCKELS, Isaac 33, Rutha 33, Allen 10, Alferd 8, Abraham 6
150. TAYLOR, James J. 22 (teamster), Elizabeth 22
151. TAYLOR, Lewis D. 30, Elizabeth 26, Hester 8, Michel T. 6, Jefferson 4, Cearlin 2 (son), Caleb 9/12 (b. Sep)
152. HINKLE, Elizabeth 65 (widow) (NC NC NC), Andrew 26 (T VA NC), John 24 (T VA NC), Charles 13 (g son), William 10 (g son); BARTER, Arigana 29 (f) (cousin) (T VA T), Lucinda 4 (cousin) (T T T)
153. HINKLE, Maryjane 44 (T VA NC), Elbert 18 (son), Lafayett 10, Charlie 7, James 4, Elizabeth 1
154. CROW, Thomas 45 (teamster), Elizabeth 41, Isaac 20 (horseler), William 18, Samuel 17, Mary C. 9, Mandy 6, Andrew 2

Page 18, Dist. 10

155. HINKLE, William F. 23, Mary Jane 20, George W. 1, Julia C. 2/12 (b. Apr), Thomas 16 (cousin)
156. BERRY, Murry S. 24, Mary 18, Rutha 11/12 (b. Jul)
157. JENKINS, William 26, Catharine 23, James 2, Frances 1
158. BOY, Andrew J. 53, Maryann 52, Callie 23, William 21, Laura 19; CARUTHERS, Elizabeth 85 (aunt) (VA Ire Ire)
159. PETERS, Benjamine 40 (divorced) (carpenter), Samuel 17 (apprentice carpenter), Cornelous 14, Margret 12, Mary 10, Lillie 8
160. BUCKELS, William jr. 36, Eliza 33, Luvina 12, Rebecca C. 8, Elizabeth 6, William A. 4, Daniel W. 2
161. BERRY, Alferd 32 (T T NC), Sarah 30, James H. 10, Benjamine B. 8, Mary C. 5, John Allen 2
162. BERRY, James 28 (T T NC), Callie 20 (wife), William 1, Margret 24 (sis) (T T NC), Mary 67 (mother) (NC NC NC), Alferd 20 (nephew); MYERS, Mary 32 (cousin)
163. BOWERS, David 41, Martha 41, Mary 17, Sarah 13, Ruth 10, Ulysus Grant 8

Page 19, Dist. 10

164. BUCKELS, Levi 41, Jane 40, Emma 17, William 16, Catharine 12, Jennie 7, John 5, Benjamine 2

Hh#	Page 19 (cont'd)

165. OLLIVER, Christian 40, Luvica 42, William 20, Carrie 18, Isaac L. 14, Jemima 11, Thomas 8, Nancy 6, Minnie 2, Alferd 9/12 (b. Sep)
166. PEARCE, Cameron 28, Amanda 21, Lillie 3, Houston 4/12 (b. Feb)
167. WILLIAMS, Thomas 21, Nancy 21, Isaac 9/12 (b. Sep)
168. NIDEFFER, Isaac 51, Levica 45, William 13, Carter 9, Adaline 8, Nancy 3; WILLIAMS, Eveline 17 (stepdau)
169. BOWERS, Landon H. 48, Lucrecia 48, Martha 20, Emmert 18, John 14, Rebecca 11, Eveline 3
170. WILSON, George 33 (miner), Mary 32, James W. 13, Minda 11, Susanah 8, Thomas 3, Mary 2
171. BOWERS, Alferd 24 (tonsil eltes), Rebecca 20, Theodocia 4, Lucy 2

Page 20, Dist. 10

172. JENKINS, Angeline 44 (widow), Levi 21, Emma 17, Noah 16, Joann 14, Mary 12, Phebe 10
173. JENKINS, Robert 20, Mary 18
174. BOWERS, Isaac 31, Rachel 40 (wife), Callie 9, Minnie 6
175. NAVE, William S. 59, Margret 45, John 26, David 23, James A. 20, George 17, Mark 15, Sarah 12, Daniel 7, Pherby 4, Louisa 19 (dau in law); LIPPS, Nancy 78 (mother in law) (T VA SC)
176. TAYLOR, Thomas 22, Lucinda 24, Rebecca E. 1
177. LOWE, David K. 21, Mary C. 19, William H. 6/12, Rebecca 66 (mother in law)
178. NIDEFFER, George 33, Elizabeth 30, Nancy J. 7, William A. 5, Marcus D. L. 3, Manda H. 2
179. MILLER, Nicholas 78 (NC NC NC), Catharine 73 (T T NC), Mary 33 (dropsy), William 13 (g son); FLETCHER, Manda 16 (g dau); BLEVINS, Robert 20 (nephew); HINKLE, George 56 (cousin) (colier)
180. COLBOUGH, Henry 49, Levica 50 (crippled), Margret 14, William 11

Page 21, Dist. 10

181. TAYLOR, Luny 25 (miner), Eliza Jane 22
182. NAVE, Mark 40, Malinda 37, Margret 8, William 6, Minnie 3; PANE, John 9 (nephew); PEAVER, Armstrong 28 (teamster); McKINNEY, Joanah 25 (servant), Theodocia 3
183. CHRISTIAN, Wiley M. 43 (dry goods merchant) (T T GA), Julia 38 (T LA T); BARNANELL, Allen 19 (nephew) (clerk in store) (T NC T); WYLEY, Mary Jessie 14 (niece) (T T GA); ARMON, Margret E. D. 15 (sis in law) (T LA VA); MOSS, Frances (B) 30 (servant) (T NC NC)
184. FAIR, Samuel 33 (teamster), Annie 24 (T NC NC), James H. 8, Margret 5, Robert L. 2, Sheffey 9/12 (b. Sep) (son)
185. REDICK, Ester (B) 65 (widow) (SC___), Africa 18 (son) (VA__ SC); GREENLIEF, David 13 (VA___)
186. RUSSEL, George 55 (colier) (OH VA OH), Nancy 38 (wife) (T KY__), Nancyanne 14, James 12, William H. 10, Watters 8 (son), George W. 6, Henry 4, Boston 2, Minnie 1
187. OLLIVER, David 35 (colier), Jane 30, William 5, Mary 5 (twins), John 3, Carrie 1
188. CHANCE, Nancy 70 (widow), John 38 (idiotic), William 32 (idiotic), Amanda 30 (helpless--idiotic), Mary 25, William P. 5 (g son), Lucyanne 2 (g dau)
189. CHANCE, Christian 36 (idiotic), Elizabeth 38; GRIFFETH, Mary C. 13 (step dau) (T __ T)

Page 22, Dist. 10

190. FORBES, Daniel 41 (widower) (T NC T), Eveline 16, Rachel 13, Marion 10, Elizaann 9, Nancy C. 8, Lyddia 6

Page 22 (cont'd)

191. NIDEFFER, Robert 19 (miner), Elizabeth 15

Page 1, Dist. 12

1. TAYLOR, George 35, Levice 33 (wife), Millie 10, William 7, Jennie 6, Eliza 3, Susanah 4/12 (b. Jan); ELLIOTT, Susanah 68 (mother in law)
2. TAYLOR, Andrew 52, Harriet 41, Joseph 20, Nancy 18, Sherman 14, Peter 11, John 7, Michal 4
3. LIPPS, Nelson 68 (T NC NC), Elizabeth 64 (T NC NC); MARKLAND, Elizabeth 15 (g dau)
4. LIPPS, Daniel 31 (works for Knox Car W Co.), Mahala 24, Martha 7, Phebe 6, William 4, Isaac 1
5. ELLIOTT, Michal 35 (farmer and JP), Martha 39, Samuel 11, Eliza 9, Thomas 6, Wheeler 4, David 1
6. TAYLOR, Alvin 39, Sarah 34 (T NC T), Nancy 16, Fanny 12, Charles 9, Eliza 6, Lillie 1/12 (b. May)
7. ARENT, William 29 (divorced) (blacksmith) (NC NC NC), Martha 10 (T NC T), John 6, Daniel 4; TAYLOR, Amanda 18 (step dau), Mary 12 (step dau)
8. MARKLAND, Nelson 54 (T NC T) (crippled), Lukinzie 44 (wife), Mary 17, Angeline 12, Millie 7, Daniel 21 (married within yr) (works for Knox Car W Co.), Mary 18 (dau in law)

Page 2, Dist. 12

9. PIERCE, Louis 35 (carpenter), Dorotha 28, Julia 8, James 5
10. LEWIS, Nicholas 28 (teamster & constable), Angeline 30, Eliza 9, Fanny 7, Sarah 6, Julia 4, Delia 2
11. LEWIS, Louis D. 68 (T VA SC), Fanny 55, Hasten 21 (son) (works for Car W. Co.), Delia 19, Eliza 17, Sarah 13
12. STOVER, Samuel 56 (physician), Amanda 20 (wife), Claude 1
13. PIERCE, Sion 52 (miller) (T NC NC), Sarah 45 (T VA VA), John 21, Carrie 19 (divorced), Rogan 14 (teamster), Flora 12
14. ARCHER, Nancy 62 (widow) (T NC T), Rebecca 18, Joanna 16, Sarah 12, Nelson 9, Andrew 7, Mary 2
15. COLE, Amanda 38 (divorced) (T NC T); CAMPBELL, Robert 9; OVERHOLSER, Samuel 73 (boarder) (blacksmith) (T VA VA)
16. MARKLAND, William 49 (works for Car W Co.) (T NC T), Merinda 38, Amanda 16, Elizabeth 14, Isabel 12; PETERS, Henry 16 (son)
17. MARKLAND, James 45 (works for Knox Car W Co.) (T NC T), Sarah 38, Eliza 10, Susan 9, Francis 7, Henry 5, Nancy 1

Page 3, Dist. 12

18. MARKLAND, Henry 32 (works for Knox Car W Co.) (T NC T), Mary 26, Amanda 9, Levice 8 (dau), Wilburn 6
19. MARKLAND, David 29 (works for Knox Car W Co.) (T NC T), Amanda 28, Elva 7, James 6, Elizabeth 5, William 3, Henry 10/12 (b. Aug)
20. WHITE, Robert 23 (works for Car W Co), Julia 18
21. MARKLAND, Philip 40 (T NC T), Eveline 28, Melvin 13, William 11, Wiley 7; OVERBEY, Sally 6 (step dau)
22. WHITE, Susan 39 (divorced), Seraphina 62 (mother), Josephine 29 (sis), Daisy 6 (niece), Lennis 10/12 (b. Aug) (niece)
23. HEADRICK, John 25 (brickmason), Ann 33, Charlic 11, Bertie 8 (dau), William 6, Josephine 5, John 2, Sarah 1/12 (b. Apr)
24. CHRISTIAN, James 41 (supt for Knox Car W Co), Mary 39 (T VA VA), Hugh 7 (nephew); DEAL, Charles 30 (boarder) (coal yard clerk) (MD MD MD); BYNON, Joshua 35 (boarder)(pattern maker) (PA PA PA)

33

Hh#	Page 3 (cont'd)

25. HURT, Robert 43 (works for Knox Car W Co) (VA VA VA), Mary 44, Sally 15, Charley 9, George 7, Emma 5
26. TAYLOR, John 28 (works for Knox Car W Co), Loretta 22, David 7, Sarah 4, Daisy 1

Page 4, Dist. 12

27. HINKLE, David 24 (works for Knox Car W Co) (T VA T), Mary 22, Belle 3, William 1
28. HURLEY, Wright 26, Sarah 25, Samuel 4, Sarah 1/12 (b. May)
29. HATCHER, James 30 (wagon maker), Martha 25, Leander 4
30. SMITH, John 55, Elizabeth 51, Mary 22, Charles 20 (physician), John 17, Lillie 14, Daisy 8; PETERS, Catherine 22 (servant)
31. PIERCE, Henry 26 (works for Knox Car W Co), Elizabeth 21, Joseph 5, Margaret 3, Orlena 11/12 (b. Jun)
32. BRASWELL, William 46 (carpenter) (NC NC NC), Louisa 42 (T NC NC), James 17, Joseph 14, Margaret 8, William 6, Amanda 2; ALLISON, Nancy 24 (sis in law) (T NC T)
33. CAMPBELL, Thomas 26 (works for Knox Car W Co), Eliza 24, Susanah 4, Amanda 2; NIDEFFER, Mary 20 (sis in law)
34. ARNOLD, Murphy 25 (works for Knox Car W Co), Elizabeth 24, Nicholas 4
35. ARNOLD, William 25 (works for Knox Car W Co), Ellen 20, Samuel 2
36. DUGGAR, James 48 (married) (crippled)
37. DUGGAR, John 22 (works for Knoxville Car W Co), Nancy 51 (mother) (married), Elizabeth 27 (sis), Jane 25 (sis), Hannah 21 (sis), Landon 15 (bro), Melvina 12 (sis), Lillie 3 (niece)

Page 5, Dist. 12

38. HURLEY, William 54 (T NC NC), Ellen 40 (wife), Nicholas 19, Seraphina 15, John 10
39. BLEVINS, Daniel 23, Amanda 20, William 1/12 (b. May); ELLIOTT, Alice 2 (step dau)
40. ROBINSON, Sampson 59, Louisa 41 (wife), Loretta 16, Mahala 3, Susan 2; RAINS, Nancy 14 (step dau)
41. GRINDSTAFF, William 38, Mahala 42, David 9, Susanah 7, George 3, Sarah 1; ROBERTS, Mary 17 (step dau); ROBINSON, William 25 (boarder) (physician)
42. GRINDSTAFF, John 52, Clara 45, Mary 23, Jennie 23, Nancy 18, Samuel 16, Matilda 11
43. CAMPBELL, John 30 (works for Car W Co), Ura 30 (wife), Charley 14, Stephen 11, Rebecca 9, William 6, James 4, Julia 10/12 (b. Aug)
44. CAMPBELL, Michal 32, Nancy 32, Nancy 6, Luna 5 (son), Martha 4, Riley 1, Matilda 7/12 (b. Nov)
45. FRITZ, Christian 25, Mary 26, James 5, Lucy 5/12 (b. Dec)

Page 6, Dist. 12

46. ELLIOTT, David 19, Hetty 21
47. ELLIOTT, James 30, Sarah 23 (NC NC NC), Rodalia 5, Emanuel 1/12 (b. Apr); LAWS, Thomas 11 (servant); BIRD, Emanuel 23 (boarder) (NC NC NC)
48. TAYLOR, Samuel 34, Sarah 29, James 5, Nancy 2
49. ESTEP, Isaac 27, Docia 28
50. ELLIOTT, Joseph 52, Sarah 63 (wife), Peter 21, Sarah 19, Joseph 9/12 (b. Sep) (g son)
51. ELLIOTT, John 25, Cornelia 21, Julia 2, Martha 11/12 (cholera morbus)
52. ESTEP, William 34 (works for Knox Car W Co), Maria 34, Sarah 13, Robert 7, Eliza 5, Mary 2
53. BLEVINS, William 45, Debitha 39, Nancy 13, Matilda 11, Lydia 5, Hester 2, John 1/12 (b. Apr)

Hh#	Page 6 (cont'd)

54. ENSOR, William 33 (works for Car W Co) (T NC T), Clara 31, Robert 9, Matilda 7, George 1
55. CRESS, Samuel 59 (T VA VA), Mary 47 (NC NC NC), James 8 (son)
56. PHIPPS, Peter 33 (works for Car W Co) (VA VA VA), Elizabeth 33, Charley 11, David 9, John 7, Amanda 5, Daniel 3, Jane 3/12 (b. Feb)

Page 7, Dist. 12

57. ELLIOTT, Daniel 27 (works for car W Co), Eveline 24, Joseph 5, Margaret 1; BARTEE, Delcena 30 (sis in law) (seamstress), Mary 1 (niece)
59. LEWIS, William 29, Nancy 28, Lewis 6, James 5, Nicholas 2
60. EAKLE, Eliza 30 (widow) (NC VA PA), Eliza 11 (step dau) (T VA T), Corle 10 (dau) (T VA NC), Nancy 8, John 5; FORBES, Rachel 14 (niece) (T T NC)
61. ARCHER, Sarah 45 (widow), Serena 18, Eliza 17, Ella 12, Allen 2
62. PLEASANT, James 63 (blind) (VA VA VA), Elizabeth 59 (PA PA PA)
63. WHITE, Thomas 26 (forks for Car W Co), Frances 19 (T VA PA), Verdia 1, James 2/12 (b. Mar); CULBERT, Henry 29 (bro in law) (works for Car W Co), Armitha 19 (sis), Seraphina 9/12 (b. May) (niece), Matilda 1/12 (b. May) (niece)
64. GRINDSTAFF, Andrew 45, Nancy 47, Michal 23, Clara 16, David 12, Martha 9, George 6

Page 8, Dist. 12

65. ESTEP, Samuel 20, Mary 20
66. TAYLOR, Francis 27 (works for Car W Co), Martha 24, Mary 3, Susan 2, Jacob 1
67. ESTEP, Isaac 52, Elizabeth 52, Mary 29, Caroline 24, Susanah 18, Milburn 15, Lawson 12, Edith 9, Mahala 7 (g dau), William 1 (g son); OVERBEY, Robert 7 (nephew)
68. RICHARDSON, Hiram 30 (NC NC NC), Freelove 27, George 7, William 3, Isaac 11/12 (b. Jun)
69. ESTEP, Julia 40 (widow), William 19, Shadrach 17, Andrew 14, Sarah 11, John 8, Murray 5, Joseph 2; GARLAND, Sarah 75 (mother) (KY NC NC)
70. ESTEP, Levi 21, Eveline 29 (wife) (married within yr); GARLAND, Sarah 4 (step dau), Catherine 8 (step dau)
71. RICHARDSON, Margaret 45 (widow), Hannah 21, Caledonia 17, Daniel 15, Matilda 11, Charley 8, Phebe 4, Charles 9/12 (b. Sep) (g son)

Page 9, Dist. 12

72. ARENT, Cain 25 (NC NC NC), Amanda 25, Ceuse? 10/12 (dau)
73. DAVIS, James 41 (supt iron ore mine) (Eng Eng Eng), Sarah 30, Lorina 8, Mary 7, John 5, Sarah 4, Lilla 2, Bessie 11/12 (b. Jul)
74. WILSON, William 27 (works for car W Co), Mary 21 (NC NC NC), Thomas 5, James 3, Catherine 2, Sarah 1/12 (b. May)
75. ESTEP, Tennessee 54 (works in ore bank), Susanah 48, Edith 14, Delila 12, Matilda 10, Nancy 7, Docia 4, Wiley 8/12
76. ELLIOTT, Moses 21, Ruth 19, Joseph 1
77. NIDIFFER, Robt. 51 (works in ore bank), Emmeline 47, Melissa 18, Harrison 16, John 14, Delcena 12, Mark 10, Edith 6, OVERBEY, Edith 84 (mother in law) (widow), William 7 (nephew)
78. NIDIFFER, Levi 23 (works for Car W Co), Margaret 23, Samuel 3, Orlena 1/12 (b. Apr)
79. HODGE, Ollie 47 (f), Louisa 20 (dau), Quaif 6 (son)
80. HEATHERLY, Robert 30, Sarah 23, Butler 4, James 3, Rebecca 1/12 (b. May)

34

Hh#	Page 9 (cont'd)

81. HEATHERLY, James 24 (works in ore bank) (T NC T), Elizabeth 65 (g mother) (T NC T), Margaret 25 (aunt), Lindon 19 (bro) (T NC T)

Page 10, Dist. 12

82. LIVINGSTON, George 36 (works in ore bank) (NC NC NC), Nancy 25, George 1
83. RICHARDSON, Canada 29 (works in ore bank), Jane 21, Johnson 4, Hattie 1
84. CAMPBELL, Isaac 21, Atlantic 21 (wife)
85. GARLAND, Frank 36 (T T NC), Nancy 35, Docia 14, Sarah 10, Highly 8 (dau), John 7, James 3, Joseph 8/12 (b. Nov)
86. CAMPBELL, Icy 53 (widow), John 19, Rose-crans 16
87. GARLAND, Highly 64 (widow) (NC NC NC), Lanna 33 (NC T NC), Campbell 21 (T T NC), Lydia 21 (dau in law) (VA T NC)
88. GARLAND, William 52, Delia 40 (T T NC), Luna 15, Elizabeth 12, Ellen 10, Sally 8, Wheeler 5, Quiller 1 (son)
89. WILSON, Poe 52 (NC NC NC), Nancy 51, Mary 31, Smith 23, Martha 18, David 16, Hannah 14, Alexander 12, Dempsy 10, Daniel 8, Amy 6, George 11 (g son), Andrew 7 (g son)
90. GARLAND, Volantine 39 (farmer & J.P.), Margaret 36, Isaac 18, Ingerton 11, Nancy 9, Susan 7, Jesse 5, Serena 3, Minerva 8/12 (b. Oct); BLEVINS, Seraphina 14 (dau) (married within yr)

Page 11, Dist. 12

91. GARLAND, John 23, Alzena 25
92. HURLEY, Andew (sic) 31, Nancy 27, Nellie 4, Matilda 1; ESTEP, Ruth 19 (sis in law), Elvira 1/12 (b. Apr) (niece)
93. HODGE, Simon 45, Caroline 36, Murphy 20 (works for Car W Co), Eveline 18, Nancy 14, Littleton 12, Caleb 10, Volantine 8, Serena 3, Davis 1/12 (b. May)
94. HURLEY, Harden 61, Nancy 65 (T T NC), Murphy 24, Isaac 8 (g son); COLE, Nancy 21 (g dau)
95. HURLEY, Alvin 29 (works in ore bank), Matilda 33, Harden 12, Adkins 7, Hamilton 5, Robert 2, James 1/12 (b. Apr)
96. TAYLOR, Jacob 51 (millwright), Rachel 43 (T VA VA), Jesse 20, Peter 17, Charley 15, William 11, Elizabeth 4
97. TAYLOR, Jacob L. 26 (carpenter), Seraphina 24, Mary 2, Martha 1; CAMPBELL, Mary 18 (sis in law)
98. GARLAND, Mordecai 55, Mary 50 (T T NC), Sarah 38 (sis in law) (T T NC), David 7 (nephew), Nancy 5 (niece); HEATHERLY, George 13 (nephew); WILSON, Eliza 15 (niece); CAMPBELL, John 79 (father in law)

Page 12, Dist. 12

99. ESTEP, William 31 (T T NC), Rebecca 42 (wife), Sheridan 10, Martha 8, Margaret 7, Ellen 4; ARNOLD, Phebe 19 (step dau)
100. ESTEP, Shadrach 65 (T MD NC), Nellie 55 (NC NC NC), Mary 24, Sarah 2 (dau)
101. PETERS, William 19, Sarah 19 (SC NC NC), John 2/12, Alvin 21 (bro)
102. RICHARDSON, John 73 (T NC NC), Matilda 58 (wife) (T NC NC); ASHER, William 12 (nephew)
103. GARLAND, David 56, Minerva 35 (wife) (T NC T); FLETCHER, Nancy 14 (stepdau)
104. HEATHERLY, Thomas 82; PIERCE, William 24 (son in law), Elizabeth 33 (dau); WILSON, Ferdinand 6 (g son)
105. BLEVINS, Luna 60 (T PA VA), Martha 61, James 37, Isaac 31, Lucretia 26, Laura 22, Mary 18, Allen 24
106. GARLAND, Isaac 70, Anna 61 (T MD NC); Eliza 21; HODGE, Sandy 11 (g son)

Hh#	Page 12 (cont'd)

107. HODGE, Levi 44, Angeline 37, William 14, Grant 12, Isaac 8, Nellie 6, Abraham 4, Jacob 1/12 (b. May)

Page 13, Dist. 12

108. HEATHERLY, Godfrey 44, Amelia 38 (VA VA VA), Thomas 17, Godfrey jr. 14, Martha 10, Jesse 6, Mary 8, Ewing 4, Amelia 1; GARNER, Thomas 27 (son in law) (NC NC NC), Margret 20 (dau), Benjamin 6/12 (b. Nov) (g son) (T NC T)
109. STOUT, Pinkney 21, Kitty 28
110. STOUT, Joseph 19, Sarah 20, Thomas 2
111. GIBSON, Henry 26, Sarah 22, William 3, Clara 1
112. BLEVINS, Allen 55, Amy 36 (wife), David 16, Clemie 13, John 12, William 9, George 7, Stinson 2
113. CAMPBELL, James 23, Sally 27, Matilda 1
114. HOLDER, Elisha 23 (NC NC NC), Martha 25, James 7, Stephen 5, Lemuel 3, David 9/12 (b. Oct)
115. COLE, Benjamine 48 (T T VA), Elizabeth 48, Pacific 14 (dau), Ulyssis 12
116. COLE, John 23, Elizabeth 23 (VA VA T), Samuel 4, Noah 2, Minerva 1
117. GARLAND, David 42 (T T NC), Sarah 33, Angeline 13, Elizabeth 10, Leanna 8, Martha 7, Mary 3, Highly 1 (dau)

Page 14, Dist. 12

118. ESTEP, Henry 34, Martha 38, Mary 12, James 10, Moses 4, Martha 2, Sarah 3/12 (b. Feb)
119. ESTEP, Moses 31, Mary 24, Catherine 3, Nancy 2, Robert 2/12 (b. Apr)
120. GARLAND, Nathan 24 (T T NC), Rhoda 27; ESTEP, John 13 (nephew)
121. GARLAND, John 35, Lettie 32, Eliza 13
122. COLE, Benjamin 72 (miller), Della 73 (VA VA VA), William 13 (g son); STOUT, Selah 51 (dau) (widow)
123. COLE, Thomas 38 (asthma) (T T VA), Eliza 43, Sarah 17, Dilla 13, Flemie 11, Charley 8, William 4
124. VAUGHN, Benjamin 29 (T NC VA), Fanny 32 (T T NC), Lettie 5, James 1
125. STOUT, Benjamin 26, Louisa 28, David 1
126. GARLAND, William 32, Nancy 28, Mary 9
127. RICHARDSON, Sampson 25 (T T NC), Nancy 27, Noah 4, Losson 2 (son)
128. COLE, Selina 32, Sarah 7, William 5, Winnie 3, James 1

Page 15, Dist. 12

129. CAMPBELL, Henry 21, Selah 27 (wife), William 3, Amelia 4/12 (b. Feb)
130. COLE, Joseph 32 (T T VA), Docia 34, Currener 14 (dau), Andrew 12, George 2
131. COLE, Jesse 36 (baptist minister) (T T VA), Eliza 43 (wife), Thomas 16, Sarah 12, Alfred 7
132. RICHARDSON, James 30 (teacher) (T T NC), Nancy 26 (NC VA PA), Alverda 9 (niece), Elizabeth 4 (dau), Walter 2 (son), Willie 6/12 (son)
133. RICHARDSON, William 37 (consumption) (T T NC) Sarah 30, Daniel 16, Highly 14 (dau), John 13, Thomas 11, James 8, Docia 3, Mordecai 1 (diarrhea); NELSON, William 6 (stepson)
134. HODGE, Isaac 43 (T T NC), Elizabeth 29 (wife), Sarah 8, Eliza 7, William 4, James 2; GRINDSTAFF, Docia 28 (sis in law)
135. COLE, Andrew 28, Harriet 29, Charles 9, Canda 6, Joseph 4, Andrew 8/12 (b. Sep)
136. RICHARDSON, John 29 (T T NC), Nancy 35, Dicia 10, Thomas 8, Millie 6, Butler 4, Jesse 2; GARLAND, Samuel 17 (stepson), David 15 (stepson)

Hh#   Page 16, Dist. 12

137. ESTEP, Avery 29 (T T NC), Eveline 25,
         David 9, Nellie 7, Andrew 5, Elizabeth
         2, Samuel 8/12
138. RICHARDSON, Thomas 61 (widower), Henry 20,
         Elkana 18, Isaac 15, Joseph 13
139. PRITCHETT, Leander 27 (NC NC NC), Ollie
         26, Sarah 7 (NC), Alfred 5 (NC), Giles
         1 (T)
140. HURLEY, Mordecai 27, Martha 26, John 9,
         Eliza 7, William 3, Nancy 1/12 (b. May);
         CAMPBELL, Losson 29 (boarder), Lettitia
         19 (boarder), David 8/12 (b. Oct)
         (boarder)
141. TAYLOR, Murray 24 (keeping saw mill),
         Selah 18
142. GARLAND, Tabitha 35, Jesse 4 (son)
143. GARLAND, Alfred 71 (widower) (T T VA),
         Mary 33, Levice 29, Joshua 21, Seraphina
         19, Loretta 9 (g dau)
144. WILSON, John 22 (VA T T), Sarah 21 (T VA
         T)
145. SHOWN, Jesse 29, Mary 28, Martha 8,
         Napoleon 5, Jacob 2, Isaac 10/12 (b.
         Aug)
146. WILSON, Canada 29 (m) (T T NC), Eliza 29,
         William 7, John 5, Mordecai 3, Nancy 1
147. WILSON, Hannah 66 (NC NC NC), Elizabeth
         39 (dau) (T T NC), David 25 (son) (T T
         NC), Jane 23 (dau) (T T NC), George 13
         (g son) (T VA T), William 10 (g son)
         (T T T), Leonard 1 (g son)
148. WILSON, George 33 (T T NC), Rebecca 32 (NC
         NC NC), Sarah 7, David 4; ARENT, Sarah
         20 (sis in law) (NC NC NC), James 3/12
         (b. Mar) (nephew) (T T NC)
149. DINSIMORE, Nancy 46 (widow) (T T NC),
         Orpha 19 (VA VA T)

INDEX

The index applies to this booklet only. It includes
the names of all heads of household plus individuals
whose surnames differed from that of the head of
household. The name is followed by the person's age,
the booklet page number and then the household number
as it appears on the original schedules.

ADAMS, James 25, 16-223
ALDRIDGE, George 13, 14-122
    Sarah 21, 17-244
    Thomas E. 4, 28-128
ALENSTER?, Sarah 39, 18-28
ALEXANDER, James 34, 18-40
ALFERD, James 30, 30-48
ALLEN, Daniel 41, 21-123
    John F. 32, 12-180
    Robert J. 62, 27-50
    Sarah 62, 20-74
ALLISON, Nancy 24, 34-32
AMOND?, William 30, 6-51
ANDERS, James 16, 3-111
ANDERSON, JAmes 32, 28-99
    James 34, 32-129
    James M. 41, 13-63
    John A. 56, 13-68
    Susan 60, 28-98
    Wade 46, 12-3
ANGEL, Albert G. 48, 22-5
    George 35, 18-24
    James 63, 18-25
    James R. 45, 19-14
    Landon 26, 18-18
    Thomas 21, 10-102
    Thomas 31, 21-112
ARCHER, Nancy 62, 33-14
    Sarah 45, 34-61
ARENT, Cain 25, 34-72
    James 3/12, 36-148
    Sarah 20, 36-148
    William 29, 33-7
ARMON, Margret E. D. 15, 33-183
ARNETT, John 56, 7-83
    Sarah 61, 10-114
    Thomas 21, 7-98
    Timothy 22, 10-112
ARNOLD, Murphy 25, 34-34
    Phebe 19, 35-99
    William 25, 34-35
ARRANTS, Charles 4, 23-70
ASHER, William 12, 35-102
AUSBEN, John 24, 9-52
AUSTIN, Sarah 16, 6-41
AVRENTS, Martha 18, 7-81
BADGETT, Catharine 22, 6-60
    Elijah 24, 6-61
BAILEY, Henry L. 57, 2-70
    John D. 22, 2-68
BAIRD, Benj. 22, 4-167
BAKER, James 24, 20-90
    Sally 60, 17-2
BAMES, Milliara 22, 19-60
BANNAN, Frank 45, 5-9
BANNER, H. B. 39, 4-208
    Jos. L. 28, 5-34
    Wm. O. 33, 6-56
BARBER, Tilman 70, 23-56
BARKER, Bengamin 15, 10-80
    Nancy 57, 18-34
BARNANELL, Allen 19, 33-183
BARNET, Eliza 14, 6-49
    Laura B. 8, 28-128
BARNETT, Henry 56, 25-177
    Spencer 53, 5-18
BARR, David 43, 23-54
BARRY, David 75, 29-180
BARTEE, Delcena 30, 34-57
    Mary 1, 34-57
BARTER, Arigana 29, 32-152
BASH, Susan 50, 3-153
BASS, James C. 48, 6-74
BAY, Marshel 30, 11-157
BAYLESS, John 46, 21-102
BEARD, Frank 18, 29-175
BEASLY, Henry 48, 18-17
BECK, Joel L. 59, 26-20
    John 28, 21-132
BENNET, David 19, 14-117
    Lucinda 20, 24-103
BERRY, Alferd 32, 32-161
    Elbert 30, 28-122
    Frances 58, 30-31
    James 28, 32-162
    Murry S. 24, 32-156
    Thomas 27, 31-105
BICE, James 40, 7-118

BICE, John 3, 7-118
    Mary 6, 7-118
    Tennesse C. 18, 3-131
BIRD, Emanuel 23, 34-47
BIRDWELL, Nannie 42, 13-52
BISHOP, Marget 33, 28-87
    Micheal 49, 25-206
    Samuel 46, 24-128
BLACK, Jacob 27, 3-141
    John 59, 3-126
BLACKWELL, William 53, 10-107
BLAIR, Alfred 36, 16-218
    Dicy 24, 18-32
BLEVEN, Agnes 66, 13-47
BLEVENS, Jerrimiah 51, 26-235
    Melvina 3, 13-80
BLEVINS, Adaline 38, 32-144
    Allen 55, 35-112
    Charles 57, 21-122
    Daniel 23, 34-39
    David 25, 11-129
    Elisha 22, 11-128
    George 36, 30-16
    Hiley 61, 10-81
    James 14, 32-107
    John 15, 10-83
    Luna 60, 35-105
    Nancy 40, 10-83
    Nathan 6, 6-47
    Riley 25, 30-49
    Robert 20, 33-179
    Ruben 48, 30-3
    Seraphina 14, 35-90
    William 27, 26-236
    William 45, 34-53
    Willy 40, 10-103
BOLIN, Samul 25, 30-1
BOND, Mary 16, 25-173
BOOKER, Runa 30, 23-90
BOON, Birdie 4, 16-234
    Jno. F. 32, 6-45
    Margaret 40, 16-234
    Nathaniel 26, 6-46
BORDERS, Clara C. 16, 5-2
    S. H. 17, 5-2
BOREN, David 33, 17-240
    Montgomery 60, 16-239
    Wiley B. 48, 13-75
BORMAN, William 15, 9-55
BOUE, Joseph 36, 30-12
BOWERS, Alferd 24, 33-171
    Ann E. 45, 29-156
    Butler 18, 18-25
    Chrisley 29, 29-135
    Christian 44, 29-158
    Daniel E. 26, 26-7
    David 41, 32-163
    David 32, 28-93
    David B. 59, 28-94
    David F. 42, 29-146
    David S. 62, 28-95
    Elizabeth 49, 28-131
    Henry 25, 27-40
    Henry 35, 20-49
    Isaac 31, 33-174
    Isaac N. 37, 26-2
    John E. 29, 26-3
    John M. 26, 28-96
    Landon 26, 32-119
    Landon H. 48, 33-169
    Lilburn 23, 26-6
    Murry 38, 31-78
    Powell 20, 31-55
    Susan 28, 28-75
    Tennessee L. 28, 28-133
    Tetor U. 54, 28-100
    Valentine 30, 26-9
    William 48, 29-147
    William C. 52, 26-8
BOWLIN, Hugh 53, 1-26
BOWLING, Henry 23, 5-24
    Jacob 58, 8-137
BOWMAN, Harris 27, 12-14
    Henry K. 38, 22-23
    Isaac 34, 12-13
    Jacob 55, 13-90
    John 8, 17-251
    John 17, 9-17

BOWMAN, John W. 34, 13-71
    Lee 30, 12-7
    Sarah 40, 12-11
    William 74, 13-72
BOY, Andrew J. 53, 32-158
BOYD, Eliza 14, 22-40
    H. Clay 31, 18-33
    James O. R. 60, 17-8
    William 73, 13-48
BRADLEY, Charles 50, 25-173
BRADLY, Elizabeth 64, 21-128
    Nathaniel 27, 19-43
    Robert 29, 17-1
BRADSHAW, Albert 29, 15-166
BRANCH, Emma 59, 14-108
    Hannah 50, 20-44
    Sidney D. 19, 14-108
BRASWELL, William 46, 34-32
BRETT, Henderson 55, 23-55
BREWER, James E. 46, 16-209
BRITT, David P. 51, 14-111
    Ellen 24, 12-15
    Franklin 58, 13-77
    Mary 15, 31-55
    Mat 34, 21-113
    Melvina 18, 13-80
    Samule W. 38, 14-91
BROOKS, David 35, 20-48
    Elizabeth 65, 30-15
    Jackson 36, 30-30
BROWN, Bettie 56, 7-106
    Christian H. 42, 29-168
    Isaac H. 70, 29-166
    James 23, 29-167
BRYANT, Jasper N. 26, 14-127
    Peter 52, 15-171
BROYHILL, Daniel 28, 5-2
    Lee 13, 5-2
BUCK, Andrew 66, 6-41
    Barzina 50, 24-116
    George V. 39, 5-13
    Isaac G. W. 47, 12-8
    Nathaniel L. 52, 12-12
    Osborn 45, 17-269
BUCKELS, Isaac 33, 32-149
    James 39, 31-104
    Levi 41, 32-164
    Robert 60, 30-42
    Robert A. 53, 31-59
    Thomas 28, 32-121
    William 72, 32-122
    William 36, 32-160
BUCKLES, Andrew 27, 30-41
BUNCH, R. J. 53, 22-2
BUNTEN, E. J. 25, 3-111
    J. D. 31, 4-196
    J. W. 22, 4-195
BUNTIN, James C. 32, 8-158
BURCHFIELD, Lydia 16, 6-49
BURK, Elizabeth 52, 22-30
BURLISON, Oliver 40, 8-144
BURMMET, John 34, 14-108
BURNNETT, Abe 25, 20-87
BURROW, John 55, 18-29
    William 58, 19-67
BUTLER, Henry 40, 6-50
    William 44, 13-89
BYERS, Frank 23, 29-183
BYNON, Joshua 35, 33-24
CABLE, Cornelius 45, 3-119
    John J. 23, 3-148
    Noah 33, 4-187
    Richard 39, 4-186
CAGLE, Benjamin 35, 12-31
    Isaac 42, 23-60
CAKNIPES?, Henry 44, 10-86
CALAWAY, Columbus 26, 20-73
    A. A. 24, 2-105
    Columbus 26, 20-73
    Francis 8/12, 20-73
    Mary 19, 20-73
CALDWELL, Mary 13, 26-238
    Taylor 19, 23-92
CALLAWAY, John 42, 5-14
    William 36, 5-17
CALLOWAY, Giles 49, 8-147
CAMERON, James 46, 18-39
    Jane 64, 21-110

CAMERON, John 44, 19-60
    Malisy 24, 21-110
    William 24, 18-26
CAMPBELL, A. O. 13, 3-115
    C. 2, 1-45
    C. 37, 1-38
    C. N. 59, 1-17
    Calvin 48, 24-135
    Daniel 45, 31-64
    David 8/12, 36-140
    David P. 53, 15-158
    Delia 20, 24-123
    Eda 16, 21-103
    Eliza 40, 21-138
    Elizab 71, 2-56
    Elizabeth 19, 24-131
    Emma 8, 15-143
    G. A. 23, 2-54
    Georg 19, 30-42
    Hamp 22, 21-102
    Henerson 34, 8-8
    Henry 21, 35-129
    Henry 22, 21-139
    Icy 53, 35-86
    Isaac 21, 35-84
    J. A. 76, 1-32
    J. C. 20, 1-48
    J. F. 9, 3-115
    J. R. 30, 3-127
    James 23, 35-113
    James 24, 19-42
    Jeramiah 27, 4-203
    Jerry 27, 5-32
    John 79, 35-98
    John 48, 31-61
    John 83, 31-64
    John 30, 34-43
    John 36, 24-146
    John J. 37, 23-78
    John T. 36, 9-43
    Lettitia 19, 36-140
    Losson 29, 36-140
    Louise 23, 30-42
    Margret 7, 31-94
    Mary 18, 35-97
    Michal 32, 34-44
    Michael 9, 21-103
    Nat 18, 15-184
    Nathaniel 35, 9-22
    May? 48, 1-40
    Nealia 23, 9-50
    Nicholas 51, 32-128
    Robert 9, 33-15
    S. G. 58, 1-41
    S. S. 11, 3-115
    Sarah 27, 31-94
    Sarah 52, 9-40
    Susa 59, 9-49
    Thomas 26, 34-33
    Thos. 19, 1-43
    W. H. 33, 3-111
    W. J. 25, 1-15
    Welburn G. 69, 8-129
    Wilbern 28, 5-17
    William 12, 15-143
    William 25, 21-94
    William 34, 19-58
    William 31, 19-36
    William R. 50, 23-72
    Zechariah C. 38, 9-20
CANNON, Elbert 42, 30-2
    Nelson 48, 30-21
CARDEN, Ancil C. 38, 28-109
    Emla C. 38, 1-52
    Jas. W. 53, 1-34
    Ripley 65, 2-59
    Ruben 25, 27-58
    Samuel 4, 1-33
    Vinson 25, 2-58
CAREY, William 49, 23-70
CARNUTT, John 47, 4-193
CARPENTER, Rachiel 86, 10-79
CARR, Alfred 55, 25-193
    Andrew J. 20, 25-185
    Elkanah 51, 25-186
    Mary 45, 25-197
    William 47, 25-184
CARRAWAY, Ashbury 7, 8-155

CARRAWAY, Jefferson 8, 7-113
CARRIER, John 5, 24-142
    John M. 50, 25-164
    Rhoda 24, 24-142
    Washington 23, 26-243
    William 67, 10-95
CARRIGER, A. T. 56, 1-13
    Allen T. 56, 27-62
    Caleb 23, 27-36
    David N. 33, 28-84
    Godfrey 51, 28-130
    Isaac 32, 29-143
    Jackson D. 59, 29-148
    Joel N. 38, 27-65
    John R. 74, 28-106
    Niol 38, 21-92
    Rebecka 67, 28-91
    Thomas 88, 21-131
    William 24, 28-90
CARROLL, John 21, 13-55
    William C. 43, 12-21
CARTER, Frazier 45, 23-67
    Landon 53, 25-158
    William 26, 21-134
    William 59, 18-32
    William J. 30, 25-157
CARUTHERS, Elizabeth 85, 32-158
CARVER, Benjaman 23, 11-140
    George 36, 10-100
CARWAY, Charles A. 5, 10-71
CASEY, William 38, 8-16
CASS, James F. 72, 29-155
    William 58, 28-77
CASSADA, William 54, 26-219
CATES, Allen 14, 27-72
    David 22, 10-77
    Franklin 31, 14-110
    Sarah J. 56, 14-109
CHAMBERS, David 45, 19-28
    David T. 49, 26-223
    James 25, 26-221
    John 23, 26-222
    John 54, 11-126
    Mary 58, 19-29
    William 46, 11-132
CHANCE, Christian 36, 33-189
    Nancy 70, 33-188
CHANDLER, William 38, 19-65
CHEEKS, David 39, 4-204
CHESTER, C. E. 43, 4-179
CHRISTIAN, James 41, 33-24
    Wiley M. 43, 33-183
CLAIMEN, Martha 30, 23-92
CLARK, Mary 30, 4-207
    Thomas J. 52, 16-211
    Willborn 60, 11-163
    William J. 24, 12-9
CLAWSON, Amanda 17, 1-48
    J. L. 46, 4-174
    James L. 20, 4-168
    R. E. 67, 4-165
    Wm. A. 24, 4-173
CLEMENS, Benjamin 37, 28-125
CLEMONS, Martha 65, 2-73
CLOUSE, Sally 18, 20-90
COCHREN, Whit 32, 11-147
    William E. 25, 10-74
COLBAUGH, Teter N. 34, 31-54
COLBOUGH, Henry 49, 33-180
    William 24, 32-141
    William 68, 20-83
COLE, Amanda 38, 33-15
    Andrew 28, 35-135
    Benjamin 72, 35-122
    Benjamine 48, 35-115
    James 26, 30-25
    Jesse 36, 35-131
    Joanna 46, 24-139
    John 23, 35-116
    Joseph 32, 35-130
    Nancy 21, 35-94
    Selina 32, 35-128
    Thomas 38, 35-123
    Winney 50, 30-9
COLLINS, Ally 15, 20-87
    Christopher 30, 18-45
    Cordia 12, 19-35
    Elizah 49, 9-39

COLLINS, Gilson O. 52, 21-92
    Jackson 20, 28-108
    James 26, 21-100
    Jane 16, 21-100
    John 64, 29-184
    John N. 22, 29-157
    Katy 56, 19-60
    Permelia 20, 29-157
    Rebecca 23, 18-46
    Saml. 21, 19-35
    Theadotia 47, 14-100
COLLIT, Stia 56, 21-136
    Tolbert 57, 21-135
COLMAN, Francis M. 29, 9-55
COLWELL, Sarah 30, 21-133
    Thomas 2, 21-133
COMBS, Elizabeth 16, 27-71
    James T. 15, 12-17
    John M. 1, 12-17
    Julie E. 7, 12-17
    Martha P. 11, 12-17
    Mary 40, 12-17
CONSTABLE, John 35, 15-174
CONWAY, Stephen 56, 22-40
COOK, Alexander 27, 11-141
    Thomas H. 29, 2-104
    W. A. D. 44, 1-7
COOPER, Anna 77, 24-120
    David 37, 5-19
    Elizabeth 76, 17-3
    Mary 50, 23-57
    Montgomery 25, 17-255
    Rhoda 17, 18-40
    Sarah 83, 16-239
    Sarah J. 35, 24-120
    William 46, 17-241
COOPPERS, Thomas 25, 10-97
CORDELL, A. D. 35, 4-197
    Russel 44, 6-59
CORNFORTH, Charles W. 7, 14-94
    Lettie 10, 14-94
    Rosa 40, 14-94
COUSINS, Emma 19, 7-114
COX, Ann 40, 18-49
    Cany 10, 18-42
    Hugh 3, 12-40
    Nancy Ann 77, 28-77
    Richard 50, 22-42
    Robert 21, 12-40
CRAIG, Hiram 34, 20-58
CRAWFORD, Thomas 33, 17-249
CREED, William 18, 30-34
CRESS, Samuel 59, 34-55
CRIMLY, John 82, 18-17
CROCKETT, John 27, 21-140
    Loucretia A. 20, 13-55
    Pleasant 55, 17-256
    Rorda L. 18, 13-55
CROMLEY, Frederick 33, 32-115
CROSSWHITE, J. H. 28, 2-92
    M. E. 57, 3-136
    S. A. S. 23, 3-134
CROUCH, George 40, 32-125
CROW, Bessie H. 10/12, 14-98
    Daniel 26, 14-98
    Daniel S. 29, 28-107
    Ebagail 71, 27-71
    Isaac 25, 25-208
    Isaac 72, 27-51
    James C. 27, 12-181
    Jinna 7, 28-122
    John 28, 20-82
    John 49, 28-102
    Leonard 46, 26-245
    Levi 29, 26-234
    Lucy 6, 18-47
    Martin 54, 24-104
    Mary 39, 24-127
    Mary L. 22, 14-98
    Mima 52, 20-79
    Robert 17, 24-127
    Thomas 45, 32-154
    Thomas 22, 29-173
    Thomas C. 55, 27-70
    William 53, 29-172
CROY, Z. Jordon 47, 24-120
CRUCK, Napoleon 26, 30-5
CRUMLEY, James 28, 30-187

CRUMLEY, William 41, 23-99
CRUMLY, George 45, 17-7
    William 50, 18-21
CULBERT, Armitha 19, 34-63
    Henry 29, 34-63
    James sr. 74, 30-7
    James jr. 24, 30-32
    Mary 21, 30-18
    Matilda 1/12, 34-63
    Seraphina 9/12, 34-63
    William 18, 30-30
DANIEL, Greene B. 59, 22-16
    Mary E. 35, 22-20
    Ryley B. 46, 24-113
DANIELS, Green 48, 17-280
    James 22, 12-25
    Mary A. 1, 12-25
    Sarah F. 27, 12-25
    Sylva 40, 17-277
DATSON, Albert 40, 10-76
DAVENPORT, Elizabeth 44, 16-202
DAVENPORT, Patsey 76, 15-185
DAVIS, Ann 27, 21-133
    Axey 60, 29-162
    Brownlow 33, 23-66
    Charles 20, 10-80
    David 26, 29-163
    George W. 66, 25-181
    James 41, 34-75
    Jefferson 58, 7-120
    Lank 30, 7-121
    Samuel 35, 30-15
    William 29, 25-211
DEAL, Charles 30, 33-24
DEBOSE, Rebecca 19, 22-26
DELOACH, James 38, 20-61
    John 30, 20-63
    Kanada 25, 16-206
    Nathan 63, 20-64
    Pheby 50, 20-59
    Saml. C. 35, 1-39
    Susan 50, 26-11
    Thomas 65, 20-62
    William 34, 20-60
DEMPSY, James 19, 23-76
    Melina? 56, 23-59
DENNY, Georgia 6, 19-59
    Mary R. 8, 19-59
    Myrtle 12, 19-59
    Saml. F. 10, 19-59
DIAL, Pleasant 50, 15-167
DICKSON, John 35, 13-88
DINSIMORE, Nancy 46, 36-149
DOBY, Isham 72, 5-2
DONNELLEY, M. E. 26, 2-88
DOUGLASS, John 13, 14-136
    Mary 21, 15-184
DOUGLESS, Susan 48, 19-2
DOUHARTY, James 10, 13-64
DRAKE, David 68, 25-154
DUFFIELD, Eliza 60, 24-138
    James W. 1, 23-53
    Mary 16, 23-53
    Nannie 30, 24-138
    Nelson 23, 16-217
    William 35, 20-57
DUGGAR, James 48, 34-36
    John 22, 34-37
DUGGER, Caroline 13, 4-165
    Charlotte 35, 4-176
    David 62, 27-60
    David A. 26, 27-53
    James W. 27, 3-140
    John 23, 26-15
    John F. 50, 3-139
    Martha 80, 27-61
    Martha 20, 2-73
    Mary A. 18, 2-73
    Monroe 22, 7-119
    Nancy 69, 1-2
    Susan C. 46, 1-33
    Thomas 31, 27-39
DUGLAS, James 31, 15-165
    Landon 22, 32-131
DUGLASS, Alexander 45, 15-169
    William 41, 15-143
DUNBAR, George 31, 24-126
DUNCAN, Alfred 10, 24-111

DUNCAN, Thomas 24, 17-252
DUNGAN, William 65, 29-159
EAKLE, Eliza 30, 34-60
EDENS, David 26, 21-109
    John 48, 21-108
    Matilda 18, 16-224
    Matilda 20, 21-141
    Samule 20, 16-224
EDMONDSON, William 30, 19-64
EFFLER, Sarah 47, 20-89
EGGERS, Alexander 46, 3-128
    Lillie A. 40, 3-133
ELDON, Joseph 32, 6-40
ELIETT, David 36, 11-152
ELISON, John 40, 11-133
ELLIOTT, Alice 2, 34-39
    Daniel 27, 34-57
    David 19, 34-46
    James 30, 34-49
    John 25, 34-51
    Joseph 52, 34-50
    Michal 35, 33-5
    Moses 21, 34-76
    Susanah 68, 33-1
    Thomas P. 46, 30-37
ELLIS, Arnold 45, 26-229
    Daniel 53, 19-33
    Daniel 26, 21-121
    David W. 40, 6-75
    Deborah 13, 7-109
    Dempsy 3, 7-109
    Haynes 37, 24-144
    Jane 49, 29-161
    John 46, 22-10
    Joseph 44, 30-26
    Radford 74, 25-188
    Radford 21, 19-31
    Solomon 48, 26-242
    Tipton 34, 25-189
    William 21, 14-94
EMMERT, Caleb 37, 18-43
    Delcenia 60, 25-207
    Fannie 50, 23-100
    George 52, 18-55
    George W. 20, 23-98
    Jeremiah 53, 23-96
ENSOR, John K. 75, 15-150
    Preston 39, 15-151
    William 33, 34-54
ERVIN, Charles 65, 19-41
    Charles 28, 24-134
ESTEP, Andrew J. 49, 26-248
    Avery 29, 36-137
    Elvira 1/12, 35-92
    Harvy 25, 1-49
    Henry 34, 35-118
    Isaac 27, 34-49
    Isaac 52, 34-67
    John 13, 35-120
    Julia 40, 34-69
    Levi 21, 34-70
    Martha 51, 28-88
    Moses 31, 35-119
    Ruth 19, 35-92
    Samuel 20, 34-65
    Samuel M. 43, 27-52
    Shadrach 65, 35-100
    Tennessee 54, 34-75
    William 34, 34-52
    William 31, 35-99
ESTEPP, Eliza 22, 26-237
    John 21, 17-261
    Samuel 20, 26-237
FAIR, Bethul 31, 22-6
    Cordelia 27, 24-116
    George 5, 17-9
    George W. 31, 31-101
    James 21, 20-45
    James D. 69, 16-238
    James N. 56, 16-222
    James N. 23, 23-52
    Joseph 31, 21-111
    Lafayette 4, 24-116
    Louisa 6, 24-116
    Mary 9, 24-116
    Samuel 33, 33-184
    Shadrack 72, 28-119
    William C. 51, 23-86

FANDREN, Albert B. 32, 9-32
    William 66, 9-29
FAUBUS, Charles 2, 11-128
    David 20, 10-120
    Fannia 30, 11-128
FEATHERS, Andrew J. 27, 23-79
FELLERS, John G. 60, 21-139
FERGUSON, Andrew 51, 30-17
    Benjamin 43, 30-18
FIELDS, Elbert 22, 8-168
    Wm. H. 25, 5-4
FINE, Alfred 46, 15-164
FINNEY, Philip 56, 2-106
FISHER, Cathrine 60, 9-47
FITZSIMMONS, Eliz. 49, 18-37
FLETCHER, James 30, 18-14
    James B. 33, 9-36
    John 28, 31-74
    Lauson 19, 31-72
    Lavinia 62, 9-20
    Manda 16, 33-179
    Nancy 14, 35-103
FLOYD, Rosencrans 17, 23-86
FOLSOM, Ellen 19, 21-105
    Henderson 47, 18-31
    William J. 60, 9-42
FONDREN, Nancy 42, 21-140
    Saml. 3, 21-140
FONDRON, Susan 10, 18-16
FORBES, Daniel 41, 33-190
    Rachel 14, 34-60
    Robert 31, 31-77
FORD, Millie C. 37, 2-71
FOSTER, Elizabeth 23, 8-145
    Emma 2, 8-145
    Horton 30, 8-159
    Nancy 87, 28-127
FOUST, Back 25, 22-35
    Daniel 45, 22-12
    Eva 13, 25-158
    Samuel J. 25, 23-81
FOX, Susanna 66, 6-71
FRANKLIN, Nancy 31, 6-62
FRASIER, Alexander 44, 29-186
    Harry 19, 28-116
    Jacob 38, 32-132
    John W. 40, 32-146
    Marget 42, 29-185
FREEMAN, Joseph 45, 7-99
FRIELDS, Esabel 30, 29-179
FRITTS, George 30, 15-170
FRITZ, Christian 25, 34-45
FULKERSON, Abraham 56, 29-164
    William 63, 22-36
FULLER, Elizabeth 35, 31-89
    John 13, 17-265
GAITER, David 14, 13-78
GAMPBELL, G. F. 29, 1-50
GARDNER, John 40, 9-59
GARLAND, Alfred 71, 36-143
    Catherine 8, 34-70
    David 42, 35-117
    David 15, 35-136
    David 56, 35-103
    Frank 36, 35-85
    Highly 64, 35-87
    Isaac 70, 35-106
    John 35, 35-121
    John 23, 35-91
    Mordecai 55, 35-98
    Nathan 24, 35-120
    Samuel 17, 35-136
    Sarah 75, 34-69
    Sarah 4, 34-70
    Tabitha 35, 36-142
    Volantine 39, 35-90
    Voluntine 35, 32-127
    William 32, 28-97
    William 35, 35-126
    William 52, 35-88
    William W. 28, 22-24
GARNER, Benjamin 6/12, 35-108
    Margret 20, 35-108
    Thomas 27, 35-108
GARRISON, Jane 33, 27-23
    John 24, 21-119
    Samuel 15, 26-18
GAUGE, Calvin 20, 11-148

GAUGE, David 26, 12-176
    John 49, 9-66
    Ruben T. 33, 11-135
    Susa 72, 9-65
GAUNT, Sarah J. 14, 3-139
GEAVER, Jackson 21, 31-81
GEISLER, George W. 24, 14-93
    William D. 26, 14-97
GENTRY, Andrew 29, 31-97
    John 31, 31-98
    Mary 50, 31-71
    Sarah 58, 31-65
GIBBS, Edgar 16, 18-37
    Frank 34, 14-129
GIBSON, Catherine 43, 24-118
    Elbert 27, 23-88
    Henry 26, 35-111
    John 32, 24-117
    Pleasant 64, 22-39
    Sharlot A. 16, 29-155
    William B. 24, 22-25
GILBERT, Edmond 25, 3-138
    John 71, 11-159
GILES, James A. 51, 22-41
    William H. 39, 14-96
GILLAM, Matilda 13, 14-112
GILLILAND, Hamilton 58, 9-60
    N. J. 18, 5-152
GILREATH, Enos 47, 2-66
GIPSON, Mary 17, 18-26
GLASS, Smith S. 30, 12-6
GLENN, James S. 18, 23-84
GLOVER, Belle 23, 12-42
    Elbert 25, 19-35
    Granville 22, 25-182
    James H. 24, 1-44
    John 46, 21-95
    Peter G. 24, 16-203
    Richard 40, 15-181
    Rutha A. 22, 22-14
    Vinnie 24, 24-110
    William 15, 6-77
    William 25, 1-42
GODFREY, William 27, 10-113
GOINS, Jessie 56, 7-123
    John 57, 9-23
GOODWIN, A. L. 64, 4-189
    C. A. 14, 1-52
    J. L. 36, 1-47
    J. M. 33, 4-182
    L. H. 44, 2-81
    M. A. 18, 1-52
    M. D. 22, 1-46
    Nancy 59, 1-45
    R. E. 41, 2-86
    S. H. 24, 4-191
    T. M. 31, 4-192
    W. W. 13, 5-81
GORDON, Dema 55, 16-230
GORMAN, Amanda 6, 12-38
    James 10, 12-38
    Jane 2, 12-38
    Mary E. 5, 12-38
    Ritchard 13, 12-38
GOUGE, Allen 44, 7-108
GOURLEY, Adam 49, 16-200
    Dora 2, 13-71
    George F. 23, 15-182
    Joseph 18, 24-121
    Mary A. 34, 16-202
    Mary A. 55, 14-98
    William 25, 15-187
    William 26, 12-37
GOURLY, Alford 22, 16-205
    Charles 45, 20-51
    Ellen 21, 27-64
    Nathaniel 16, 20-53
    Thomas 25, 19-9
    William 34, 14-99
GRAGG, Abner 25, 7-91
    Daniel 18, 1-6
    James 60, 3-108
    James C. 20, 3-113
    James W. 28, 7-103
    M. E. J. 25, 3-110
GRACE, Elijah 21, 20-72
    Margaret 22, 20-72
    Rhoda 2, 20-72

GREEN, David C. 33, 3-130
    Joseph W. 34, 3-137
GREENE, Timothy 40, 24-106
GREENLEE, Howel 21, 10-80
    James 4, 21-126
    Miles 30, 11-132
    Rufus 15, 11-132
GREENLIEF, David 13, 33-185
GREENWAY, James K. 35, 22-42
GREENWELL, F. E. 62, 3-113
GREER, James 26, 7-114
    James A. 29, 5-29
GRIFFETH, Mary C. 13, 33-189
GRIFFIN, Hages 30, 17-278
    James 30, 6-80
    Sallie 26, 6-80
GRIFFITH, James 24, 31-71
    James 73, 28-121
    Thos. D. 25, 1-24
GRINDSTAFF, A. S. 34, 26-4
    Andrew 45, 34-64
    David 29, 19-17
    David 29, 32-112
    Docia 28, 35-134
    Elvy 21, 27-69
    Franky 23, 12-182
    George M. 49, 26-16
    Isaac 38, 8-15
    John 52, 34-42
    John 52, 20-65
    John 69, 27-34
    John H. 22, 14-124
    M. C. 72, 8-9
    Michel 40, 32-111
    William 44, 30-8
    William 38, 34-41
GROGAN, Isaac 53, 5-215
GUIN, Amos 24, 10-111
    Andrew 21, 10-80
    Isaac 40, 11-142
GUINN, A. J. 21, 4-157
    Elizabeth 24, 5-220
GUY, Elizabeth 50, 15-160
HALE, James 30, 16-229
HALL, Oliver 51, 12-182
HALLEY, James 37, 10-87
    Robert J. 40, 9-31
HAMBRICK, David 20, 13-65
HAMBY, Allen 70, 2-72
    Allen 56, 4-201
    D. M. 23, 5-218
    Elizabeth 20, 2-71
    Landen C. 21, 4-202
    Landon 21, 5-33
    Thomas 50, 5-217
HAMILTON, Joshua 43, 30-20
HAMMER, Laina 18, 20-91
HAMMET, George D. 24, 12-22
    Newton 79, 13-59
    Samule 42, 12-46
HAMPTON, Andrew C. 30, 8-139
    Francis 49, 6-40
    Lanon 66, 26-225
    Lauson 28, 5-20
    Marget 70, 9-21
    Samuel 25, 32-147
    Sarah 47, 9-37
    Thomas 24, 21-111
HAMS, John 50, 19-58
HANGER, James A. 25, 8-145
HANN, Martha 55, 14-132
HARDEN, Alvin 38, 32-142
    Andrew 30, 32-135
    Daniel 50, 29-141
    Eli 39, 9-48
    Elijah 78, 27-30
    Elijah D. 45, 27-24
    George 34, 26-19
    Isaac 64, 27-27
    Jacob 19, 30-48
    John 21, 31-51
    John H. 35, 27-28
    John N. 72, 28-124
    John W. 37, 27-32
    Lydia 44, 32-143
    Onijah J. 35, 28-123
    Sallie 20, 31-51
    William 52, 27-31

HARDIN, Margaret 55, 8-161
HARDY, Sewell 29, 5-8
HARMON, A. J. 42, 4-169
HARRIS, William 25, 24-111
HARRISON, Henry 56, 5-5
HART, Abraham 69, 24-127
    Cam R. 45, 21-127
    Christly 35, 24-123
    George 26, 24-115
    Leonora 44, 24-114
    Peter E. 34, 29-181
    Solomon 72, 24-125
    Thomas C. 42, 24-124
HARTLEY, Albert 24, 3-154
    Cal 26, 3-153
    Elvira 19, 3-153
    Jas. 2, 3-153
HATCHER, James 30, 34-29
    Martha 54, 21-96
    William 23, 21-93
HATELEY, John F. 42, 2-98
    W. S. 33, 3-129
    William 72, 4-158
    Wm. C. 19, 4-159
HATHAWAY, E. C. 54, 1-48
    John 31, 20-71
HAUGER, Cornelius 23, 8-140
HAUN, Geroge A. 47, 13-76
HAWLEY, Frank 46, 23-87
    John 24, 23-68
HAYES, Elbert 15, 29-176
    James 45, 26-237
    Martin W. 1, 6-57
    Robert 47, 14-115
HAYNES, Dicy 6, 16-212
HAZLEWOOD, John 47, 8-12
    N. J. 6, 1-8
    Pleas 27, 2-95
    Richard 34, 9-18
    Tabe 22, 9-26
HEAD, Cement D. 58, 10-85
    Johnathan 28, 10-83
    Joseph A. 32, 10-75
    Sarah C. 12, 10-76
HEADRICK, Chas. 33, 18-35
    Chas. 57, 20-69
    John 25, 33-23
HEATHERLY, George 13, 35-98
    Godfrey 44, 35-108
    James 24, 35-81
    Robert 30, 34-80
    Thomas 82, 35-104
HEATON, E. W. 16, 7-83
    Edward T. 33, 26-10
    Elkana 38, 7-82
    G. W. 52, 3-151
    Isaac M. 29, 27-26
    John W. 51, 26-5
    Johnson 45, 7-97
HELFEL, Daniel 39, 11-164
HELTON, Robert 7, 21-128
HEMPHILL, Margie 54, 8-150
HENDERICK, Elizabeth 8, 15-145
    Emaline 28, 15-145
HENDRICKSON, E. D. 37, 6-78
HENDRIX, Harrison 67, 23-84
    Jacob R. 31, 22-13
    John 57, 23-64
    John S. 14, 22-49
    Solom H. 39, 22-14
    William 52, 17-243
HENNIGER, George 29, 18-19
HENRY, James 24, 21-100
    John 25, 19-6
    Russell 23, 18-50
HENSELY, Thomas 22, 20-89
HESS, David 72, 27-64
    John B. 52, 22-7
HESTER, John R. 27, 9-45
    Mary 18, 20-87
    Mary 58, 9-46
    Sally 14, 1-26
HEWITT, Anna 16, 24-121
HICKS, David 67, 4-171
    Jane 37, 29-162
    Louvella 7, 7-85
    M. A. R. 18, 4-175
    Mira B. 11/12, 7-85

HICKS, Nancy 49, 7-92
    Samuel 20, 2-95
    Wm. W. 38, 7-107
    Willy 13, 29-162
HIGGINS, Gilbert 30, 16-228
    Isaac 26, 23-89
HIKS, Mathias 47, 3-109
HILL, Albert 34, 10-84
    Alexander 20, 2-60
    Ezakial 60, 10-70
    John 54, 9-64
    Robert 57, 10-71
    Samuel 38, 10-72
HILS, Henry 30, 10-121
HILTON, David 57, 18-20
HINES, Christema 70, 23-55
HINKLE, David 24, 34-27
    Edgar 3, 18-52
    Elizabeth 65, 32-152
    Elizabeth 32, 30-47
    George 23, 31-57
    George 56, 33-179
    Lotta 4, 18-54
    Maryjane 44, 32-153
    Micheal 33, 17-286
    Nancy 46, 31-51
    William 6, 18-54
    William 26, 30-40
    William F. 23, 32-155
HINTOR, Thomas E. R. 51, 28-128
HISE, Jacob 49, 5-25
HIX, Daniel 35, 11-144
    Sarah 60, 11-143
    William 60, 11-146
HODG, John M. 23, 32-113
HODGE, Dusky 17, 17-8
    Isaac 43, 35-134
    Levi 44, 35-107
    Nathan L. 27, 24-133
    Ollie 47, 34-79
    Rowe 18, 14-131
    Sammy 30, 5-22
    Sandy 11, 35-106
    Simon 45, 35-93
    William R. 55, 7-127
HODGES, Waitsel 37, 15-157
HOLAWAY, J. A. 32, 2-63
HOLDER, Elisha 23, 35-114
HOLLY, David 45, 20-54
    David 15, 15-165
    James 70, 20-78
    Julia A. 20, 15-165
HOOPER, Mary 39, 13-53
HOOPWOOD, _____ 37, 14-94
HOPSON, Isaac 29, 11-124
    Sarah 48, 11-125
HORVEL, William M. 36, 11-127
HOSS, James H. 35, 8-154
    Walter 11, 14-114
HOUN, Flonunc 18, 18-47
HOUSLEY, Harison 51, 32-109
HOUSTON, Finna 32, 22-21
    H. Basher? 28, 22-11
    Mimie 3, 5-13
    S. E. 18, 5-13
HOWARD, Dorcas 65, 7-124
    Maria? 30, 18-12
HUGHES, Albert 47, 12-41
    Charles 60, 6-49
    David 25, 17-248
    James 56, 12-42
    John 19, 23-80
    John 60, 17-246
    Joseph 33, 17-268
    Louis 33, 6-48
    Margret 40, 24-112
    Mitchell 20, 7-90
    Sandy 76, 24-105
HUMPHREY, Eliza 61, 20-73
    France 25, 21-103
    John 82, 21-99
    Pinkney 25, 21-97
HUMPHREYS, Curly 20, 16-193
    David 45, 22-37
    George 21, 17-259
    Jessie 71, 17-244
    John 49, 17-258

HUMPHREYS, Lecy 66, 22-33
    Marion 20, 22-38
    William 42, 22-33
    William 22, 17-262
HUNLET, Eugene 33, 20-91
HUNTER, John W. 29, 29-151
    Robert 21, 29-151
HURLEY, Alvin 29, 35-95
    Andew 31, 35-92
    Harden 61, 35-94
    Irvin 16, 30-49
    Mordecai 27, 36-140
    Nicholas 19, 30-41
    William 54, 34-38
    Wright 26, 34-28
HURLY, Ham H. 22, 8-131
HURT, Robert 43, 34-25
HUTSON, Miles 77, 22-27
HYATT, Allen 17, 22-36
    Lucinda 60, 22-36
    Sis 11, 22-36
HYDER, Andrew F.? 34, 14-122
    Ann 48, 15-176
    Caswell T. 51, 14-126
    Daniel 25, 19-8
    Frances U. 42, 15-183
    Hannah 56, 24-107
    Henry 38, 16-195
    Henry 33, 14-134
    J. H. 68, 21-100
    Jacob 38, 15-180
    James E. 61, 19-10
    Jesse 47, 15-172
    John L. 42, 9-47
    John W. 56, 16-194
    John W. 59, 15-147
    John W. 71, 11-161
    Joseph 24, 15-139
    Joseph 70, 15-186
    Joseph 46, 19-7
    Josephine 15, 5-34
    Loss F. 36, 21-101
    Martha 16, 15-153
    Micheal E. 35, 14-131
    Nathaniel 18, 16-229
    Nathaniel 31, 15-173
    Nathaniel 18, 16-229
    Nathaniel K. 36, 11-150
    Nelson 62, 15-175
    Rosanah 57, 14-125
    Samule 19, 16-229
    Samule W. 62, 14-133
    William 25, 15-177
    William 34, 15-184
INGRAM, Nancy A. 40, 10-105
    David 24, 10-94
INGRIM, Thomas 68, 10-98
IRICK, Alice 12, 5-214
    George W. 21, 4-213
    John 15, 5-214
ISAACS, Marion 29, 3-112
ISEHOUR, Sol 45, 7-84
JACKSON, Andrew 29, 13-67
    James 38, 9-30
JAMES, Nancy 77, 9-24
JENET, Ashbury 68, 8-155
JENKINS, Abe 25, 19-16
    Angeline 44, 33-172
    Ann E. 25, 29-157
    Catherine 75, 24-149
    David 24, 18-50
    David 50, 20-85
    Eliza 17, 20-89
    Fannie 53, 28-117
    Hugh 53, 20-66
    Martha 24, 28-118
    Martha 28, 19-11
    Parele 15, 28-77
    R. J. 29, 1-12
    Robert 20, 33-173
    Samuel 23, 32-117
    Samuel 29, 9-35
    William 22, 19-12
    William 53, 19-13
    William 26, 32-157
JESTUS, Harvy 39, 13-61
JOBE, Abraham 62, 21-117

JOBE, Ethelbert K. 31, 16-231
    Margret 61, 26-232
JOHNSON, Albert M. 44, 6-55
    Alfred 69, 6-79
    Andrew 24, 8-4
    Carter 35, 12-27
    Charles 32, 12-32
    Enoch L. 18, 12-25
    George 44, 17-274
    Henderson 34, 8-165
    Henry 3, 9-66
    James W. 29, 7-81
    Jane E. 5, 9-66
    John H. 27, 9-38
    Mary A. 15, 12-25
    Nancy 61, 21-116
    Rachel 54, 8-11
JOINE, Hannah 50, 8-167
JONES, Ambros 25, 16-224
    Ambrose C. 44, 4-206
    James H. 44, 5-1
    John A. 21, 1-23
    Kate P. 60, 29-160
    Rebecka 44, 27-33
    Robert 31, 27-54
    Wesly 30, 16-225
JORDEN, Cany 21, 18-52
JULIAN, Henry 32, 7-90
    Wm. M. 42, 6-38
JUSTICE, Elkanah 37, 8-13
    Frank 36, 7-100
    Louisa 18, 6-73
KEATON, Peter 18, 5-15
KEEN, John V. 31, 12-26
    Jonas H. 65, 25-190
    Mary 62, 12-25
    William M. 42, 13-73
KELLER, James 6, 5-217
KELLEY, Alfred 23, 26-230
KELLY, Nancy 48, 24-142
KENT, James 64, 11-158
KEPPLER, Christopher C. 61, 22-43
KEYS, William 26, 16-236
KIDWELL, Richard 47, 22-15
KINCHELOE, Harriet 15, 23-68
KING, Callie 35, 22-23
    John 38, 17-251
    Vina 30, 22-3
KINNICK, H. H. 44, 3-149
    J. C. 23, 2-103
    John 66, 2-102
KIRK, Elizabeth 41, 13-52
KIRKPATRICK, J. T. 27, 5-216
KITE, Alvin 36, 16-198
    Andrew 18, 15-158
    Catherine 36, 15-189
    Malden 60, 4-198
    Mary 57, 16-199
    Nancy 16, 15-158
    Russel 34, 5-3
KITZMILLER, David 47, 29-149
KLINE, Sarah 35, 12-39
KUHN, Andrew J. 50, 15-138
    Joseph 46, 25-209
    Millard 29, 25-210
LACY, Albert K. 33, 22-28
    Alexander 30, 10-99
    Andrew J. 39, 22-22
    Ann 65, 24-140
    James 35, 26-244
    John L. 25, 10-96
    John M. 25, 23-94
    John W. 64, 29-175
    Joseph 22, 24-141
    Lou 2, 15-156
    Mary A. 4, 15-156
    Samul 28, 22-29
    Sarah 18, 15-156
    Sarah 1/12, 15-156
    Sarah 90, 9-21
    Sarah 79, 22-27
    William S. 47, 26-233
LANDRETH, Henry 17, 13-74
LANDY, Thaddius 35, 15-142
LANE, Joseph 25, 17-264
LaRUE, Jesse V. 69, 14-94
    Latia 71, 14-94

LATY, James A. 20, 14-94
LAWRENCE, William 39, 24-136
LAWS, George W. 29, 6-66
　　James 23, 6-68
　　Joel 53, 6-70
　　John 35, 6-67
　　Marion 18, 6-72
　　Thomas 11, 34-47
LEDFORD, Isaac 22, 8-146
　　Thos. 60, 8-149
　　William 25, 8-142
LEE, Alexander 40, 18-36
　　Louisa 50, 25-170
　　Tabitha 13, 25-166
LEFTWICH, Horace 30, 21-130
LENARD, John 45, 17-245
LEWIS, Alfred 24, 20-70
　　Amy 55, 28-83
　　Ann 42, 3-111
　　Eliza 10, 32-109
　　Ephraim 52, 31-68
　　Frederick J. 38, 30-24
　　Gideon 41, 31-67
　　Gieon? 65, 2-93
　　Hampton H. 43, 11-155
　　Hasten J. 45, 30-22
　　Isaac 51, 29-154
　　James 24, 28-120
　　James F. M. 46, 32-106
　　James L. 24, 2-107
　　James L. 27, 31-80
　　John 22, 31-69
　　John 48, 29-153
　　Joseph 25, 29-142
　　Lawson L. 46, 2-82
　　Louis D. 68, 33-11
　　Lydia 57, 28-76
　　Mary 72, 2-84
　　Mary J. 36, 2-85
　　Muny 24, 30-33
　　Nancy 25, 20-87
　　Nicholas 28, 33-10
　　Samuel 33, 32-133
　　Sarah 40, 16-197
　　Stephen 36, 31-72
　　Susan J. 40, 2-61
　　Thomas G. 22, 2-94
　　William 29, 34-59
　　William L. 39, 1-53
　　Wm. S. 20, 2-83
LILLEY, John S. 43, 22-18
LINDAMOOD, James 25, 25-194
　　Susan 63, 25-180
　　Thomas 55, 25-201
LINEBACK, Sarah 47, 7-119
　　Wm. H. 19, 6-41
LINSEY, George 30, 14-92
LINVILLE, John 35, 15-159
LIPPS, Daniel 31, 33-4
　　Nancy 78, 33-175
　　Nelson 68, 33-3
LITTLE, Andrew J. 23, 22-44
　　George W. 37, 22-43
　　Henry 74, 22-43
　　Rabecca 18, 16-233
LIVINGSTON, George 36, 35-82
　　Murray 30, 14-133
LIVINGSTONE, Eliza 42, 19-24
　　John 42, 20-72
　　Saml. 33, 19-18
LOGAN, Joseph 42, 20-80
LONY, William 20, 15-146
LOUDERMILK, Jacob 62, 17-279
　　James 41, 16-233
　　Noah 24, 17-273
LOUDY, Catherine 47, 17-281
LOUR, George J. 34, 30-11
LOVE, Alexander 34, 16-220
　　Alexander 70, 16-212
　　Eliza 13, 24-105
　　Eva 18, 23-89
　　Franklin 10, 16-234
　　Georgianna 1, 16-212
　　Henry 50, 16-210
　　Henry A. 5/12, 24-106
　　Jacob 37, 17-10
　　James 18, 30-34
　　Kittie 18, 16-229

LOVE, Margret 20, 24-106
　　Molly 18, 18-49
　　Richard 17, 24-105
　　Samuel H. 1, 23-89
LOVELACE, John 32, 28-114
　　John 31, 32-124
LOVELESS, Allen 24, 27-22
　　Elijah 27, 27-21
　　Letta 57, 15-185
　　William H. 26, 26-17
LOWE, David K. 21, 33-177
　　Martha 39, 31-99
　　Stephen 28, 32-138
LUNSFORD, A. 20, 4-180
　　Enoch 62, 4-181
　　J. E. 36, 4-209
　　J. F. 38, 4-210
　　Mary E. 22, 4-190
　　S. A. 26, 4-211
LUSK, John A. C. 49, 16-228
　　Tennessee 19, 16-201
　　Tennessee H. H. 53, 16-227
LUTHER, Jordan 55, 3-132
LYLE, Daniel 17, 17-286
　　George 33, 17-285
LYON, Ezekiel 22, 25-191
　　Henry 36, 26-220
　　Jerimiah 27, 25-212
　　Martha 45, 25-213
　　Thomas 47, 25-183
　　William B. 39, 25-195
LYONS, David S. 10, 13-52
　　George 26, 29-165
　　George E. 13, 13-52
　　James B. 15, 13-52
　　John 26, 25-166
　　Joseph 39, 15-163
　　Mary J. 18, 13-52
　　Thomas 24, 29-177
MACKROY, Joseph 65, 28-127
MAKESSON, Spencer 54, 10-79
MANNING, James 28, 9-41
MARKLAND, David 29, 33-19
　　Elizabeth 15, 33-3
　　Henry 32, 33-18
　　James 45, 33-17
　　Nelson 54, 33-8
　　Philip 40, 33-21
　　Susan 45, 19-57
　　William 26, 20-88
　　William 49, 33-16
MARLER, David 30, 24-143
MARSHAL, Landon 35, 17-275
MARTIN, James H. 57, 13-85
MASTEN, George W. 48, 13-66
　　Joseph 24, 16-235
MATHERLY, Jane 40, 19-5
MATHERSON, John C. 34, 2-75
　　Wm. A. 50, 2-74
MATHESON, Ella 16, 27-68
MATSON, Frances 26, 18-49
　　Thomas 32, 18-49
MAYES, Andrew 32, 26-249
McCATHRINE, James 66, 20-68
McCORKLE, Joseph 34, 26-228
McCRAW, Napoleon B. 75, 12-18
McDANIELS, Alford 43, 17-270
McELRATH, Elizabeth 23, 13-68
McFALL, John 13, 17-282
McFARLAND, Elizabeth 66, 18-51
　　Nat 31, 18-50
McGINNIS, Newton 38, 4-163
McINTOSH, Adiline 37, 8-6
　　David 47, 13-79
McINTURFF, John 31, 12-10
　　Mary 15, 16-230
　　William 25, 16-230
McKEE, Smith 29, 32-108
McKEEHAN, Addie 16, 14-133
　　Arzilla 42, 14-125
　　Elizabeth 16, 14-106
　　Landon 52, 14-116
　　Martha 17, 14-125
　　Rosa 21, 14-125
　　Samule 47, 15-144
　　Thomas 18, 14-125
　　Wiley W. 61, 14-136
　　William 53, 15-140

McKEEHEN, Cinthia 65, 14-101
McKERSEY, Eliza 60, 14-114
McKERSON, Annie 16, 8-135
McKINNEY, Joanah 25, 33-182
　　John 38, 19-27
　　Joseph 32, 27-46
　　Martha 37, 27-29
　　Samuel 35, 11-153
　　Theodocia 3, 33-182
　　Thomas 28, 15-176
　　William 47, 30-188
　　William 21, 11-174
　　Wilson 33, 20-56
　　Wilson 66, 11-156
McKINNY, William 28, 11-168
McLEAN, Newton 23, 6-58
McLEOD, Rutha 79, 18-37
　　Tillman 30, 7-87
McNABB, W. G. 52, 7-115
McNEAL, Thos. 42, 7-122
McNEELY, Square 65, 2-80
MEREDITH, Hugh 46, 8-164
　　John 25, 8-167
　　William 46, 21-124
MERRIT, James 41, 15-190
　　Edgecomb 55, 19-3
MERRITT, John 50, 19-23
　　Leonard 37, 19-20
　　Rebecca 75, 19-23
MESSIMERE, J. A. 40, 2-79
　　Jane 69, 2-92
MILERUN?, Calvin 46, 11-122
MILLER, Absolom 72, 8-135
　　Adie 13, 12-28
　　Alexander 17, 12-28
　　Alice 18, 1-25
　　David H. 28, 6-77
　　Delilah 62, 7-128
　　Dora 1, 7-84
　　Francis 38, 7-94
　　Hannah 33, 10-78
　　Hily 14, 11-165
　　Jacob 21, 7-109
　　Jacob 27, 7-102
　　Jacob A. 35, 8-136
　　James 36, 10-88
　　Jerry B. 45, 18-15
　　John 58, 14-112
　　John S. 50, 5-26
　　Johnson 35, 9-63
　　Lafayette 52, 25-161
　　Lorenzo 33, 8-148
　　Moses A. 63, 14-105
　　Nicholas 78, 33-179
　　Rachel 75, 19-59
　　Rachel 18, 7-84
　　Rebecca 22, 5-29
　　Robert 58, 12-36
　　Susan 66, 26-226
　　Wesly 38, 8-156
　　William 50, 11-137
　　William A. 20, 10-115
　　William H. 36, 10-108
MILLHOM, Alice 18, 21-139
MILSAPS, Maniel 60, 10-114
MINTON, Griffon 33, 29-182
　　Rufus 43, 26-239
MOLLER, Lear 25, 21-113
MONROE, John 84, 22-15
MONTGUMERY, S. W. 48, 4-212
MOODY, Martha 18, 16-238
MOONY, Eliza 60, 20-52
MOORE, Clayton 18, 16-214
　　John 47, 11-139
　　Luvania 18, 11-145
　　Mary 23, 16-214
　　Mary 60, 11-145
MOREFILD, Thomas J. 22, 9-33
MORGAN, Adeline 30, 6-74
　　Elizebeth 58, 10-110
　　Giles 55, 20-50
　　James 23, 8-134
　　John 32, 7-111
　　John 20, 3-155
　　Thos. 25, 8-132
　　Thomas 36, 9-56
　　W. D. 52, 4-156
MORGANGAS, D. 25, 4-170

44

MORLAND, Mary 70, 8-138
MORRATTA, Eliza 42, 31-80
    Margret 20, 31-80
MORRELL, Alzenia 39, 28-106
    Caleb 62, 27-71
    Edlet 25, 21-106
    Isaac 24, 27-44
    John S. 66, 22-47
    Joseph P. 30, 22-48
    Thomas 30, 10-92
    William 34, 29-150
    William E. 27, 22-49
MORRILL, Carry 14, 29-161
    John W. 27, 29-161
MORRIS, David 24, 26-215
    Franklin 33, 25-203
    Henry 63, 25-204
    Henry 31, 25-159
    Jefferson 30, 26-214
    Jefferson 64, 27-63
    John 33, 25-202
    Mary 59, 25-163
    Virgie 42, 20-67
    Rosa 75, 17-246
MORTON, Alexander 35, 8-14
    David N. 57, 11-173
    George F. 69, 8-5
    Jacob S. 24, 11-174
    Merieth Y. 28, 11-151
    Zechariah 32, 8-7
MOSELY, Julia 37, 21-125
MOSLEY, John D. 24, 14-109
    Margaret 24, 13-54
    Samule 35, 15-161
MOSS, Frances 30, 33-183
MOTHORN?, John 24, 20-55
MOTTEM, George 68, 24-131
    George W. 32, 22-46
    Henry D. 22, 23-61
    Isaac H. 40, 24-132
    John H. 28, 24-122
    William 37, 23-77
    William 51, 22-45
MOTTEN, George 6/12, 24-141
MOURLEY, David 32, 1-1
MOURTON, M. Y. 65, 1-51
MOYERS, Samuel M. 23, 28-113
MULER, Isabell 23, 7-83
MULL, Elleck 23, 27-70
    Manual 56, 17-283
MURAY, David 23, 20-79
MURRAY, Andy 34, 20-79
    Simon 63, 17-272
    William 41, 15-145
MYERS, Elijah D. 24, 26-18
    Harmon 27, 31-95
    Henry 31, 31-70
    Martha 56, 27-25
    Mary 32, 32-162
    Pheby 57, 28-123
MYRES, William 28, 10-118
NAVE, Abraham 46, 14-120
    Allice 30, 29-171
    Britty 3, 17-2
    Daniel L. 43, 26-1
    David F. 26, 27-68
    Henry 24, 14-121
    Henry T. 33, 27-55
    Isaac N. 37, 27-59
    James A. 28, 27-69
    Jemiah 52, 27-45
    Julia 30, 17-2
    Levi 22, 27-35
    Luvicy 73, 27-31
    Mark 40, 33-182
    Mark W. 62, 21-98
    Peter 26, 29-144
    Pleasant 42, 30-36
    Samuel C. 31, 27-56
    Sary A. 53, 27-66
    Thomas 29, 27-67
    William H. 57, 27-57
    William S. 59, 33-175
NAVY, Elias 23, 13-61
    William E. 19, 13-61
NEATHERLY, William 18, 29-159
NELSON, William 6, 35-133
    William H. 45, 10-115

NETHERLY, Hiram 15, 14-94
    John 17, 14-94
NEWTON, James 68, 26-238
NIDEFFER, Elihu 34, 32-107
    Elizabeth 47, 30-46
    George 33, 33-178
    Isaac 51, 33-168
    James 37, 31-66
    James 17, 30-46
    James C. 28, 30-43
    Luvica 15, 30-49
    Mark 69, 32-140
    Martha 14, 32-106
    Mary 20, 34-33
    Robert 19, 33-191
    Samuel 27, 32-136
    William 35, 30-28
    William 24, 32-139
NIDIFFER, Calvin 26, 29-138
    Elizabeth 51, 29-157
    Jessee 21, 27-51
    Levi 23, 34-78
    Permelia 18, 27-51
    Robt. 51, 34-77
    Thomas 27, 29-145
OAKS, Chas. G. 53, 8-162
    Daniel 67, 5-16
    David 51, 6-73
    William A. 27, 6-64
OBERHOLSTER, James 20, 1-8
OBRIEN, Julia 16, 16-231
OBRIENT, Andrew 3, 26-8
    Martha 21, 26-8
OBRION, B. M. G. 64, 21-125
OFLARITY, Patrick 55, 17-250
OGLE, Lillie V. 16, 8-139
OLIVER, Chrisley 29, 28-111
    Elijah D. 36, 28-103
    George 47, 1-37
    Isaac 28, 29-134
    Jackson 41, 28-112
    James 34, 28-92
    James 62, 28-104
    John 35, 25-168
    John 72, 27-43
    Luvica 38, 28-105
    Marion 40, 25-175
    William 68, 28-110
    William I. 25, 1-36
OLLIVER, Cary 16, 31-70
    Christian 40, 33-165
    David 35, 33-187
    George 36, 31-63
    George W. 38, 31-83
    Mary 82, 19-62
    Nancy 68, 31-70
ORENS, Nancy 48, 17-276
ORENT, Lewis 33, 24-137
ORR, Brownlow 19, 19-25
    Jackson 54, 8-133
    James W. 48, 5-6
OVERBEY, Edith 84, 34-77
    Robert 7, 34-67
    Sally 6, 33-21
    William 7, 34-77
OVERHOLSER, Samuel 73, 33-15
OVERHULSER, William 41, 21-115
OWENS, Hamilton 45, 14-101
PAINE, Mary A. 16, 2-95
PANE, John 9, 33-182
PARDIEW, Cilas 67, 3-121
    Genetta 56, 3-118
PARDUE, Lurand 51, 3-114
PATTER, Sarah 30, 21-98
    Saml. 17, 21-98
PATTERSON, Robert 36, 26-218
PATTON, Drury M. 40, 13-86
    Joshua M. 40, 14-106
    Thomas Y. 37, 14-107
PAYNE, Aubra 8, 13-66
    James I. 35, 14-123
    Nathaniel 23, 15-148
    William 25, 13-49
PEACKS, Alfred C. 34, 29-178
PEAKS, Eli 61, 26-240
PEARCE, Alferd 38, 31-60
    Armstrong 52, 30-29
    Cameron 28, 33-166

PEARCE, Catharine 8/12, 30-44
    Lilburn 79, 32-123
    Mary 22, 21-140
    Mary 20, 30-44
    Nathaniel 47, 32-116
    Richard 65, 31-100
    Robert 24, 30-38
    Tennessee 61, 30-19
    William 58, 31-79
PEAVER, Armstrong 28, 33-182
PEMER?, Samuel 35, 31-76
PENIX, Elizabeth 6, 24-145
    Miles 44, 22-9
    Sarah 10, 24-145
    Sherman 13, 24-145
    Susan L. 16, 24-145
PEOPLES, Andrew J. 51, 12-5
    Emma 31, 20-85
    John W. 27, 13-58
    Kenada 44, 17-254
    Nathaniel T. 37, 13-74
PEREGRY?, John 50, 18-44
PERKINS, Geo. W. 24, 4-205
    J. L. 6, 4-164
PERRY, Albert W. 53, 5-23
    Andrew J. 28, 25-160
    David A. 27, 8-151
    George 25, 25-199
    George M. 33, 18-27
    Isaac 23, 26-231
    James 66, 18-41
    Jane 50, 22-34
    Joseph 28, 8-153
    Julia A. 9/12, 28-87
    Nancy 66, 25-196
    Saml. 19, 19-8
    Saryfine 17, 28-87
PERSINGER, John H. 38, 23-74
    Lewis 30, 23-73
PERSON, Alexander 35, 13-70
PERY, David 28, 25-178
    William 38, 25-179
PETERS, Alerd 62, 31-53
    Alferd 27, 30-46
    Benjamine 40, 32-159
    Catherine 22, 34-30
    Chrisley 33, 28-76
    Daniel 17, 31-96
    David 34, 29-139
    George F. 25, 8-3
    Henry 16, 33-16
    Henry T. 22, 32-137
    James 65, 31-52
    Marget E. 19, 27-65
    Micheal S. 41, 28-129
    Mollie 17, 30-20
    Pleasant 17, 27-62
    Rheubin 52, 5-219
    Ruben B. 35, 32-134
    Thomas 56, 8-2
    Thomas 30, 30-20
    Thomas W. 56, 5-221
    William 19, 35-101
    William M. 28, 29-137
PHARR, David 33, 28-88
    Jackson C. 30, 25-155
    Joseph 79, 24-151
    Sally 6, 27-53
PHILIPS, Wm. O. 27, 1-6
PHIPPS, Peter 33, 34-56
PIERCE, Chrisly A. 33, 27-37
    Elizabeth 33, 35-104
    Francis M. 47, 1-2
    Griffin 25, 1-4
    Henry 26, 34-31
    Henry C. 55, 1-8
    Henry C. 72, 27-38
    Jenne U. 10, 27-61
    Joseph 39, 1-31
    July A. 10, 27-58
    Lillie I. 4, 1-10
    Louis 35, 33-9
    Rhoda J. 16, 27-56
    Samuel 4, 1-9
    Sarah E. 16, 27-57
    Sion 52, 33-13
    William 24, 35-104
    William A. 50, 27-41

PIERCE, William C. 44, 1-3
PILKINTON, C. 23, 4-181
    Enoch 26, 4-184
    Letha 50, 4-183
PINN, George 45, 22-17
PIPPEN, Westley 24, 27-73
PLEASANT, James 63, 34-62
PLESS, James I. 29, 1-14
PLOT, Caroline 60, 2-91
PLOTT, Ellen 16, 23-69
POLAND, Catherine 15, 24-142
    William 24, 25-172
POTTER, Carie N. 34, 4-199
    Damiel W. 33, 11-136
    Daniel 73, 5-214
    Daniel 31, 6-80
    Elihu B. 29, 3-115
    Eliza 36, 28-75
    Ezel A. 30, 3-145
    John M. 54, 4-164
    Johnson 74, 4-160
    Margret 60, 25-192
    Martha 16, 3-148
    Mary A. 49, 4-161
    Nathaniel 4, 28-75
    Noah J. 40, 4-177
    Peter 81, 4-178
    Peter H. 50, 3-150
POWELL, Joseph 4, 8-151
    Joseph 32, 6-53
    Nathan 56, 20-84
POWERS, Avery 23, 28-78
    Isaac N. 24, 28-86
    John L. 49, 27-47
PRESSNEL, Alfred 22, 1-9
    Anna 53, 3-135
PRESTON, Pleasant 54, 21-133
PRICE, Charles 30, 15-168
    James P. 42, 12-19
    Joseph D. 65, 14-113
    Redman 73, 11-167
    Thomas 37, 11-166
PRITCHARD, Jerry 27, 7-89
    Nathan 25, 7-95
    Thre. 25, 7-96
PRITCHETT, Leander 27, 36-139
PUGH, David W. 7, 12-25
    Hester A. 43, 12-23
    Zachariah T. 32, 12-24
RADER, Rebecca 11, 2-72
RAINS, Nancy 14, 34-40
RAMSOMS, John 32, 5-7
RANGE, Alfred 50, 23-92
    Ann 40, 18-49
    Elizabeth 50, 17-272
    Elkanah D. 56, 23-75
    Harrison 41, 17-242
    Henry 62, 23-91
    Jacob 58, 23-65
    James C. 59, 12-29
    Jerimiah B. 43, 23-93
    Johnathan 54, 16-204
    Kelly 7, 29-160
    Landon 39, 17-271
    Sarah F. 40, 16-201
RANKIN, Mary M. 54, 5-35
RASON, Rubin 24, 30-4
RASOR, George W. 53, 30-10
    Vaught 55, 30-6
    William 30, 31-55
RAY, Hamilton 54, 5-28
    Samuel 39, 7-126
READY, John 23, 23-102
REDICK, Ester 65, 33-185
REESE, D. N. 40, 22-19
REEVES, Elizabeth 30, 23-87
RENFRO, Henry M. 54, 24-138
    Joseph 51, 30-14
    Sarah 18, 9-42
REYNOLDS, Elizabeth 56, 25-187
    Mary 23, 23-70
    Pompy 37, 19-39
RHUDY, Levi H. 31, 29-160
RICHARDS, Benjamin 35, 25-205
RICHARDSON, Andrew 23, 32-130
    Canada 29, 35-83
    Eleana 55, 30-23
    Hiram 30, 34-68

RICHARDSON, James 30, 35-132
    John 29, 35-136
    John 73, 35-102
    John 42, 32-110
    Margaret 45, 34-71
    Sampson 25, 35-127
    Thomas 61, 36-138
    William 37, 35-133
RICHESON, William 23, 7-110
RICHIE, Jemima 61, 28-115
    Martha 42, 29-155
    Susan 72, 28-132
RICHISON, Jos. H. 34, 5-12
    Linda 55, 7-112
RIGGS, James 33, 23-95
RITCHARDSON, Spin? 28, 16-214
RITCHER, David J. 41, 31-56
RITCHIE, Carerick 26, 32-145
    Elbert 28, 30-35
    James 37, 30-27
    William 23, 32-126
ROBERSON, Mosses 34, 10-91
ROBERTS, Alen H. 24, 10-118
    George 34, 18-38
    George 22, 23-70
    John 62, 10-117
    John 37, 18-13
    Mary 17, 34-41
    Nancy 64, 18-30
    William 27, 18-22
    William 49, 9-61
ROBERTSON, David 20, 30-50
    John C. 36, 22-1
    William 29, 22-8
ROBINSON, Mary 46, 8-1
    Sampson 59, 34-40
    William 25, 34-41
ROBISON, John 52, 16-232
ROCKHOLD, Mary 45, 25-173
    Walter 15, 25-173
RODDIE, Eva 16, 25-190
RODGERS, Joseph 26, 16-192
ROGERS, Nicholas 70, 30-1
ROGGERS, Hugh 29, 19-40
ROWE, Thomas Y. 39, 13-84
    William H. 40, 11-162
ROYSTON, Marion 22, 26-247
    Mary 75, 26-246
RUSH, Benjamine 25, 20-79
RUSSEL, George 55, 33-186
    Thomas 61, 16-221
    Emma 22, 18-45
RUSSELL, Theopolus 27, 19-1
RUTLEDGE, William 45, 29-152
RYON, Elizabeth 42, 18-56
SAMS, Owen 37, 25-200
SANDERS, Richard 35, 14-130
    Susan A. 22, 14-114
SAPES, Cahun? 22, 10-80
SAULTS, Mary 19, 29-175
SAYLOR, Henry 23, 17-282
    Noah 48, 17-284
SCALF, Adlaide 21, 23-101
    David 60, 26-223
    Elizabeth 32, 26-224
    Jessie 1, 23-101
    Nancy 36, 26-225
    William 43, 23-97
SCOTT, James 45, 20-87
    Sarah 52, 22-31
    William 60, 16-217
    William M. 32, 22-32
    William T. L. 43, 12-1
SELLERS, John 50, 29-151
SHARP, James K. 29, 29-170
SHAW, Drewre 51, 8-10
SHEETS, Ellen 22, 19-38
    George 24, 3-117
    Young 51, 3-116
SHELL, Alfred C. 50, 6-62
    Alvin P. 41, 23-85
    Andrew 23, 14-104
    Aron 48, 14-103
    Elkanah 47, 23-83
    Emeline 60, 23-58
    Finly 50, 5-31
    James 35, 23-57
    James 22, 6-76

SHELL, John 39, 18-52
    John A. 58, 5-27
    John L. 32, 6-44
    Mary A. 35, 8-157
    Milton 39, 8-160
    Nathan 29, 7-93
    Robert P. 37, 24-119
    Saml. 37, 20-53
    Virginia A. 11, 24-103
    William 62, 18-54
SHEPPARD, L. J. 30, 4-185
SHERFFORY, Annah 9, 13-67
SHEWMAKE, Mary 60, 12-175
SHOEMAKER, George 51, 13-78
SHORTS, David 64, 17-253
SHOUN, Frederick 39, 30-45
SHOWN, Jesse 29, 36-145
SHUFFIELD, A. K. 24, 3-124
    George 76, 3-125
    John C. 45, 3-122
    Wm. D. 40, 3-123
SHUFFIELED, W. S. 26, 3-120
SHULL, Andrew 51, 9-28
SILUS, Elizabeth 21, 14-136
    Margaret 2, 14-136
SINERLEY, Christey? 39, 9-19
    David 42, 12-178
    Eligah 59, 9-33
    George 36, 1-30
    Henry 88, 9-25
    Jacob 66, 12-177
    James 29, 11-134
    Johnson H. 29, 9-44
    William 18, 11-169
    William 26, 11-138
SINERLY, Ellen 35, 19-19
    John M. 30, 15-146
SINES, Salina 18, 9-25
SIMMONS, Flavious J. 44, 13-81
    Lewis A. 28, 13-82
SIMMS, Charles 19, 15-199
    Henry 30, 15-188
    James 2, 15-180
    John 45, 16-191
    Mary 24, 15-180
    Milburn 1, 16-202
SIMS, Emmer 3, 2-72
    Francis 9, 2-72
    Martha 12, 2-72
    Susan 86, 19-4
    William 12, 19-7
SIMULY?, William 28, 7-101
SINGLETARY, Maryann 72, 18-56
SIREY, George 11, 3-128
SIZEMORE, George 36, 6-69
    Nat 24, 10-101
SLAGLE, Abner 46, 25-167
    John 39, 24-150
    Levi 49, 24-130
    Peter 75, 25-165
    Peter 44, 25-162
SLOAN, Joseph 15, 7-118
SMALLING, Alfred B. 30, 23-69
    Duke W. 69, 12-43
    Martin 26, 14-118
    Robert 56, 24-103
    William 35, 13-47
SMITH, Alfred 16, 24-103
    Alice 19, 22-15
    Andrew 20, 13-164
    Anlisha 23, 26-226
    Carter 27, 6-42
    D. H. W. 28, 2-57
    E. J. 62, 1-27
    E. J. 34, 4-200
    Edgard 8, 26-226
    Elbert 35, 3-129
    Eliza J. 52, 3-138
    Elizabeth 74, 22-34
    Elizabeth 37, 8-166
    Elizabeth 17, 8-164
    Ellen 64, 12-40
    Ezekiel 69, 1-18
    Francis M. 36, 1-11
    G. H. M. 21, 20-46
    George W. 43, 5-21
    Hamilton 60, 21-118
    Hamilton W. 35, 2-55

SMITH, Henderson 33, 5-36
Jacob 25, 8-164
Jacob 61, 15-141
Jacob A. 65, 2-76
James 59, 21-107
James 50, 17-255
James 19, 30-34
James G. 66, 21-120
Jerinereta 5, 10-115
John 5, 26-226
John 55, 34-30
John 38, 26-227
John 25, 8-163
John C. 35, 21-141
John H. 64, 1-20
John K. 49, 8-152
Joseph 32, 26-12
Lafayett 5, 2-70
Lawson M. 59, 1-25
Lovena 56, 8-141
Maggie 11, 26-232
Margaret 20, 8-164
Mary E. 62, 1-29
Matha 40, 10-115
Melissa C. 33, 2-77
N. T. 35, 2-67
Nathaniel 40, 15-178
Nicholas 69, 5-11
Racheal 6, 25-202
Robert 1, 26-226
Robert 34, 19-61
Robert L. 36, 1-15
Safrona 28, 18-14
Sarah S. 28, 2-70
Thomas 9, 25-202
W. B. C. 31, 20-84
W. G. B. 29, 1-19
William 12, 13-83
SMITHPETERS, Ann 14, 21-92
Eliza 40, 20-47
William 75, 16-209
SNAPP, Alfred 33, 22-26
SNODGRASS, Cornelia 27, 14-137
James 18, 15-149
John 52, 13-53
Lucy B. 10, 15-147
Thomas 25, 12-45
William 30, 12-44
SNYDER, Alexander 29, 14-128
Henry 21, 20-91
Henry 26, 14-94
Henry 52, 18-49
Solomon 32, 5-30
SONGER, George 45, 20-86
SORRELL, William 28, 9-17
SOUTH, Nella 71, 27-63
Rahchel 34, 27-63
SPEARS, Franklin 20, 25-174
Marion 4, 23-59
SPENCER, Elizabeth 40, 16-235
STALLING, James 50, 25-198
STAPHINA, Mikiel 33, 10-116
STEFFEY, John 48, 18-16
STEPHENS, Charles 52, 11-171
John 50, 31-92
John 40, 11-172
Joshua 70, 11-170
STEPP, George O. 30, 24-129
Silas H. 55, 14-102
STONE, Mary C. 17, 29-148
STOUT, Anderson 22, 26-217
STOUT, Andrew L. 56, 8-130
Benjamin 26, 35-125
David 26, 7-117
George 46, 30-34
Granville W. 60, 4-213
Henry D. 65, 26-216
James R. 33, 3-152
Jefferson 7, 5-3
John 35, 26-241
John L. 19, 4-166
John R. 59, 3-147
Joseph 19, 35-110
Kizey 67, 31-62
Lemuel 5, 1-6
Logan 21, 4-162
Lourana 40, 6-80
Mary A. 28, 2-62

STOUT, Pinkney 21, 35-109
Saml. 25, 17-5
Selah 51, 35-122
STOVER, Alexander 25, 28-81
Cam. 63, 28-80
Damil 6, 24-127
Elizabeth 12, 24-127
George 70, 25-156
John 4, 24-127
Lamarr? 47, 20-77
Maynard 2, 24-127
Nathaniel 49, 21-114
Robert 30, 16-208
Samuel 56, 33-12
Solomon 68, 29-174
Thomas 56, 21-131
William 10, 24-127
William B. 21, 25-152
STRALY, Josaphine 14, 16-230
STRATHER, Daniel 35, 20-50
Eliza 1/12, 20-50
Margaret 24, 20-50
STREET, Johnathan 25, 11-160
Samuel 42, 11-154
Simon 24, 5-37
STROTTER, Daniel 38, 29-168
STUART, Burten 14, 16-230
SUTHERLAND, Kisy 40, 21-137
SUTTON, John 55, 27-72
SWAMER, Amon 50, 12-2
George W. 43, 12-4
SWANNER, Joseph 70, 13-64
Joseph 37, 15-154
William 13, 13-58
SWINEY, James jr. 35, 25-176
James sr. 70, 25-175
John 41, 25-169
Martha 33, 24-145
Westley 44, 23-71
TADLOCK, Robert 25, 21-105
TATE, Andrew 45, 12-38
TAYLOR, Alvin 39, 33-6
Amanda 18, 33-7
Andrew 52, 33-2
Andrew 38, 15-156
Barsha 55, 17-265
Caswell C. 35, 15-149
Daniel 26, 31-85
Danul W. 27, 24-109
David 45, 16-196
David 44, 21-97
David 54, 30-49
Deliah 75, 16-212
Edmond 50, 14-119
Eliza 23, 29-186
Elizabeth 72, 31-95
Francis 27, 34-66
General 25, 31-90
George 35, 33-1
Henrietta 7, 16-217
Henry 9, 17-10
Isaac 34, 17-267
Isaac N. 50, 12-20
Jacob 51, 35-96
Jacob L. 26, 35-97
Jacob V. 34, 30-39
James 29, 23-82
James J. 22, 32-150
James M. 42, 13-51
James P. 35, 24-110
James P. 52, 17-260
John 28, 34-26
John 38, 16-215
John 25, 13-68
John W. 22, 31-86
John W. 53, 31-87
Joseph 4, 7-85
Julia 13, 16-220
Levi 35, 31-96
Levi 81, 23-101
Lewis D. 30, 32-151
Luny 25, 33-181
Margret 77, 30-47
Martin 27, 17-263
Mary 12, 33-7
Mary 37, 19-63
Murray 24, 36-141
Nathaniel 60, 16-230

TAYLOR, Nathaniel 88, 17-269
Nathaniel L. 62, 24-108
Robert 24, 7-85
Robert 27, 32-148
Rufus 60, 12-28
Sally 8, 17-2
Samuel 34, 34-48
Scott 27, 17-266
Starling 70, 16-207
Tener 50, 16-216
Thomas 22, 33-176
Thomas F. 45, 31-88
Thomas H. 49, 31-102
Vonnie 9, 19-58
William 26, 31-93
William 41, 16-219
William 22, 21-109
William 31, 21-110
William 55, 16-234
William B. 60, 31-94
William B. 39, 22-20
William T. 27, 31-103
TEAGUE, Avery 37, 1-28
James 23, 10-104
Logan 56, 9-58
Robert A. 30, 1-22
THOMAS, John O. 47, 16-229
Licy 30, 24-147
Strawberry 50, 6-43
William S. 55, 26-250
THOMPSON, E. M. 21, 22-4
Rebecca 40, 2-72
Samuel 44, 23-76
William 37, 22-51
TILSON, Nathaniel 30, 16-226
TIMS, Amos 64, 1-21
James A. 26, 1-10
TINNER, Alexander 34, 7-125
TIPTON, Albert 62, 21-129
Harriat 16, 16-209
Isaac 70, 20-75
John W. 31, 19-66
Nancy 75, 10-91
Nancy 41, 17-9
Thomas 24, 20-76
William 18, 8-155
TONCRAY, Alexander 34, 18-42
Charles 43, 21-140
William 41, 18-46
TONEY, Samuel 36, 28-126
TOUCHPOINT, Nat 4, 16-221
TOWNSON, Calumbus 22, 10-73
John 40, 9-34
William 29, 10-93
TREADWAY, Benj. 62, 19-37
Eliza 21, 15-173
Julie 17, 14-131
J. Hampton 24, 24-121
Jacob 49, 19-34
John 24, 19-21
John 50, 19-38
Letta 80, 15-185
William 35, 15-155
TREDWAY, Lawson 10, 27-73
Robert 45, 28-85
TRIBBETT, Nicey 39, 6-60
TRICE, Jackson 30, 11-149
TROXWALL, Mary 66, 24-118
TROXWELL, James 24, 25-171
TRUMAN, Adline 20, 1-22
J. R. 26, 1-23
TRUSLER, Margret 78, 25-197
TRUSSEL, George 24, 30-44
TUCKER, Addie 6, 14-121
Annie 6, 14-127
Edmon 20, 14-127
Emma 18, 14-95
Martha 16, 16-205
Mary 12, 14-122
Sarah 12, 14-127
TUMER?, Rutha 63, 17-4
TURBYFIELD, Jas. P. 49, 6-63
John W. 19, 6-65
TURNER, John W. 35, 18-23
TWIGG, Daniel 23, 7-104
John 56, 7-105
VANCE, Abner 60, 5-10
Abner H. 22, 7-106

VANCE, Andrew 25, 7-88
        Jane 20, 7-107
        Sallie 17, 7-107
VANDEVENTER, Jacob 68, 31-84
        Joseph 36, 31-58
        Mary 47, 25-176
        Martha 24, 29-159
VANHUSS, Daniel S. 45, 27-48
        Joseph P. 47, 27-60
        Thomas 56, 27-49
VANOVER, Maron 22, 1-6
VAUGHN, Benjamin 29, 35-124
        Lutiarn? 49, 31-65
        William 33, 25-153
VAUGHT, James 25, 1-5
VEST, Archibald J. 35, 22-50
        Susanah 64, 23-63
        William J. 41, 23-62
VINES, Thomas 20, 4-172
VUNCANON, A. 47, 2-96
        A. B. 46, 3-143
        J. L. 25, 3-144
        Nancy 73, 3-142
WAGNER, Andrew J. 29, 4-194
        David A. 20, 2-89
        Jas. 1. 24, 2-97
        Mollie 19, 29-152
        N. C. 48, 2-87
        Nancy N. 17, 2-90
WALKER, Benjamine 70, 14-128
        Emaline 52, 15-162
WALLICE, Elizabeth 22, 21-138
        William 7, 21-138
WALTERS, Barby A. 21, 27-48
WARD, William 23, 10-106
WASHAM, Hugh 7, 33-24
WATES, Odam 24, 9-62
WATSON, Eliazor 75, 12-17
        John 13, 23-91
        Wiley 40, 14-135
WEAVER, Russel 23, 31-82
WEBB, John C. 27, 7-86
        Rod 42, 20-81
        Sarah 18, 6-56
        William 56, 6-39
WELCH, Agness 37, 19-60
        John 39, 18-53
        Mary 6, 20-52
        Mat 2, 19-60
WEST, Elizebeth 60, 9-27
        John 29, 28-74
        Sarah 9, 25-190
WHALEN, Julie E. 25, 22-30
WHALEY, Rachel 46, 2-64
WHISENHUNT, Loucinda 50, 12-16
        Mary 18, 12-12
WHISHUNT, Noah 49, 10-119
WHITAKER, Susan 30, 28-82
WHITE, Boston C. 11, 2-77
        Daniel L. 6, 2-77
        David W. 35, 2-86
        John A. 8, 2-77
        John V. 31, 2-78
        Lawson 24, 2-101
        R. C. 31, 2-100
        Robert 23, 33-20
        Robert 62, 31-60
        Sabry 54, 2-99
        Susan 39, 33-22
        Thomas 26, 34-63
        Thomas C. 42, 1-16
WHITEHEAD, Andrew 30, 9-51
        Charles 21, 6-43
        James 60, 11-130
        John 51, 9-57
        Marth J. 42, 3-131
        Mary C. 13, 2-64
        Nancy 18, 6-43
        Thomas 56, 10-82
        Thomas A. 50, 9-53
        Wm. C. 48, 2-60
WHITEHOOD, Mary 21, 13-79
WHITESIDE, William 32, 29-176
WHITHEAD, David A. 40, 10-69
        James 26, 10-90
        James 80, 9-68
        James C. 32, 10-109
        Larkin 70, 10-89

WHITLOW, James 55, 17-255
WHOSHORN, Frank 30, 15-179
WIGHT, Landon 17, 29-180
WILBOURN, Maggie 29, 18-11
WILCOX, Canick 26, 6-59
        David 49, 18-47
        James 25, 18-48
        John 32, 18-34
WILLIAM, Russel R. 30, 9-54
WILLIAMS, A. M. 24, 3-146
        Alexander 41, 26-13
        Alfred 44, 21-104
        Alfred M. 28, 27-42
        Alphonzo 63, 12-30
        Archibald 46, 13-62
        Arthur 36, 31-75
        Caroline 6, 28-78
        Elihu 33, 32-120
        Elijah 30, 19-22
        Elizabeth 47, 17-6
        Eveline 17, 33-168
        George D. 77, 13-54
        George E. 52, 12-35
        George T. 32, 14-95
        Harriet 75, 13-78
        Harvey 23, 29-136
        James M. 35, 15-153
        John 26, 32-114
        John B. 52, 2-65
        John H. 35, 28-89
        John Q. 60, 16-237
        John P. 22, 12-1
        Joshua 71, 13-55
        Levi 22, 32-107
        Lorenzo 49, 32-118
        Mandy 55, 17-247
        Margaret 30, 14-125
        Matt? 57, 19-32
        May C. T. 24, 12-1
        Nathaniel 44, 13-50
        P. J. 25, 2-66
        Pinkney P. 66, 13-60
        Pleasant 72, 16-205
        Pleasant 59, 31-73
        Pleasant 26, 19-30
        Redding 55, 23-53
        Samuel L. 14, 12-1
        Samuel W. 45, 15-152
        Samule 36, 13-57
        Thomas 21, 33-167
        Thomas E. 27, 12-34
        William 39, 26-14
        William 30, 28-79
WILLSON, Elbert 21, 28-131
        James 42, 29-179
        Sarah 40, 28-101
        Tenny 70, 29-140
WILSON, Canada 29, 36-146
        Elijah 62, 13-83
        Eliza 15, 35-98
        Emanuel 35, 24-148
        Eveline 30, 30-42
        Ferdinand 6, 35-104
        George 33, 36-148
        George 33, 33-170
        Hannah 70, 8-143
        Hannah 66, 36-147
        Jack C. 45, 7-116
        James 26, 19-15
        James F. 20, 4-184
        James M. 48, 1-35
        John 22, 36-144
        John 23, 30-13
        Poe 52, 35-89
        Solomon 27, 31-91
        W. D. 39, 6-60
        William 27, 34-74
WINTERS, James A. 25, 6-54
        Martin 53, 6-57
        Stephen 52, 6-52
        William 59, 7-113
WISHON?, David 25, 19-26
WISSENHUNT, Rhoda 12, 13-54
WITEHEAD, Marget 42, 12-179
WOLF, George 16, 29-159
WOODS, Alphatine 3, 32-140
        Elizabeth 34, 32-140
        Henry 2, 32-140

WOODY, Lenoir 50, 29-169
WORD, Keren H. 49, 2-69
WORKMAN, Martha 48, 6-74
        Martha 44, 8-152
WRIGHT, James 24, 13-69
        Thomas 56, 12-33
        Wesly 46, 11-131
WYETT, Elizabeth 57, 13-56
WYLEY, Mary Jessie 14, 33-183
YOUNG, Alfred 48, 21-126
        Daniel 32, 9-67
        Henry 57, 16-213
        Jackson 70, 23-89
        John W. 47, 13-87
        Rachel 20, 5-13
_____, Leonard 68, 19-25